Creating the Academic Commons

Guidelines for Learning, Teaching, and Research

Thomas H. P. Gould

THE SCARECROW PRESS, INC.
Lanham • Toronto • Plymouth, UK
2011

Published by Scarecrow Press, Inc.
A wholly owned subsidiary of The Rowman & Littlefield Publishing Group, Inc.
4501 Forbes Boulevard, Suite 200, Lanham, Maryland 20706
http://www.scarecrowpress.com

Estover Road, Plymouth PL6 7PY, United Kingdom

British Library Cataloguing in Publication Information Available

Library of Congress Cataloging-in-Publication Data

Gould, Thomas H. P., 1953–
Creating the academic commons : guidelines for learning, teaching, and research / Thomas H. P. Gould.
p. cm.
Includes bibliographical references and index.
ISBN 978-0-8108-8108-2 (cloth : alk. paper) — ISBN 978-0-8108-8109-9 (ebook)
1. Education, Higher—Computer network resources. 2. Education, Higher—Effect of technological innovations on. 3. Internet in higher education. 4. Distance education. I. Title.
LB2395.7.G68 2011
378.1'7344678—dc22 2011000525

∞™ The paper used in this publication meets the minimum requirements of American National Standard for Information Sciences—Permanence of Paper for Printed Library Materials, ANSI/NISO Z39.48-1992.

Printed in the United States of America

Contents

Preface

I am, unabashedly, a lover of libraries. I also love universities. To stroll across these beautiful places, such as the University of Oklahoma or Georgetown University, and, of course, my own home at Kansas State University, is to appreciate not only the care given to native landscaping and urban design but also the very uniqueness of community that is part of all learning institutions. Universities are not just the special places of learning for all countries and all peoples. They are—at their best—a self-contained escape from the mundane world. They attract those seeking what is missing. Of course, that "missing" is a mere degree of qualification for some. But for many others, it is something far more, an indescribable sense of belonging to a noble quest. I defy anyone to stroll the streets of Cambridge and not sense what has preceded, what has been learned, and what has been shared in those classrooms and courtyards.

At the heart of every university is its multidisciplinary access point to all information: the library. For denizens seeking information, their quests begin and end here. Whether it is the catacombs of the stacks, the vast expanse of tables and new technology tools, or even the special smell that all libraries share, these are special places filled with special people. These are the gathering points of learners, scholars, and teachers. In my days at the University of North Carolina at Chapel Hill, I spent entire days wandering through the graduate library looking here and there for what I had not found and never knew even existed. I spent hours in special rooms set aside for graduate students, surrounded by books and journals that would remain until I returned. Seems so old-school today, but that room was a quiet place within a quiet place. I doubt they are even used today. I looked patiently through dust-covered volumes of Sociological Abstracts, amazed when I found what could not be located using FTP or other (now primitive) online search tools available at the time.

What is still present in all libraries is information and access to untold "pages" of information I could not even imagine twenty years ago. This book is, at its core, about information, information storage, and those we have designated as the experts in how all this information will be retrieved. But it is also about a special type of library and a special type of librarian: the millennial library and millennial librarians who can offer unique assistance to students, teachers, and researchers in an age when the sum total of all available information exceeds what can be found by any one person. This work cannot pretend to be the final word on what a millennial library will look like in even five years (as the included case study updates illustrate). It does not suggest that every possible service or software application is listed here. It is the paean of one lover of libraries who sees the unfolding new library as a natural consequence to thousands of years that precede it.

ABOUT THIS BOOK

Let us all agree that technology in 2011 is a moving target. A very quick, vague, hard-to-track moving target. I fret in my dreams that the moment I consign this work to production, something momentous will occur. I fret in my waking hours that something is already happening somewhere that I have missed or overlooked. I ask only that my gentle reader take into account that this topic is a moving target.

The book is divided into three sections: supporting students and faculty, the supporting elements of an academic commons, and the evolving issues facing the academic commons movement.

Section one addresses three types of academic commons already in place at some universities: learning, teaching, and research. To my knowledge (remember: moving target), no university library is addressing learning, teaching, and research commons as three separate units. Some have mixed parts of each together. Again, to my knowledge, none has a single overarching commons concept that addresses all or incorporates a fourth commons I offer later in the book. I may be in error and can only say that if you feel your library has accomplished this, then bully for you—and please let me know!

Section two delves into archiving, e-reserves, the fate of books, libraries as publishers, and issues swirling around access, security, and sustainability. No doubt some of these will raise eyebrows: Libraries as publishers? Librarians as archivists? Electronic books (and their accompanying reading devices)? As I note in several places in this section (and others), little is settled as we try to understand not only where we are now but especially where we will be in a few years. Some libraries are already acting as publishers, with universities looking to their central storage facilities (read: e-reserves) as a step in that direction. Some librarians are already wrestling with the issue of what to save and what to ignore. This challenge is made more manifest by the rapid drop in electronic storage costs: It is now possible to store everything, if we want. But just because we can, should we? And though the Kindle and iPad have most certainly raised the level of discourse regarding electronic books, much is left to be chewed on as we move more and more toward a new delivery scheme for our printed tomes.

Section three addresses the issues likely to be confronting librarians and their administrators in their quests to establish the commons outlined in section one: copyright, intellectual rights, and (perhaps the newest issue) privacy. This part of section three is presented in a policy approach intended not to wade through the voluminous forest of pertinent cases but to look at the overall landscape and potential outcomes. This section also attempts to look at how a university library administration can "sell" the idea of its academic commons to the public: students, faculty, and university administrators. And, finally, as might be expected from a book such as this, I attempt to peer even further down the road to what might occur in the near term in the areas of the academic commons: university turf wars, acceptance of change by staff, and the need for a fourth academic commons, one devoted to librarians themselves. This "LibTech commons" is envisioned as a worldwide commons shared by librarians at every library. In its way, it can be seen as a precedent to a global library. It would also be the foundation for the creation of a new idea that grows directly from existing library practices: searchology. The need is clear: In a forest of trillions of trees, we will more and more depend on a professional who can find the right tree (or trees), thus facilitating research collaboration on a scale we have never enjoyed.

All of this will be made possible only if a university sees its library as central to the long-term success of its students, educators, and researchers. The successful university will shun the too-often traditional habit of assigning various portions of what is discussed in this book to various offices within its bureaucracy. One central location of information and knowledge creation already exists at all universities: the millennial library.

Acknowledgments

This book is the product of many, including the multitude of librarians who helped me find obscure sources, track down even-more obscure references, and, generally, put up with the needs of a very needy graduate student-turned-professor. I thank them all for their patience and their insights. They navigated me to what I needed when I had all but given up the hunt. I would especially wish to thank a librarian whose name I cannot dredge up out of my memory, but who tolerated a very needy, very freckled-face child at Savannah High School's makeshift library all those years ago. You made your room less mysterious and a much-needed haven for me. Thanks.

I would also like to thank the librarians at the various libraries I contacted for information included in this book. Some of the places and information did not make it into the book, such as that provided by Thomas Moothart, coordinator of Onsite Services at Colorado State's Morgan Library, and Brian W. Rossman, associate dean of libraries at Montana State University. Though many of the details of what has happened and will be happening at your libraries did not make it into this book, your advice shaped the final product.

I also thank Scarecrow Press and Martin Dillon for allowing me to take longer than I should have, possibly writing more than I might have, and dwelling far too long on what must have seemed to be the least important. All authors rely on editors. Lucky authors are assigned to great editors of the ilk of Martin. In addition, I would like to thank the precision and (almost scary) accuracy of Kellie Hagan at Scarecrow Press, who found more errors and vagaries than I care to admit.

Finally, and most important to the creation of this book is my wife and true love, Carol, who not only tolerated my hours at the computer, whether at home, at work, or in the mountains of Colorado, but also kept my thinking on track and my writing relevant to a less-than-clear topic. I thank her also for reminding me that, though I am not a librarian, I have much to say about them and their role at the heart of all universities. And, I thank her for pointing out when I tended to digress, which was often.

Introduction

The Millennial Library

The need to collect and preserve information has been a key element in the success of civilizations for centuries. Ensuring the long-term viability of storage areas for information, or libraries, as they came to be known, preserves key information regarding the patterns of nature, such as rain, floods, droughts, early winter snows, and late spring frosts. Information of scientific advances continue to be closely guarded and highly valued. Cultural artifacts and histories help preserve a nation's identity—and they continue to be the glue that binds peoples together. While great paintings and sculptures have found their places in museums, books, plays, poetry, music, film, and science, most important for universities, are the stuff of libraries.

The strategic gathering and storing of "data" led to the construction of monuments to information, libraries on the scale of that in Alexandria, Egypt. And, yet, the Library of Alexandria and the much more recently constructed U.S. Library of Congress were created to serve a limited elite: the former the world's leading thinkers and rulers; the latter, members of Congress. Not just anyone was expected to use these special libraries, and even fewer were allowed to see all of their contents.

In the age of modern libraries, especially those at universities, the storage of research—both in the data that is used to create the final works and the works themselves—became the central goal. Over the ages, with the rise of science and the refinement of scientific methods, as well as the increasing reliance on past discoveries by new researchers, the university library became the vital resource for stored information and data. Systems of storage and retrieval were created, such as Dewey's and the Library of Congress. Over time, researchers and graduate students came to know the stacks by categories, carefully exploring and committing to memory areas within the library relevant to their work. And faculty and some graduate students would be allowed to create their own minilibraries—monographs and journals—for ready access within reserved carrels in the library itself. This relationship between users and the library grew into a well-grounded understanding and mutual respect. Librarians collected and arranged. Researchers mined the collections for much needed information and data.

The elite nature of some very special libraries persists today. But, for the most part, libraries are now intended to be public, accessed by all manner of individuals seeking information. As access to books became more common, with commercial stores on every other corner, the library also grew to include more services to researchers. And, the vast majority of modern libraries have evolved far beyond the cataloging of scrolls or monographs. Not surprisingly, these changes have occurred in concert with the decreasing costs of information storage, starting with the technology breakthrough of digital tape in the 1960s. The pace of change within technology has increased decade by decade, and now year by year, and with that the amount of information stored per square foot of a library has skyrocketed. Since the days of "platter" information delivery via CD-ROM in the 1980s, individual libraries have grown gateways of vast amounts of electronic data in archives accessible worldwide at the speed of light. Even the movement of sharable materials between libraries today takes seconds and minutes to complete, not the former days required by the postal service.

But perhaps as important, the actual amount of information available both within the library itself—in cooperation with other libraries and through its electronic access to hundreds of databases—has increased dramatically over the past decade. Rather than being restricted to paper indexes generated annually, such as Sociological Abstracts, virtually all information created in all forms post–circa 1980 is available through a library's Internet connection. In part this also has been made by possible by the dramatic and rapid increase in online access speeds, as evidenced in Figure I.1, as well as the increases in computer speeds (Figure I.2) and corresponding drop in prices (Figure I.3). For an expansive report on library purchases and holdings over the period of 1986 to 2008, refer to the American Research Library's 2007–2008 report.[1]

The decline in the costs associated with the preservation of digital objects has rekindled the age-old debate as to what to save and on what basis that decision should be made. Indeed, the Library of Alexandria's greatest patron, Egyptian ruler Ptolemy Soter, sought to ensure the collection included at least one copy of all known works of art and science. Librarians in those times rarely strayed into the realm of determining what was appropriate to save or into the evaluation of the properness of the works archived. That was and is the world of archivists. For the librarian, all was saved, all was preserved. Today, "all that is created" amounts to massive amounts of data. For example, in April 2010, the

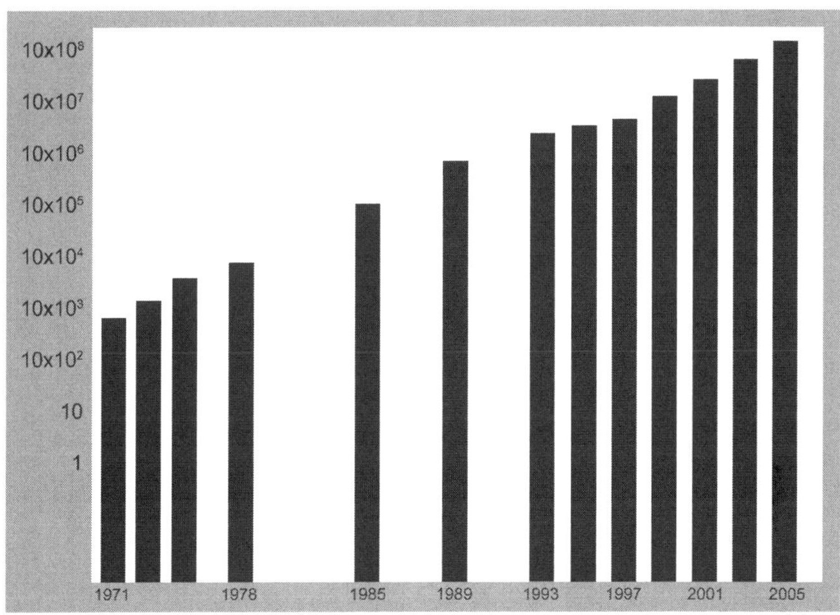

Figure I.1. Moore's Law: Transistor Speeds, 1971–2005 (log scale)

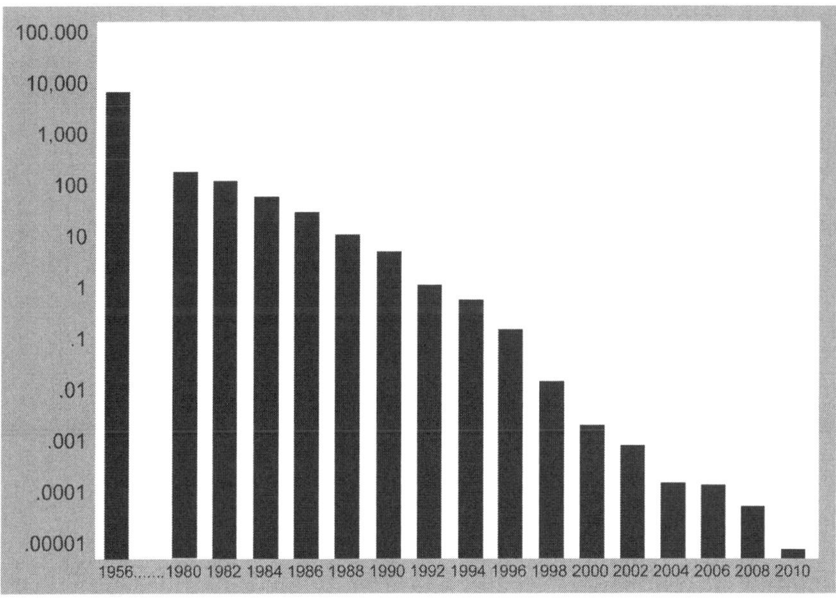

Figure I.2. Cost per megabyte for information storage: 1956–2010 dollars (log scale)

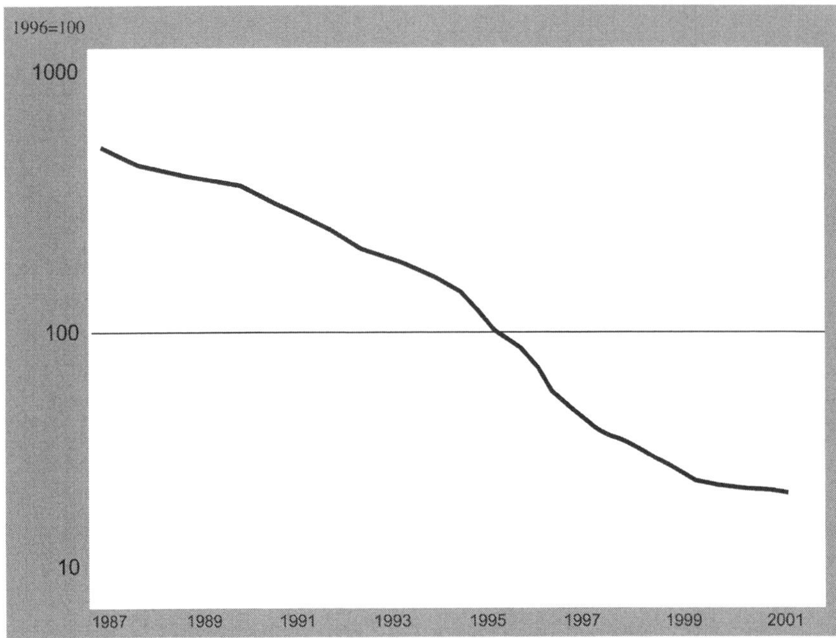

Figure I.3. Computer Price Declines, 1987–2001 (index log scale)

Library of Congress announced it had reached an agreement with the owners of Twitter to archive the billions of postings made since the online message board's inception in March 2006. Matt Raymond posted news of the deal on Library of Congress's blog. "Today we hold more than 167 terabytes of web-based information, including legal blogs, websites of candidates for national office, and websites of Members of Congress," Raymond noted.[2]

Preserving all of this data, especially online formats, has itself raised concerns, both inside and outside libraries. The ultimate destruction of Alexandria's library (and the similar fiery fate of the first Library of Congress) surely helps crystallize the concerns that information not only be collected, but also safely preserved and protected, as well as easily accessible. The accessibility was assured to researchers with the creation of collections of printed volumes within the stacks of university libraries. That is, accessibility was synonymous with preservation, and preservation was synonymous with print. The preservation of these printed works led to notable advances in the science of archiving, perhaps starting with the creation of a longer-lasting acid-free paper. It also fostered a hierarchy within libraries: Those institutions with more highly valued printed works were ranked higher in prestige to their university patrons. These higher-ranked institutions became known as research one libraries and are still held in special regard.

As improvements in technology lowered the cost of data storage, more and more information has been moved from print to online, an easily accessible area. In the latter portion of the twentieth century, data moved to digital archives known as e-reserves. Since the turn of the century, information has moved another step into an online "cloud"—a storage system reliant upon tens, perhaps hundreds, of thousands of servers. To a large part, this constant move to provide information has been driven by access: The goal being to provide as much, as fast, to as many people as possible.

The fear among some—especially senior faculty members—concerning the loss of this ephemeral electronic data in e-reserves and within clouds has not lessened. If anything, the anxiety has increased. Those who create information, as well as those who rely on the certainty of being able to access information, demand that it be secure, unchanged, available, or more specifically, *findable*. For it is one thing to create millions and millions of pages of digital material, but if a desired set of data cannot be accessed, it is as good as lost.

Additionally, without a clear set of guidelines for digital information storage, researchers have little assurance that what was created will remain intact and safe from malicious or unintended modification. Notably (and obviously), this possible threat of research modification is far less of an issue with print, whether monograph or journal. Digital records can be modified far more easily than print, especially given the creation of hundreds of thousands of copies of books and journals that represent a findable, reliable, and accurate record of what has been created and when it was created.

However, the change that now faces all libraries, and especially those within universities, goes far beyond debates over the nature and form of archives. Having previously been ordained as the repositories of all information, including that found in science, social science, and humanity archives, librarians have for decades seen their role as much more vital than that of collectors and catalogers. To no small degree, the academic community is finally beginning to understand the role of the modern library is that of a catalyst for information sharing. Librarians are working directly with students, creating special tools for researchers, and assisting teachers in the delivery of information to students. And, all of this is coalescing within a relatively new concept: the academic commons.

THE ACADEMIC COMMONS AND UNIVERSITY LIBRARIES

The academic commons is the latest advance directly addressing the concerns of access, reliability, and storage, and this will come to house all innovation, all research, and all collaborations. Already a handful of university libraries have and are moving to create these academic commons. In many ways, the term "academic commons" is a branding process—it creates a name and face for a variety of activities that have been occurring at different levels at many universities, as well as, more importantly, brings into sharp focus a need for standards and best practices. It is an online place, a portal that supports researchers, enables collaboration, and enriches pedagogy by providing to academicians software, training, and a "space" for all this to occur and reside. The academic commons opens to library patrons the opportunity to share information in a hyperdynamic, real-time environment, regardless of where the collaborators are physically. It also provides for a long-term storage of information in new forms. These academic commons—already becoming the mark of modern librarianship—are the heart of a new library, a facility that will be called here the "millennial library."

As is always the case with any innovation, this new role for libraries and their librarians has been the subject of much discussion and research internationally for the past decade or more. Part of this discussion has included not just the nature and potential role of an academic commons, but also the future impact of new information platforms within these online areas, platforms that are facilitating the publishing of research, as well as robust critiques of these works. As stated in the Keystone Principles of the Association of Research Libraries (ARL) and the Online Computer Library Center (OCLC):

1. Scholarly and government information is a "public good" and must be available free of marketing bias, commercial motives, and cost to the individual user.
2. Libraries are responsible for creating innovative information systems for the dissemination and preservation of information and new knowledge regardless of the format.
3. The academic library is the intellectual commons for the community where people and ideas interact in both real and virtual environments to expand learning and facilitate the creation of new knowledge.[3]

The future role of the academic commons, its various forms, and its impact on researchers, educators, and students will be discussed later in this introduction. But first, what of the professionals who will make the millennial library a vital and relevant resource?

A New Librarian: Millennial

Librarians already have expanded their roles and activities to more directly engage with students, teachers, and researchers, both within the library and in academic departments and classrooms. New services have been and are being developed to assist these groups, including the identification, facilitation, and adoption of newly created software and hardware tools. In many libraries, these new services and software packages are being placed within an academic commons. Librarians—the "search and preserve" professionals who have acted as our guides in finding information for centuries—are now at the forefront of this movement. This is in part because librarians are well trained in information collection and retrieval and because such skills have been a part of the core courses at most schools of information and library science (SILS) for decades. It is only logical that the task of the creating and updating of an academic commons should equally be entrusted to the hands of those who will maintain a university's millennial library. The two are inseparable spatially, historically, and philosophically.

However, few guides exist to assist libraries in establishing an academic commons. Recent surveys of university libraries reveal that while many have a well-established or recently established academic commons, few exhibit a predictable pattern, either in structure or services offered. They are in a scattered array of form and function. Some academic commons have been created as clearinghouses to assist students in learning via the posting online of research and teaching guides. Others have been established to provide teachers with pedagogical resources, such as syllabi and outcome measurement tools to improve learning assessment. And still others have been created to assist academics in research. All of these are laudable and worthy purposes. They need not, however, be mutually exclusive, as they often appear to be at some universities nor located at various places within a university's administrative structure.

The millennial library, as will be defined and outlined in this book, is a singular place where all of the activities associated with helping students learn to learn, teachers learn to teach, and researchers learn to conduct research, collaboration, evaluation, and publication will be gathered within one portal. It will also be a place—both physical and online—where research is evaluated, archived, and distributed. It will be dynamic, modifying its purpose and services to accommodate changing technology, new software, and an ever-increasing "online, all-the-time cloud" environment. The days of libraries waiting for patrons to come in and seek a book from their dusty shelves are long past, if they ever existed. The millennial library and its academic commons will act as an educational community builder, and will be, as it always has been historically, the heart of every university.

But is it too late for libraries? Has technology overtaken university libraries? Has the need to use the services of a librarian been marginalized by the very technology that makes an academic commons possible (and necessary)?

The Millennial Library and the Academic Commons as the University's Information Source and Teacher

The examples abound. Until recently, if you lived in Kansas and wanted to read about the news in New York City's Gramercy Park neighborhood, you would be required to find a vendor who carried the local edition of a New York paper. Now, the inquisitive reader simply logs onto the *New York Times* website, and searches for the neighborhood's news. It is more than a matter of convenience. The *Times* is changing from its traditional role as a news source for New Yorkers, to an information center for a global community. Its difficulties, economically, revolve around its attempt to shift away from the traditional local print customers, to global online users, many of whom are interested in the comings and goings of Gramercy Park. Ignoring its local market would be tantamount to surrendering its responsibilities to the hundreds of other "reporters" who are ready and able to report online the activities within Gramercy Park.

So it is for libraries. A library in New York or in Kansas is no longer the library for patrons in those geographic areas, but to all of those potential patrons residing anywhere on the planet. Consider that not long ago university libraries stood as individual units, solitary, apart from each other. What a user of a particular library could find was what was in that user's library. And, to some extent, the holdings of a university's library were a mark of the institution's academic excellence, setting out a mark of a campus-wide commitment to learning, teaching, and research. Universities used the size of the holdings in their libraries, such as the nine million monographs at the University of Texas–Austin, as a tool to recruit both students and faculty and, perhaps, administrators. Much of this value on a library's holdings was based on geography, though the issue of "membership privileges" was also a factor. Local faculty, for instance, had more available services than visiting professors.

But sometimes the local holdings were not sufficient. Researchers seeking more information than was present in the holdings of their own particular university library were forced to travel many miles to access the sought-after materials at another institution. Some of these pilgrimages continue, in many cases, to view firsthand special collections that do not travel well and are rarely shared between libraries even today. Yet, even in this area of special collections, libraries are working to provide online digital records. For example, the University of Washington lists more than eighty special collections available online. As noted on the library's website:

> Our online collection comprises a unique presentation of selected primary source material for a variety of research needs. Researchers who are studying the historic and contemporary life of the region, as well as, those who need

> digital access to samples of our rare materials will find a selection of unique and unpublished artifacts such as photographs, architectural plans, historical maps, artwork, correspondence, pamphlets and ephemera.[4]

Today, the digital delivery of information contained in most libraries eliminates the need to travel to any particular physical location, other than to an Internet-ready computer. That is not to suggest all nine million monographs in Austin are available online, though that library is one of several institutions working with Google Books to make some of its holdings available electronically.[5] In addition, other libraries are moving in this direction, including the University of Michigan, Harvard University, Oxford University, the New York Public Library, Stanford University, the University of California libraries, the University of Wisconsin–Madison, the University of Virginia, the Complutense University of Madrid, the National Library of Catalonia, and the Library of Congress.[6]

This issue is raised because one of the primary roles for a university library's academic commons is to completely nullify geographic barriers and by doing so foster more collaboration regardless of the location of the researcher, the cohorts, or the local university library's holdings. In a way, this collaborative scheme has already been used millions of times using interlibrary loan (ILL). Conceptually, the cooperative agreements among libraries to share books and journals through ILL have allowed a researcher and publisher in one geographic area to work more closely with another at some distance. Yes, this one-way flow of information has existed since a researcher created the first citation. And, yes, the rapid delivery of materials via library-to-library electronic data sharing may be a harbinger of what is to come: multimodal sharing of "live" research in real time within an academic commons area online.

Yet, libraries have found that ILL is a double-edged sword. Yes, it can be used to quickly fulfill the needs of their patrons, far more quickly compared to physical travel to the source. Yes, library patrons can receive information at a click of a mouse via e-mail in the case of journal articles and some sections of books. The result in some cases, however, is that many of these patrons may believe they need never set foot within the library itself. This false belief must not be allowed to stand. If a library—or its academic commons—is nothing more than a delivery mechanism, then all that we have created is another reason not to know and use the full potential of the millennial library. A major part of the scheme proposed in this book is that drawing the patron to the brick-and-mortar library is a critical part of an academic commons and critical to academic success. Focusing just on the academic commons as an online vehicle for students and faculty overlooks the vast potential of millennial libraries, and, as a result, reduces the quality of learning, teaching, and research, and, by extension, threatens the university and social progress.

The role of the library as a mecca for students, teachers, and researchers, complete at some universities with the previously mentioned carrels, is in the midst of a deep and pervasive change. The impact of the delivery mechanism on the relevancy of the university library—left unaddressed by university administrators—has the potential of pushing the academic library into the shadows. The library is a building, to be certain. And, to some, its role is entirely transparent: it is an anonymous catalyst in the research ritual of data gathering. At some universities this "transparency" has led to a gap between the library and its patrons, whether they are students or faculty. Studies such as Frade and Washburn's "The University Library: The Center of a University Education" in 2006 have been published seemingly as a balm against the fears that libraries will no longer be relevant.[7] Even Basbanes's correct contention that "Libraries will remain important to colleges and universities"[8] seems to suggest that worries and doubt to the contrary exist inside and outside academic libraries. Frade and Washburn conclude that,

> Continuing change in the landscape of academia—such as the use of course management systems, hybrid course development, increased digitations of materials, changes in scholarly communication patterns, distance education programs, and new uses for personal assistance devices—will challenge the library to develop new ways of meeting the changing needs of faculty and students in order to remain central to the academic life on campus.[9]

All this argues for a more deep-throated call by university libraries to their constituencies, a call emphasizing the dynamic role libraries have already taken on and are expanding upon. Call it a reintroduction of faculty and students to a resource in which they rarely delve very deeply. Call it a reeducation of researchers—faculty, graduate students, or undergraduates—to the proper methods and best practices of online data mining. Term it an awakening of Web users to the reality that the best information is not found in a simple search of a tool, such as Google Scholar. Total access to all information, without training and guidance, renders research a hit or miss experience, with little or no standards. Not all information is equal in value, and the value must not be based purely on ease of access.

Millennial librarians will step forward and make their case to their patrons in a clear and unified voice: the path to the best research outcomes goes directly and unavoidably through its academic commons. This new millennial library requires a new branding, a new image, a new outreach to those who would miss the vast resources that are within its academic commons.

The Millennial Library and the Academic Commons as Gatekeepers

It is the very flood of information that is already upon us all that requires more involvement of and reliance on the modern millennial library. As noted by Bazillion in 2001, librarians must play an even more central role in judging what is preserved, especially given the possibility of direct-to-e-reserve publishing. "Gatekeeping is vital if we are not to be overwhelmed by the volume of self-publication present on the Web." Bazillion goes on to note that with the changing roles of the library, "the leap must be made if recorded knowledge is to be preserved and transmitted in an age when storage media are in flux."[10]

But this crisis in relevancy and purpose is only an issue if the library's role is restricted to the collection and storage of information. This is clearly not the role many libraries are accepting. In a time of rapidly growing online databases, online storage, and online libraries, such as ibiblio.org, the modern librarian is the keeper as well as the finder of information. Information regarding some rare detail—perhaps advertising history for a term paper—might have been found a decade ago in a few specific journals and within a shelf of monographs. It is now on a few pages buried somewhere within millions of websites. It takes a professional tracker to find the right data for students. It takes a millennial librarian with a learning commons. It also takes a millennial librarian to help faculty find the best pedagogical practices available within a teaching commons. Academics will look to the librarian of today to locate the best sources, the latest data, and most rare collections within a research commons. Finally, a specialized library will be required to help colleagues stay abreast of the latest tools available for use within these three academic commons. Keeping the millennial librarian on the leading edge of technological advances will require a LibTech commons.

The Millennial Library and the Academic Commons as Learning Catalysts

Libraries are no longer the "calm and quiet places" they were immediately following World War II.

> Information resources [then] were predominantly stable and static, resident on paper and microfilm. The innovations of that era included automated typewriters to produce catalog cards, book approval plans, photocopiers, and an increasing number of publications in microformat. Changes in collections and services came mainly by growth rather than metamorphosis.[11]

As the library underwent rapid changes and added new weapons to its repertory in the later part of the twentieth century, the institution also became "a resource for many and a partner of none . . . increasingly isolated in a decentralized, diverse, and competitive world."[12] Simply acting as an archive—print or electronic—will not reverse this trend that is isolating some libraries from the university patrons they serve.

To overcome this gap between patrons and libraries, an increased emphasis must be placed on library outreach and research services. Many libraries have instituted classes on new research gathering software and techniques, services such as computer-to-computer electronic information delivery of material housed at the library. The installation of such mundane but very popular coffee shops and dining areas targeting students are signs of outreach intended to reestablish a physical relevancy. The millennial library will constantly be filled and refilled with new archives, new tools, new jobs, and new expectations. Today's photocopiers create portable document format (PDF) files—then paper copies of selected research items. The created electronic documents are then e-mailed to the requesting researcher. Yes, we, seasoned academic researchers, know about this tool. But do all faculty? Do students? More importantly, do they know how to use these tools properly and efficiently?

Libraries have used subject-focused librarians for some years. Today, however, these subject-focused database experts are also engaged in directly working with classes of students in researching particular topics. This includes not only hosting training sessions within the library, but also visiting classes. This is a small step away from the old, pedestrian brick-and-mortar library, but represents a huge symbolic move for the millennial library.

All of this may be necessary to close whatever perceived gap exists between librarians and their patrons. The ability of researchers and students to use tools such as Google Scholar can allow some to remain ignorant of the highly specialized, efficient, and valued search techniques possessed by research librarians. As some research has suggested, young researchers are more likely to avoid any information databases that require modest registration. The fear is that rather than searching past these ephemeral barriers researchers will opt out to the easy-and-quick access to research findings. The result would be faster publishing, but lower research value. This is more than a question of esthetics: Progress relies on researchers accessing the best, most relevant information.

For students, the perceived value of the millennial library as a structure with computers, soft chairs, and hot coffee sells short the larger role the library is already playing in undergraduate learning. Students' success is higher when they feel confident they know where to look for research. Ironically, it may be that average graduate students understood this far more twenty years ago than they do today. As noted by Troll, very few of today's "get it now" students press beyond the first level, or "surface," of the Web. This surface level contains only 7 percent of the data appropriate for academic work. Few students dig deeper into the Web, into areas that are not indexed by search engines, into areas that contain information that is "1,000–2,000 times better in quality than the surface web."[13] Add to this the inability of commercial search engines to index much more than one-sixth of the surface Web, that students rarely use more than one search engine, and that they inaccurately presume that they are reaching the best information, and it is obvious why now, more than any time in history, future academic success will rely more and more on librarians.

Enter the Millennial Librarian

Direct interaction between faculty and librarians is more than just a matter of providing service to teachers and researchers. As suggested by Dilmore, when faculty experience direct, one-on-one interactions with librarians, the perception of the library as a valuable part of the university—and, most importantly, each faculty member—increases. Further, the degree of positive reactions increased in the study when the interactions between faculty and librarians also increased. Some of this may be simply a matter of people knowing each other, knowing their background and personality. But it is also a function of being able to put a face on a place. This new library will come to be more of a person, rather than just brick and mortar.[14] It is the personification of this new millennial library and its millennial librarian that will result in creation of an even more important role for both in the success of the hosting institution.

The emerging populations of millennial librarians that have appeared at universities worldwide understand this gap and are reaching out to students and faculty, offering exciting new tools and new services. We are witnessing a redefinition of what a library is, a profile that librarians have been aware of (if not their patrons) for several years, if not decades. It is a role made possible fiscally and successful technologically more than ever in history. And with the dynamic, engaged, and dedicated millennial librarians, the possibilities for success in learning, teaching, and research have never been greater. This is the time for the university librarian to claim the role of catalyst and leader: a professional that is engaged in every aspect of what makes a university a global asset to students and faculty. The millennial library will not only be the center of innovation as libraries have been for many years; it will be seen as the technological resource by those who need it most: students and faculty. It will be their partner in success. It will reinsert itself into academic conversations by offering more than what some patrons have assumed (incorrectly) that it is: a remote copier (and ready operators). It will become "noisy" as some have suggested, noisy with the "sounds" of research and collaboration, just as it must have been in the days of Ptolemy. This new role is the "academic commons" and the commotion it will generate will come from project collaborations, research publishing, grant writing, and critical thinking and learning.

Libraries have always played a critical role in learning, just as they have been silent partners behind the most successful teachers and researchers. The millennial library is not just a part of the university landscape; it is the most vital, most central part of the institution's education and research success. As Frade and Washburn noted in 2006,

> Continuing changes in the landscape of academia—such as the use of course management systems, hybrid course development, increased digitization of materials, changes in scholarly communication patterns, distance education programs, and new uses for personal assistance devices—will challenge the library to develop new ways of meeting the changing needs of the faculty and students in order to remain central to the academic life of campus.[15]

And it is argued here that not only is the online nature of the library changing, but that the physical place on every campus that is designated as the "library" is also changing. In fact, rather than diminished by the digitization of information, the physical library will increase in importance as a place of innovation. As argued by Shill and Tonner in 2003, the library as a physical place on campus "serves a number of socially valuable roles." This is especially true when the library adds new services.[16] Bringing these services to the forefront will make the millennial librarian a more relevant resource by providing a competitive edge to researchers and students.

As this book progresses, keep in mind that the millennial library is both the virtual academic commons and the physical brick and mortar that comprise the world of the modern university library. And, most importantly, the success of the academic commons will depend on the millennial librarian, who will assure its relevance with constant upgrades and additions.

THE ACADEMIC COMMONS

The creation and perceived need of an academic online area within a university web network is a fairly recent phenomenon. Unfortunately, given the vague definitions that have swirled around the activity, identifying which university established the first academic commons is almost impossible. Suffice to suggest that Stanford University and the Massachusetts Institute of Technology are good bets for first on the block in the United States with an academic commons. More important than who was first, in the end, is the fair conclusion that if your university does not have an academic commons or is not considering establishing one, it is woefully behind and/or out of touch.

Part of the challenge in nailing down who set up the first academic commons may be largely linked to the wide variety of actual definitions of the term "commons." Almost all universities have launched websites within their own networks intended to serve a variety of purposes that address their own interpretation of an academic commons, including:

- An academic area for students, with specific research-support tools and services
- A home for a university library's online collection of electronic archives that might include faculty research, publishing, and possibly data sets stored in a common language
- Research and teaching support for academics, enabling efficient sharing of data and information with colleagues both inside and outside the university

Included in this book are examples of universities that are either operating or implementing an academic commons. These include not just the larger schools, such as the University of Michigan and those in the California state system, that are perceived—rightly or wrongly—as able to afford such a service as an academic commons. This text will explore academic commons projects at smaller schools, such as Ohio University, Colorado State University, and Montana State University.

Supporting Student Learning

Academic learning commons intended to assist students have sprung up in the new millennium at dozens of universities worldwide.

> The room, located on the ground floor of the library, reflects a change in approach by the University of Texas Libraries towards creating spaces that meld current technologies with environmental comforts in a way that accommodates the needs of the modern library user.[17]

The goal for what are being labeled an information commons or learning commons is to encourage improvements in undergraduate research, writing, and group tasks. Students are assisted by subject-specific librarians, who tutor students on the most efficient strategies for accessing and using everything from online search engines to the library databases. These student commons come in a variety of shapes and sizes. Typically, they involve the addition of computers, the creation of group work centers, and the encouragement of students to be "noisy"—that is, talk with each other in groups. In all regards they are a significant shift for traditional libraries: no sending students into the stacks, no long hours sifting through dusty indexes, no long evenings working in isolation and silence. To some degree, with the addition of off-campus mechanisms and support tools, these student-focused learning commons are facilitating a renewed connection with students who might otherwise never engage with their university library. The student commons will be examined in more detail in chapter 1.

Supporting Faculty Collaboration: Teaching and Research

In the fall of 2007, Ohio University rededicated the third floor of its Alden Library to a new idea: a faculty commons. The purpose, according to a university press release, was to provide a "dynamic center of activity for faculty coming together from different disciplines across campus."[18] Included in the renovations were "smart rooms" enabling faculty online conferencing, media development rooms, and several centers devoted to teaching, technology, and research. In addition, specific librarians in control of such research-related areas as library collections were also housed in the faculty commons.

The Ohio University library administrators decided that an online presence could be enhanced by a physical presence, a model being employed at other forward-thinking institutions. The design of the faculty commons area was structurally little more than a reshuffling of existing resources, with the addition of new technologies, into a single unit intended to serve a specific user need. Rather than having media development on one floor, collections on another, and conference rooms on a third, all of these resources were physically moved into one area. This outside-out perspective engendered a closer relationship with faculty at the university by showing a real desire on the library's part to provide a more efficient delivery of targeted services. It also showed an understanding by the library of the technology necessary to enhance teaching and research academic outcomes.

Such a commitment to teaching and research is not solely the responsibility of the university library, though it may be best suited to accomplish the goals of such an endeavor. Drawing the university as a whole into such a project takes time and patience. As noted in a report published by the Carnegie Foundation for the Advancement of Teaching,

> Making a place for serious intellectual work on teaching and learning in higher education is a long-term agenda, and there's much still to be done and plenty of questions still to be answered.[19]

The Carnegie report went on to suggest that researchers have enjoyed a more robust tradition than teachers, whose craft "in many settings, has been largely private work, guided by tradition, but uninformed by shared inquiry or understanding of what works."[20] Creating a teaching commons is one path to encouraging the type of direct criticism and improvement sometimes lacking within an often-isolated university department. For example, rather than falling back on the overused and highly unreliable teaching evaluations produced by highly stressed students at the end of every semester, a teaching commons could offer a department chair a dynamic mechanism to gauge and improve an individual instructor's pedagogical methods and standards through training and mentor feedback.

And, although faculty have a long history of collaboration (more in the sciences than in the humanities), many faculty still seek easier ways to work within teams of collaborators located inside and outside their universities. They are looking for pathways to collaborative areas, through such tools as Skype, Wikis, and Second Life. They are demanding faster Internet connections, larger allowances for file attachments—such as is available at TransferBigFiles.com and other similar websites—and more space to store and share data and writings. And yet today, too many are even ignorant of the variety of tools a library can provide, such as self-filling online ILL forms, much less RefWorks and the vast variety of other tools already available. As part of this new research commons, faculty will be made aware of all of the tools that can assist them in their publishing, as well as tutor them on their use.

Chapters 2 and 3 will examine challenges related to the creation and maintenance of new teaching and research commons.

Data Storage, Retrieval, and Publishing

Universities for many years have maintained an electronic database of materials collected or created on campus. This activity typically involves the electronic storage of theses and dissertations, as well as electronic coursepacks used by teachers. The former activity—graduate student publication storage—was created, for the most part, as a reaction to space limitations and distance access. The latter of these activities have, at times, involved the misunderstanding and/or misapplication of the fair use portion of the U.S. Copyright Act by academics.

The nature and interest in electronic reserves increased sharply after the action in 2008 by the National Institutes of Health to require public access to funded research.[21] This decision certainly spurred many universities to create or increase use of electronic reserves. These e-reserves are intended to preserve works created by campus academicians. And, many library science researchers have focused on the best practices associated with such archives.

However, the larger challenge posed by e-reserves is the nature of publishing itself. Are e-reserves online journals? Consider that rather than shipping research articles and support data to outside publishing entities, only to eventually require these same articles be made available within a university's e-archive, some institutions and researchers are looking at publishing directly to a university commons area. These research commons lack only a few—but critical—components of online journals: editing, peer review, and formatting. For example, Kansas State University established a publishing operation in 2007 called New Prairie Press (NPP). And, in June 2009, announced that it was interested in being a home to new online, open access journals. The faculty member in charge of managing the new press noted on the NPP news page that it could not offer any editorial support, which would include, presumptively, peer review and formatting. Yet, without these vital tools that are an essential part of publishing, is NPP really a publisher? Or is it really a hosting site—an e-reserve—with a name?

Structured differently, NPP could present a type of online journal publishing operation that might support teams of individuals and associations by supplying editors, a peer review system, and Web managers capable of maintaining an open access journal. Were NPP to offer editorial support—management of the content side of the journal—it would, in fact, be a more complete publishing operation. Without these support functions, NPP cannot fulfill the role of a true publisher.

Many universities have provided an academic press, some centuries old. A handful of these academic presses are already engaged in servicing multiple journals, some within their universities. Consider the University of Toronto Press (UT Press). The *Journal of Scholarly Research* is among the many journals to which it provides editorial services. The journal's editors and editorial board review submitted articles. Accepted works are then sent to the UT Press, which carefully edits the work, provides the author galleys, and then completes the publishing process. That last process of publishing could as easily be an online journal as a printed one. As noted by Amy Desrochers, Production Coordinator at the University of Toronto Press:

> I don't think the editorial structure would change very much if journals were to go strictly online, skipping the printing stage. The material would still have to be copyedited, typeset, then checked by proofreaders and authors/editors to verify

> nothing was lost in the move from the copyedited Word file to the Design file. From there the online files would be created, which only skips one printer file in between. The process would still be the same.[22]

This raises an important question: is the role of the millennial library to also act as a university publisher? Is the act of a professor putting a nonpeer-reviewed research article within an e-reserve an act of publishing? As more and more online journals are created within operations, such as NPP, it is clear that there is a need for some best practices standards. If within a multijournal online environment, such university presses are able to provide services to these small, independent journals, will the fees be sufficient to cover the substantial costs for establishing the editorial team, the bank of peer reviewers, and the website formatters? At the level of the independent online journal, where would that funding originate? Would that funding be a reliable flow that would support the online, presumably open access, journals in the years and decades to come? This may be a dangerous quagmire for any university and its library: at what point and what level should a library or its university be engaged in publishing? More importantly, is the university committed to the long-term costs of such a new journal? Researchers and readers rely on their academic journals for many things, not the least of which is that, once started, they will remain sustainable. This sustainability must derive from something more than good intentions. Simply because one can do something does not mean one should do it. Creating online academic journals should be carefully weighed within the long-term goals of academia, not merely within the scope of what is technologically or, seemingly, economically feasible. In section 2, chapters 4–7 will examine challenges related to the creation of a new storage, retrieval, and publishing regimen.

Selling the Millennial Library to Its Stakeholders

In section 3, chapter 9 will address the need for the millennial library to increase and improve its engagement with its stakeholders. The time of the library being seen as anything other than central to the success of any university is over. The presidents and provosts who consider libraries as only a necessary cost must be brought into the light: The millennial library is key to the success of every student and faculty member at every university. Millennial librarians are catalysts for improvements in learning, teaching, and research.

Yet, while this may be evident to those familiar with the growing importance of online learning, teaching, and research, those who hold the primary budgeting roles in a university are often in the dark. Through the use of surveys, marketing techniques that stress outside-in communication, and social networks, millennial libraries will redefine their critical roles in the university and reeducate the institution's administration of the growing interconnection of the academic commons with scholarly success.

The Future of Millennial Libraries

In chapter 10, we will consider a few of the long-term challenges facing millennial libraries, including institutional politics and necessary upgrades in staffing, as well as issues of access to holdings and ongoing relevancy. The long-term sustainability of all libraries and the work of library staff have always relied on value attached to the services rendered. Perhaps one of the most challenging issues the millennial library must face is change itself: Can it be nimble enough to absorb change, increase the willingness to embrace new ideas and new methods, and ensure that the trust that will be placed in it will be sustained and rewarded? Assisting librarians in taking on the rapidly changing environment of online learning, teaching, and research should include the creation of its own commons, a LibTech commons. This fourth commons would serve the teams dedicated to keep the learning, teaching, and research commons up to date and reliable. Through the LibTech commons, millennial librarians will have their own area to share ideas on a global platform.

Those of us keenly interested in the future roles of our university libraries have witnessed massive shifts in thinking in just the past two decades. We are at the edge of a vast universe of possibilities: coordinated and sharing databases, rapid and real-time research collaboration, valued online student-mentor constructs, and many, many more. We see the rise of a global library and with it, perhaps, the creation of a new science, "searchology," and its professional "searchologist." In many ways, these searchologists will become the sages, the specially trained individuals who know where to find ancient tomes, as well as the latest breakthrough. They will be experts of not one science, except that of the search itself. But, whatever the turns that are to come, the academic commons, whether learning, teaching, research, or LibTech within the millennial library, will play a critical role in the future of the university and society.

Yes, these are heady times for libraries and librarians. Technology and the web have done to the millennial library what they have done in all other areas of progress: enlarged and expanded the impact and reach of services inside and outside the university. As we move forward, we must remind ourselves that libraries are even more important today as a physical place of learning than they have been in the past. We should also remind ourselves that many libraries and librarians have already adopted many of the suggestions that will be made in this book, as highlighted in the sidebars, and will continue to add to and improve on their roles as not only supporters of learning, teaching, and research but their own craft as millennial libraries and librarians.

NOTES

1. Martha Kyrillidou and Les Bland, eds., *ARL Report: 2007–2008* (Washington, D.C.: Association of Research Libraries, 2009).
2. Matt Raymond, "How Tweet It Is: Library Acquires Entire Twitter Archive," *Library of Congress*, blogs.loc.gov/loc/2010/04/how-tweet-it-is-library-acquires-entire-twitter-archive/ (accessed 23 April 2010).
3. Carla Stoffle, Karyle Butcher, Jerry Campbell, Betty Hahn, Sharon Hogan, Charlene Hurt, Sarah Michalak, Jim Mullins, and Lance Query, "The Keystone Principles," *Association of Research Libraries: A Bimonthly Report* (1999).
4. content.lib.washington.edu/cdm-ayp/search.php (accessed 12 July 2010).
5. University of Texas–Austin, "FAQs about the University of Texas—Google Books Library Project," www.lib.utexas.edu/google/faqs.html (accessed 10 April 2010).
6. University of Texas-Austin, "FAQs about the University of Texas—Google Books Library Project."
7. Patricia Frade and Allyson Washburn, "The University Library: The Center of a University Education?" *Portal: Libraries and the Academy* 6, no. 3 (2006): 327.
8. Steve Stanek, "Academic Libraries Thrive Amid Technology," *Chicago Tribune*, 2 March 2003, sec. *Education Today*.
9. Frade and Washburn, "The University Library: The Center of a University Education?" 327.
10. Richard Bazillion, "Planning the Academic Library of the Future," *Portal: Libraries and the Academy* 1, no. 2 (2001): 151–160.
11. Steve Marquardt, "Managing Technological Changing Performance Appraisal to Performance Evaluation," in *Managing Change in Academic Libraries*, ed. Joseph J. Branin (Binghamton, N.Y.: Haworth Press, 1996), 101–110.
12. Richard M. Dougherty, "Achieving Preferred Library Futures in the 1990s: What Is Required?" in *Research Libraries: Yesterday, Today and Tomorrow*, ed. William J. Walsh (Westport, Conn.: Greenwood Press, 1993), 49.
13. Denise A. Troll, "How and Why Libraries Are Changing: What We Know and What We Need to Know," *Portal: Libraries and the Academy* 2, no. 1 (2002): 99–123.
14. Donald H. Dilmore, "Librarian/Faculty Interaction at Nine New England Collages," *College & Research Libraries* 57, no. 3 (May 1996): 274–284.
15. Frade and Washburn, "The University Library: The Center of a University Education?" 327.
16. Harold B. Shill and Shawn Tonner, "Creating a Better Place: Physical Improvements in Academic Libraries, 1995–2002," *College & Research Libraries* 64 (November 2003): 431–466.

17. “The University (of Texas) Federal Credit Union Student Learning Commons,” www.lib.utexas.edu/pcl/commons (accessed 10 June 2009).

18. Mary Reed, “Faculty Commons Opens in Alden,” Ohio University News and Information, www.ohio.edu/outlook/07-08/September/59n.cfm (accessed 17 June 2009).

19. Pat Hutchings and Mary T. Huber, “Building the Teaching Commons,” Carnegie Foundation for the Advancement of Teaching, www.carnegiefoundation.org/perspectives/sub.asp?key=245&subkey=800 (accessed 17 June 2009).

20. Hutchings and Huber, “Building the Teaching Commons.”

21. *The National Institutes of Health Public Access Policy,* Public Law 2008 (accessed 8 June 2008).

22. Telephone conversation with Amy Desrochers, 7 June 2010.

Part One

SUPPORTING STUDENTS AND FACULTY

Millennial libraries will be active participants in the enhancement of university faculty research and teaching via new technologies, staff support, and specialized training. This is a major shift for most librarians, who have tended to be left in a passive role by university faculty unaware of the resources available in modern libraries. As part of this shift, more and more libraries have already established a commons area in which tools and data can be stored and shared. These commons are known by various names, from information commons to student commons, to those that do not use the word "commons" for what they have created. But too many stop at the student, neglecting the important role the library can play in the success of the university faculty.

For example, some have made their library staff available to assist tenure-track faculty in identifying and using new databases and online analysis tools. Many others have established training classes for faculty to learn how to use these new resources that commonly help faculty maximize their time and improve their research. A university library's research commons can provide faculty with the latest research software, including links to many online support packages located outside the campus network.

A teaching commons can also pull together the various teaching aids, providing both a dedicated online portal to the latest ideas, as well as a physical space with all the various on-campus support units supporting university pedagogy. Grading tools, assessment rubrics, and teaching enhancement videos are placed within a teaching commons that may represent the most significant codification of the multitude of various pedagogic resources created by various institutions in the past few decades. Rather than relying strictly on the limited resources available within a single institution, faculty can tap into hundreds, if not thousands of teaching improvement, measurement, and assessment guides instantly.

The enhancement of faculty performance, both in research and teaching, accrues value to every university in higher rankings academically and in more successful graduates, who then become more successful alums. In the age of new technology, such commons are not just popular add-ons to a library's function on campus, they are integral parts of the forward-moving, forward-thinking university. Carefully planning and implementing such faculty-centered research and teaching commons portals can reap enormous benefits to every university. Every university that is committed to its faculty must be equally committed to research and teaching commons. Any university committed to engendering progress by fostering the best research and the best teaching possible should be adding these three commons to their network. It is no longer a question of if but when the university administration will provide the necessary support to make their millennial library—and its learning, teaching, and research commons—a reality.

Chapter One

The Learning Commons

THE CHALLENGE TO LEARNING

The crisis in education—whether it is worries over student assessment, course outcomes, or teaching standards—has generated a lot of heat, but not much light. The discussions surrounding education can be hyperbolic at times. The state of higher education in this country has been the topic of government committees, education seminars, and report after report. One, issued every two years by the National Center for Public Policy and Higher Education, reported in 2008 that while some progress had been made since 2000, the status of the nation's students in many "areas, the center assesses—preparation, participation, affordability, degree completion, benefit to states, and learning—is inadequate."[1] Some news reports have suggested the troubles start in high school, before students enter the higher education system.[2] Researchers darkly predict that United States' leadership in areas like science is threatened by poor standards and low outcomes.[3] And still others suggest that some universities have a "revolving door" mentality, with high numbers of students dropping out of school between their first and second year, and fewer and fewer students graduating.[4] But only some, if any, have talked about the role of university libraries as part of a potential solution.

This is not to suggest that university libraries can be the cure-all for what ails incoming freshmen or juniors dropping out of college. However, it can be a resource to solve some of the most egregious problems, such as poor research practices, poor studying techniques, poor pedagogy, and a lack of understanding about what the academic library can provide in all of these areas. For example, several researchers have noted that undergraduate and graduate students are highly prone to use only the top level of the Web, what has been labeled the "surface Web."[5] For the most part, the more valuable data—especially that within proprietary databases and dynamically generated content—is not accessed. The result is that students believe that if they cannot find the information within a few clicks using a general search engine, the data does not exist. This belief by students that answers are just one or two clicks away has fueled a culture that believes quick access, easy access, and open access is the same as a deeper, more profitable database search. This is compounded by the thought that search engines, such as Google, can access everything that is online, which is patently false.

This culture of quickness over quality is compounded further by the general ignorance of most students for how to conduct data searches. As noted in a report by OCLC in 2006, when it comes to students evaluating the services offered through a library website compared to a public search engine, the latter wins out in the minds of undergraduates in several key areas. Students in large numbers believe the library is more trustworthy and accurate, but they rate search engines as more reliable, cost-effective, easy to use, convenient, and fast.[6] The report also found that three out of four students ask a librarian for help, rather than attempt to solve the problem using a library computer. Less than one in five actually rely on a computer to solve the problem. Only 2 percent of the students surveyed in this report used an available online librarian through the "frequently asked question" area. These disconnects, combined with the impatience of youth, have created an information gap that is the core raison d'être for a learning commons. This commons—dedicated to introducing students to the special services and technologies housed within the millennial library—can result in lower dropout rates and more successful graduates.

THE SOLUTION: THE LEARNING COMMONS

Libraries, perhaps more than any other entity on a university campus, are committed to new technology. Despite tight budgets resulting in a library providing access only to a modest number of computers, university libraries are still finding new ways to help students, and are reenergizing older methods, such as employing library assistants available for training incoming freshmen. The fact is libraries—even those not touting an academic commons—are far ahead in the digitizing of information and the utilization of automation compared to many other professions (medicine, law, education, museums, legislatures, and law enforcement come to mind). And, it has long been recognized in the schools of information and library science that electronic material and print are both vital parts of the modern institution's holdings.

What the millennial library will offer will be a new cyberlibrary "face"—be that a portal or redesigned website—constructed to communicate in a language and style to help new and disaffected patrons. The poor research habits mentioned earlier may require this new library, this millennial library, to reach out to undergraduates in ways completely foreign and often very uncomfortable for library specialists.

Reforming the lax habits of students in how they find information is critical. In a forest of trillions of bits of information, the millennial librarian is not just vital but irreplaceable. Information delivery, a generic activity that constitutes the core of what many libraries have long deemed their main mission, has been subsumed by electronic platforms that are a poor academic substitute. Students access websites, blogs, Twitter, Facebook, and other social networks, often believing they are conducting acceptable academic research. To counteract this trend, they need help in understanding how to access databases and books from anywhere and everywhere. Almost three out of four undergraduate students surveyed in a 2002 Pew Institute study reported they could find the research they needed without visiting their school library. In addition, "Nearly three-quarters (73 percent) of college students say they use the Internet more than the library, while only 9 percent said they use the library more than the Internet for information searching."[7] This is an unacceptable and very unreliable arrangement.

In this chapter, we will explore the various goals for libraries that are addressing the needs of the new undergraduate. These include:

1. Opening up the library as an access point to the latest and best information via a rebranding campaign
2. Teaching students the best practices to using databases, but also how to create the search terms that will produce the best results, whether online or in the stacks
3. Positioning the library as a campus-wide resource available by inserting librarians into academic departments and dorms

To meet these new goals, libraries will have to modify not only their physical environment, but also the traditional roles information specialists play in teaching. Waiting for the student to come to the library will not adequately assist learners in the improvement of their academic skills. But, simply putting database links on the library website will not work either. Undergraduates require a portal "through which students and faculty will access the vast amount of information resources,"[8] both online and in print, and through which they will rebuild an active and one-on-one relationship with their subject librarians.

This portal must guide students through the massive maze of databases and e-journals to the "deep" web, as well as the stacks, and then show them how to create the best search terms to find the best information, as well as how to use the print materials to find other sources of information. This is already happening in what some universities are calling information commons, academic commons, or knowledge banks. For the purpose of this book, we will refer to this "place" as a learning commons.

Many libraries in North America already are reacting to a demand by students that the delivery of information and the tools to analyze that data be made easier to access and faster to locate. As noted by Gardner and Eng, "Today's undergraduates are pushing the academic library to rethink the ways in which it presents its most basic services."[9] The delivery of resources that libraries have provided to students for decades now requires a new approach, a new relationship with information users. Complicating the situation, as noted by Jager, is that many students are unfamiliar with the advantages of a university library.[10] Some, especially those engaged in off-campus distance education, have no ready physical access and believe they can make their way through their years at the university without walking into the library at all. Graduate school students and paraprofessionals engaged in distance learning still see a need for the resources the library can provide, but only if they know about these resources and can quickly access them, again online, in the stacks, and at a distance. Other students, such as incoming freshmen, rarely use the library, perhaps because of some perceptions formed by their engagement with their previous high school libraries or a basic ignorance of the tools and support available. In the OCLC report, De Rosa and her fellow researchers found that college students are twice as likely to rate their university library as having worthwhile information compared to high school student ratings of their secondary school library. And, high school students are 24 percent less likely to report that librarians provide worthwhile information compared to students at a university.[11]

All of these situations—ignorance of the resources available, availability of library holdings and tools at a distance and online, and a lack of prior experience in an institutional library—require that the university library focus its outreach on the branding process employed by students. This starts by determining and describing the brand image that already exists within the minds of students (as measured by a survey or one-on-one contact opportunities), developing tools to modify this brand, and then implementing the campaign. As noted by Reeg-Steidinger, Madland, and Hagness, "the value of (customer) service must be determined by the users. Students must be able to define what they need for their success; too often academic librarians have determined what students should have to succeed."[12]

BRANDING THE LEARNING COMMONS

Call it packaging, call it simple advertising nomenclature, or call it little more than reintroducing students to what libraries have been offering their patrons for years. Whatever name a library and its university gives its learning commons, administrators must first understand that students are in control of the library's brand. This brand may include beliefs and attitudes about the library that are both negative and uninformed. Finding out the attitudes and beliefs of incoming students requires little more than a simple online survey that includes a five-point Likert scale. This survey might include questions regarding high school library usage, familiarity with online resources, and general feelings about the library.

The survey should reveal the attitudes of incoming students, giving the library a baseline to compare not only year-to-year new users, but also the progression of the group members as they matriculate through their college years. Librarians should not be surprised if they find that first term students are largely unaware of what a university library can offer. The information gap between incoming freshmen and librarians is large, according to researchers. Too many students have neglected, according to Reeg-Steidinger, Madland, and Hagness in 2005, "to turn to the library for help, thinking the Internet will solve their research needs. . . ."[13] On the other hand, many researchers have found that large numbers of students, and in some academic areas this amounts to more than a majority, still use the university library.[14] The survey can provide the library staff with a snapshot of where the needs of their particular university students are most profound and, literally, where their patrons' "heads are at."

For instance, some students fail to understand the impact a library can have on their performance in class work and tests. Rather than waiting for students to stumble upon and discover the library's resources via trial and error, "librarians must give their users a reason to want to come to the library, and this can be accomplished by a 'customer-driven' staff."[15] And, indeed, many libraries are deep into this process of outreach.

But, it need not end there. Communicating the values of the library in the language of the incoming freshman is another vital key to success. Rather than suggesting the library can help a student search for sources for a paper, the message might be more relevant if it directly addresses the patron's need: "We can turn that C paper into Gold," or "Suffering from the C Blues. We have the fix." Such research-based "advertising" can shift the brand image of the library held by all students, not just those new to campus. Of course, all of this must be accomplished in the oppressive air of static or falling budgets. Yet, with online Web 2.0 communication opportunities, the cost of such a campaign could be minimal. Above all, no library that is targeting students should believe print brochures (very costly items) are necessary or effective. The fact is, more casual, helpful language in an e-mail or through Facebook is likely to be far more effective than (stale) advertising campaigns using static and costly print materials. The library's advertising campaign should target students where the students are—online—and in a platform they are most likely to use, such as mobile devices and social networks.

THE MILLENNIAL LIBRARIAN AS A ONE-ON-ONE GUIDE

The library should never pass up the chance to ask students face-to-face what they are trying to accomplish. That is, rather than asking a perplexed student what database she is looking for, ask what question she needs to answer. Students have a better chance describing what they need in terms of what they lack than in terms of what the library can offer. "Roaming" librarians can look for those students who need help finding information, whether the patron is in the stacks or using a database. These engaged librarians—perhaps better described as guides or mentors—might be wielding handheld online devices such as iPads running Twitter and Facebook, as well as the library's databases. This is an opportunity to show immediate results: helping students find the right database or monograph for the right job to produce the best result, all in a forest of trillions of options. It can also provide the librarian with an opportunity for "customer feedback." The new dynamic is very similar to the person (library patron) who has fallen into a hole and calls for help from those passing by. Help comes when someone (the millennial librarian) jumps into the hole. The librarian patron, puzzled by this, asks why the librarian has jumped into the hole. "Because I know the way out." Millennial librarians know the latest tools, the most up-to-date databases, and the best resources. And, most importantly, they are uniquely qualified to show students how to use the best search terms to find the best information, not just that buried deep within the Internet, but also within print monographs and journals. The millennial librarian's first task might be to dissuade incoming freshmen of the notion that "if it isn't online and in the first ten sites on the list, it doesn't exist."

Offering students a newly designed and clearly purposed learning commons in terms of what matters to them can reshuffle the deck of existing attitudes. It is not only adding additional services and features, but repackaging the resulting structure in something specifically aimed at the target consumer: students. The brand will evolve from positive outcomes, but will be built on realistic expectations that can be met.

BEST PRACTICES: TEACHING LEARNERS HOW TO LEARN

Finding information is not the problem students face. Finding the right information is and guiding students to that "best" information can be a key element in a student's success on a term paper. Teaching them how to identify the "okay" sources from better sources of information on their own is key to a student's college, and lifetime, experience. The troubles often start with the task of differentiating an academic journal source from a nonscholarly magazine, or a valid book source from something posted on Wikipedia. The belief among some students that "if it is online, it must be valid" is only superseded, at times, by the immediate and instantaneous desire on the part of students to cite "something, anything." The very nature of the web is to render all information not only free but also equal, at least in the minds of some users. And, while students usually understand the noncitable nature of an encyclopedia, they are not always so clear on what is fair game online. Using Wikipedia as a source of information is perfectly valid. Using it as a scholarly source of information is usually inappropriate. As noted by Waters and Greenstein, not all information is equal.[16]

The trouble is that students often cannot determine what constitutes a valid source of information and, in many cases, simply use what is the easiest to find. Guiding students not only to the best sources, but also how to dig deeper into the research materials they find is uniquely suited to librarians. A student who cannot find any scholarly works on the impact of advertising on children will remain convinced the topic has never been researched, unless he is pointed to the right database. The student who looks for works dealing with education and the elderly in LexisNexis may indeed find some works, but not ones appropriate for an essay in a sociology class. The bottom line is that without guidance all information appears to be equal.

The seemingly constant appearance of new software platforms—such as SweetSearch (www.sweetsearch.com), a resource rolled out in 2009 mainly geared toward students in grammar and high school—requires an awareness of what is new, and possibly, what is just around the corner. If this feels like a 24/7 activity, it is. Just as researchers chase after new grants, and administrators are keenly aware of new endowments, so the millennial library must be "plugged in" when it comes to new software and hardware advances.

An up-to-date learning commons enhances the student's research activities, including access and use of databases, recognition of valid sources, writing skills, and proofing of work. To accomplish this, many libraries have crafted a combination of study/research area options blended with staff assistance targeting the student's experience (or lack thereof) with research files.

As a physical place, the learning commons can include group working areas equipped with multiscreen computers that promote collaborative work among students. Group activity may be in the commons area with other single-person stations. Often they are in separate, though not large, rooms that can be reserved in advance for several hours. Note that area private businesses, especially coffee shops, located around many universities have rooms (usually not complete with computers, but often with free wireless access) set aside for groups. And, some libraries have these rooms, but usually they are reserved for faculty and administrative committee meetings. These group rooms are specifically for students and are designed to enhance the team effort.

In some cases the software packages offered within a library network include high-end audiovisual editors, as well as other software identified as useful in the aforementioned student surveys. The specific features of these rooms, probably not found anywhere else on campus, can be designed around the student needs. A simple interface on the library's main website can manage room reservations and allow students to book the space in advance. It can also help identify in advance specific needs the groups may require for their study/creation sessions.

Of course, a learning commons may also have large, multiuser "quiet" rooms with individual workstations. These rooms can be tailored to meet the needs of specific types of students, either within large areas, such as science writing, or more defined topics such as special collections or biographies. Again, students should be allowed to reserve these workstations using a web-based menu on the library's site.

Students also expect a physical location where they can either use a supplied desktop, their own laptop, or handheld device to access the Internet.[17] This need not be a quiet corner of the library. In fact, this area may be considered the "noisy" area of the library. As a dean at a mid-eastern university noted in July 2009, the student commons area is becoming increasingly noisy, much to the concern of some older patrons, typically graduate students and faculty.[18] Few undergraduates complain, she noted, perhaps because many of these students are literally "tuned out" via portable music devices and do not hear the "noise."

The size of such a commons area is driven more often by what space is available than on an assessment of need. Some universities have taken to removing low-usage materials, such as current periodicals, to create the necessary open space. Some have sifted through their stacks, eliminating books rarely used. Some have added mobile stacks to compress storage space. Some have shifted holdings to reserve centers, sometimes in cooperation with other nearby universities. Some, as is the case with my own library, have done all of these.

What has been put in these commons areas also varies by university. In general, bench tables are lined up and either desks for computers or laptop docking stations installed. Some universities provide laptops on a lending basis. The computers are connected to the library network by "fat" wire or wirelessly. Software is either installed on each machine or provided by the network. The latter is the most popular recent trend. The actual programs provided are generally Microsoft Office and Adobe CS packages, as well as specialized tools such as analysis tools like SAS or SPSS. Again, software needs can be addressed via student surveys. Finally, while millennial students have proven to be familiar with a large number of software packages, the techniques students often employ in using these tools are inadequate and hit-or-miss. Expert assistance should be available either physically in the learning commons area within the library or available through chat or blogs via the help section of the library website, or both. A list of possible software packages, including open access options, is included in Appendix B.

In addition to computers and laptop docking stations, some university student learning commons include a dining area, with everything from coffee to donuts to sandwiches. Many university library surveys have found that offering dining on-site is a priority for students working on projects. Again, the format of these food courts varies widely, based on funding and space. They might be located in a library basement, entry area, or at a nearby site. The intent is to make the library experience of conducting research or meeting in teams comfortable and convenient.

As students work in the learning commons, they will collect data that usually requires storage for use later at other locations, such as classes or their homes. Storage of research gathered by students might require a download of the information to a memory device. Given the potential viruses inherent with memory "sticks" and other storage media, requiring the students to send their collected data to their own e-mail account may be more strategic. However, with user-supplied hardware, such as memory devices, comes the potential for viruses. Ideally, and very likely in the near future, many libraries will provide an area within the library's own server network for student work and data transfer. Given issues of infection, reliability, slow load speeds, and the size limitations for attachments using some e-mail clients, this solution is already being adopted in libraries that are blessed with the necessary funding. Such online storage of information allows students to seamlessly move back and forth between online research areas (and computers) and offline reading and writing. Having space on the library server for student work in some ways harkens back to the student carrels of the previous century, where library materials (e.g., books, journals) could be stored for later use. The new online carrels, however, would be available to students from within the library, as well as in their homes or at other locations. And given the very low cost of online storage these days, petabytes of data could be accommodated.

But none of what we have discussed thus far will amount to much without a key ingredient: a new kind of mobile, techno-savvy librarian.

THE MILLENNIAL LIBRARIAN: TRAINED AND MOBILE

In the summer of 2008, Google search engine technologists "stopped in awe" at encountering a very large number of unique URLs: one trillion.[19] This number is not just a large forest of information: This is an impossibly large forest of information. Sifting the good from the bad, the reliable from the suspect, the right paths from the wrong choices are not only difficult tasks; they are ones that escape even the best, most up-to-date researcher. The solution for some researchers is to rely on peer opinion, presented within online communities that promote sharing and verification of new information and ideas. These e-communities grow, thrive, die, and change. They join with others, split off from previous large groups, and, consequently, exhibit a constant state of flux. And, while of value to trained researchers, these online communities remain inaccessible to the average student. What these students require is a guide, a person who can help them navigate the Web.

The millennial librarians are new state-of-the-art sifters, catalogers of information, sponsors of group learning activities, and teachers of the techniques that students need to find the best research. Without a guide, the forest of information can too easily mislead the best researcher, much less the neophyte student, to whom the mass of trees would be daunting. Even a well-seasoned researcher may tend to stay in areas of the Web's most common, well-known ground. Sampling from the edges of the forest is not what is required in this new century. We need to plunge in deep to find the best information as we seek to create the best knowledge.

The millennial librarian has three tools to assist in this journey: single classes (if full-term courses are not feasible) on how to use online information sources; sites that provide ongoing assistance, as well as peer advice; and, finally, an awareness that the millennial librarian is a constant and willing presence to be tapped by students for guidance.

Courses and Classes on Searching for Information

It is not surprising that many university libraries offer classes to students that specifically address how to use databases. What is surprising is that these classes routinely are not part of courses required of all university students. Finding information in the millennial library is not simply a pattern of searching a few databases or following some subject guide handouts. The complexity of one trillion Web pages is not solved by a Google search, no matter how refined the search terms used. It is a constant effort of searching, searching within results, and using what is found to search even deeper. The deeper the search—if properly defined—the richer the results, or so researchers suggest. The nature of information has changed so persuasively since the days of social science abstracts that any university not assisting students to understand the cross currents of online databases could be arguably faulted for education malfeasance. At the very least, such a library-sponsored research course would be evidence that a university understands the complexity of modern research and the great diversity of research databases, and the degree to which both of these have changed in the past decade. Students are asked very early in their educational experience to research, evaluate, and write about what they have found from databases accessed through a library website. In most universities they are rarely taught how to use these databases. This is especially disturbing, given that these databases constitute the largest repositories ever conceived. It should not be a surprise then that these students—having developed poor research techniques—may stick to those methods, however unreliable, for the rest of their academic and professional lives. Indeed, without intense reeducation, these university graduates not only will miss out on how to conduct a successful search, they may remain ignorant of their own inadequacies in this area. Many university libraries offer classes, typically one-hour, noncredit skills sessions aimed at training faculty on new software and hardware devices. Two major drawbacks can render these classes less effective than they should be for students: They are promoted and structured in a style and language librarians are most familiar with, and they are disconnected from each other. Librarians might teach about a particular research tool, such as RefWorks or Write-N-Cite, but these teaching sessions are sometimes presented in such a style and manner that presumes the targeted participant is at least as knowledgeable as a faculty person and that this person must have some prior understanding of the Web and research sites.

Students should not be presumed to be as research savvy as faculty, nor as familiar with online research databases. These young learners can and must be treated as the early adopters they are.[20] Freshmen will benefit not only from training in research tools, but will develop the mind-sets necessary to apply these tools in later classes. Further, these valuable "first" classes should not be the responsibility of university faculty to teach in individual classes. Only the library can step in and provide the unique leadership with regard to teaching information search techniques. Without this central teaching focus, the resulting hodgepodge of methods taught by various faculty in various departments in various ways will either confuse and frustrate students or leave them unaware of the potential benefits to their education that are available at their library.

These classes and courses in research methods should be backed up by a library website that reflects an "outside-in" approach to organization and presentation. Rather than structuring the site based on the nature of the library organization, the millennial library website will be organically grown from the perspective of the users. For example, student users should not have to wander around looking for the information that resides in specific electronic databases, such as LexisNexis. Many library websites presume that a certain understanding exists among students of what is an electronic database. Students often do not possess an understanding to determine which of these tools is appropriate. In some cases, students can go through their entire academic career without developing any understanding of what information is available in these databases or how to use them. Simply bringing a research librarian to address a class about a particular database can generate mixed results: Those students already familiar with the database in question reap the lion's share of the benefits, and those not familiar may walk away untouched.

Library science is uniquely qualified to lead this effort to ensure students learn from day one how to effectively search the massive database of the web. For example, the multidisciplinary nature of libraries ensures students will not be restricted to the search terms found within one discipline—that is, those defined by a single curriculum. Librarians can provide the broader perspective and the best practices that lead to desired results. A university seeking to generate the greatest learners would find the resources to fund the teaching of the techniques that lead to the highest outcomes, whether in learning or in research.

Such a course in mining the Web would, of course, change from semester to semester, as the web itself constantly changes. The course would require constant attention and research on the part of library staff. And, team teaching could take advantage of the various subject-focused professionals within the library. A suggested syllabus might include basic techniques, followed by specific research resources in the form of subject-targeted databases. But even more important, the class would promote user-generated content (UGC), as we will discuss in greater detail in chapter 2. Students trained to use UGC as a group learning guide to the appropriate resources might bypass the sometimes unreliable, and often impenetrable, world of peer-review academic journals. At the very least, a group learning environment can provide students with a sense of community and camaraderie, as they struggle with completing their research projects.

In addition, leveraging the proclivity of new undergraduates to rely on online tools such as YouTube, libraries might provide video resources as guides to the "where-it-is" and "how-to-use-it" challenges posed by students. Such videos need not be high-end productions. Nor should they be more than a few minutes long. Breaking up a topic, such as using ILL, into its components will be a far more useful—and used more often—tool than a thirty-minute "lecture."

Mentoring Guides, Classes, and Sites

Researchers have found that students respond favorably to information offered by their peers.[21] This may be because of the shared experiences of students, as well as their shared language. Whatever the basis, librarians can improve outcomes of undergraduate research experiences by using the affinity of students to the ideas and suggestions offered by other students identified as "peer experts." Such student peers can literally "float" through the physical learning commons, providing instruction and encouragement to cohorts wrestling with an assignment. They can also provide immediate assistance through instant messaging, chat sessions, or blogs on the library website.

Libraries also may, based on recent research, find that student–peer mentors may provide cost-effective "lab" assistance in broadening the impact and scope of such a research methods course.[22] Students are attuned to the social network of fellow students far more than the average library professional. What these students lack in precision and accuracy, they can more than make up for with the ability to connect to the undergraduate patrons. A peer undergraduate or graduate student can provide human-to-human guidance, a personal intervention that may lead to improved research outcomes.

Selecting peer guides at a university with a SILS is obviously far easier than on campuses lacking a SILS. Looking for likely candidates might include familiarity with research databases, some advanced computer skills (though this need not include coding), and a true interest in helping other students. Training these candidates to work with other students is one of the keys to success of a learning commons, and can be a ready solution for institutions facing tight budgets. In many libraries, funds are simply not available to add professional staffing to offer these training services.

> Ideally, the [information commons] would be staffed by professional reference librarians and highly trained technology staff to provide the best quality service

> for users. In reality, that goal can be difficult to implement. The costs of providing double staffing or for training library staff to adequately handle technology issues can be too great for a library to consider either option feasible.[23]

For many commons, the team of student guides is not only their best option but, given the "always open" nature of most university libraries, is an especially appropriate solution to effectively "reach" students. Properly trained mentors would be in a unique position to assist students in a nonthreatening way that is difficult to replicate with professional staff.

All things change, but the Web changes faster than any other library resource. Peer mentors must be kept up to date on the latest tools, websites, blogs, and other resources, just as they must be trained to rely on each other to solve what they cannot deal with alone. Most of all, they must be trained to avoid reflecting any sense of elitism that often creates negative experiences for students and could prevent future interactions. The millennial library is a team sport with student mentors working with other students and library faculty working with both. Within the new university-required research methods course, these student mentors (some universities refer to them as "ambassadors") could act as lab assistants, helping students with class assignments. Libraries that implement such a peer system must ensure that their student guides are not only up to date on current technology, as mentioned previously, but routinely evaluated on performance by their patrons. These student mentors must be mentored themselves by one or more library staff persons in a team atmosphere.

Given that most library staffs are already stretched to their maximum, team teaching student research training classes would also maximize the intersection of students and librarians, as often as possible, in the crucial first few months of a student's experience at the university. Early introduction and bonding of freshmen and librarians are vital and can generate long-term relationships that can positively impact the overall learning experience of students in their university lives. This bonding can also reverse existing negative beliefs and attitudes students may hold about libraries. Such positive interactions are more effective and far more lasting than any marketing campaign and can provide a snowball effect, as these positively impacted students relay their experiences to their peers.

THE LIBRARY WEBSITE AND VIDEO AND UGC

In addition to a restructuring of the university library website, the importance of including video and UGC pages to reach students cannot be overemphasized. Too often websites present valuable information in a "push" format, shoving materials to the student. A more effective approach for a library website would be to employ a "pull" philosophy that guides students, but ultimately gives them the sense they are in charge of what they learn, when they learn it, and in what order. Video should be at the core of this model.

Students of this century are keenly attuned to video and prefer such works over other media (like books), no manner how "slick" the production values.[24] Some research, in fact, suggests that the more "un-slick" the production, the more believable the information will be for students, especially first-year students. Just as many faculty are using video posted on YouTube (and posting video themselves online), so can libraries use video to capture the most important parts of these research methods classes, especially those sections that discuss step-wise implementation of such things as software installation and specific techniques. Further, the videos need not be stored locally. That is, rather than taking up space within the library's server, the videos can be posted at a video storage area, such as YouTube, with the source code embedded into a library Web page for student viewing on demand.

These videos serve to connect a "real" person—a librarian—to the student and faculty population at large at the university. Add to this a UGC path, and students can step forward to work with each other. Such feedback pages can act as an instantly created and constantly updated frequently asked questions (FAQs) page. Yes, they will require some monitoring. But students providing feedback on classes, in-library experiences, and online research challenges provide their cohorts with some of the most valuable and immediately useful information and solutions.

All of these tools and practices will not only help students learn (and learn to learn), but will also improve their perception of the library itself. Rather than a remote, at times daunting monolith, the library becomes a group of people—students, librarians, and educators. But, some university libraries are also looking at another technique to bridge the gap they may have with students and faculty: an in-department presence.

Outreach: Visiting Departments

For many libraries, waiting for students to come to the reference desk for help ceased as an outreach option a few years ago. Researchers outlining the new roles the millennial library will play in academia invariably see real, in-department outreach as a key component. Many sources suggest this. See Dewey, Hardesty, McClure, and Walters as recent examples, along with those researchers that they cite.[25] For some universities, ensuring that students and faculty are aware of changes in the access and nature of research materials is key to the long-term success of the library, researchers, and teachers.

Outreach includes the posting of new materials, typically by e-mail, to departments, and, in some cases directly to targeted student groups, such as majors or freshmen. Libraries use printed materials, such as posters, to announce special events, speakers, or classes. And some librarians, especially those attached to a particular curriculum, are asked to speak to classes.

The placement of a librarian physically in a department is a relatively new idea, as noted by Dewey in 2004.[26] These visits can include everything from social gatherings, such as student clubs, to attending faculty meetings, to actually moving into an empty office or in a corner of a hall in a department. The intent is to transform the student's perceptions of the library—a place somewhere on campus that includes lots of desks with lots of unapproachable people—into a person as a real resource. With the librarian in the hall or in an office one or two mornings a week, students learn that this resource will be available to answer questions and offer advice in person. This can play a large role in the student's individual success with writing and research assignments. A personal contact will assist the student, who may have problems even putting the challenge into words. It is hard to ask a question without some basic understanding of the problem. Library databases, while somewhat familiar to faculty, are often a mystery to students. Deciphering which e-resource is the best, most appropriate, and most likely to generate the much-needed information is more than just teaching how to select search terms, though that is an important start. Students, by and large, are unfamiliar with the differences between EDUCause and ERIC, or between LexisNexis and federal reports.

The key to a successful research experience for the novice can often hinge on the first few encounters with a search engine. A single-day "injection" of information is not enough for students to absorb the best practices. While faculty should be keen on this challenge that many of their students face, how to use library resources may not be a key feature of their curriculum. One-on-one or one-on-a-few direct encounters with a librarian in a department's library or reading area can generate both a sense of comfort among the tutored students and provide a personal connection to the library itself. It is, again, putting an actual face on the library.

Equipped with a laptop, the visiting librarian can show students, in their own departments, how to find the right database or journal, how to use ILL, how to use various technologies (e.g., scanner stations), how to refine search terms, and how to overcome other barriers to academic success. The actual physical comfort level of the encounter occurring within the student's "territory" cannot be overstated. Students can feel overwhelmed when visiting a library for the first time. Encountering the large numbers of students in a library seemingly already familiar with the facility can render the newcomer unwilling to ask for help. Meeting in the more familiar environs of the student's department lowers the stress level.

Finally, increasing the opportunity to interact with students also increases the opportunity to introduce students to their own learning commons. Rather than relying on students finding their own way—those who are already comfortable with the library need little assistance in accomplishing this—the library can reach out to new users and draw them into the research world of university-supplied information. Too often the library research of their patrons is filled with surveys of existing users, tracking the behavior of those already in the library. Certainly this is useful. However, in the face of declining patron visits, libraries must ask those who do not see a value in the library as a building, those who did not visit the library or pose a question to a librarian.

However, asking nonusers what they want may generate vague information: How do they know what they want if they do not know what they are missing? In addition, patterns that users see as successful may have already created barriers to thinking of the library as anything but a building of books. The education of nonusers must start by showing what they can accomplish with the tools available in the learning commons. Showing students concrete solutions will generate far more positive involvement than lecturing them on what they should to be doing or how their use of Google may not provide the results they are expecting. Yes, this is an uphill battle. But undergraduates have already developed deeply embedded habits before they attend their first class at the university. Providing them with their own learning commons portal creates a sense of community and belonging but also a gateway to the tools in student-speak—a UGC language they already understand and can readily integrate.

Support Sites: A Student Portal

Collecting all the necessary materials to support student learning and use of library resources might be best placed in one online area. A website portal that respects the user, avoids frames, and loads quickly with narrow, subject-defined pages will be used far more effectively than a site that attempts to treat the learning commons as a course or textbook. Information should be presented and labeled to answer questions the students have, not based on the internal structure of the library or the learning commons staff. Short videos and imaging should be created to answer one question or problem. Handheld personal digital assistants (PDA) placed near equipment, such as specialized scanners or high-end computers, can provide specific walkthrough solutions to a variety of challenges students might encounter.

The portal site should also provide students with an opportunity to look at FAQs, help areas, and problems/solutions posed by cohorts, as mentioned earlier. Access to sites outside the library's website, such as Google Scholar and other similar tools, would extend the library's impact at no budgetary costs. This requires that the learning commons staff pay careful attention to the portal site and keep it updated. This includes checking the site's internal and external linking. Research estimates that the half-life of links within a site is somewhere around four to six years. That is, half the links on a website will fail to work over a period of sixty months. What is referred to as "link rot"—the failure of a link within a site—renders resource links unusable and often results in students simply giving up on finding a particular reference. Bottom line, any site created is a site that deserves constant maintenance. We will discuss some of the issues and solutions surrounding link rot later in chapter 10.

As mentioned earlier, this student portal also should provide space for sharing group projects, allowing all members group access to updating and editing. This may be the most difficult task for any library. Student use of such an online storage area must be carefully and dutifully monitored. Abuse, such as using the commons as a media-sharing platform, must be stopped as quickly as possible. Requiring authentic log-ins and no anonymous postings should keep such misbehavior in check. However, as many universities have discovered, their students can be quite clever when faced with a challenge. Stiff fines and extended exile from the learning commons for offending patrons may also dampen such urges.

HOW MUCH DOES THE LEARNING COMMONS COST?

Funding of any university project is always an issue. Whether the necessary dollars come from existing university accounts, state legislatures, private donors, or private foundations, libraries can expect budgets running anywhere from roughly $1 million at schools such as the University of Iowa, to $30 million at George Mason University. As noted by MacWhinnie, "there is no common funding pattern for establishing an information commons."[27] Each library's budget will be driven by its own needs, be these additional staffing, equipment, or maintenance.

As noted at a land grant university in the Midwest, the first step in creating an argument to seek funding for an academic or learning commons at a library is convincing the library's own staff of the need. This can fall along demographics, with younger staff more interested than older, well-established library faculty. However, this is not always the case. Given the nature of the commons as being seen as collaborative in nature, the issue of perceived need may fall along academic lines. That is, while professors in the hard sciences have been early adopters of new web tools (after all, it was a physicist who invented the web), those laboring in the humanities are catching up, as noted by Ireland in 2008.[28] Knowing where the fault lines are can provide the library administration guidance in how to craft the argument. The argument may come down to a matter of perceived relevance to the mission of the library within the various parts of the university. Some faculty may still be solidly behind the idea that a university library is for collecting and storing. This group, also wary of new technology tools, may never be fans of a learning commons, no matter how helpful such a site may be. And, these professors may be part of a solid, unmovable university community that does not use e-mail and will not post their syllabi online.[29]

Finding the funding source to meet the budget rests upon the library to convince its university administration and faculty that such a commons would generate significant improvements in student learning. Given the limited, zero-sum nature of resources inside and outside universities, any new project would likely take funds that might be made available to a different project. Thus, the library must make a substantial argument to its own university first, before expecting to attract the attention of an outside funding source.

Part of the challenge for any library in justifying substantial funding, such as that necessary for an academic commons, is overcoming internal resistance and political fiefdoms inherent to all universities. How will the library find room for the learning commons? Will it require eliminating books and journals? Which subject areas will be addressed? Who will control the electronic side of the project? As encountered at one major mountain state university, at least three university committees in 2009 were in the process of establishing various components of an academic commons with little or no cross-coordination.[30]

Ideally, the university that is ready to seek funding—from the government or private entity—will have resolved the major issues. One of the most challenging barriers to any academic commons within universities relates to technology development and management. For an academic commons to be successful, control of technology on campus must be synchronized with the library's need to access servers fluidly, without interference. Committees working on an academic or learning commons should be controlled by one entity—the library—and report their findings to one governing body, the library dean. Such arrangements can be significant challenges to existing power grids within universities. But, it should be noted that, historically, these divisions often were created without an overarching technology plan. This lack of planning is understandable given that knowing where technology and innovation is heading is difficult if not impossible. Thus, technology at universities tends to be developed by independent groups, usually under the banner of information technology (IT), with priorities that may clash with the library's view of an academic or learning commons. For example, one solution that might lower the budgetary impact would be to look to outside, open access resources to augment on-campus software, rather than creating on-campus versions. However, creation of these on-campus technologies falls in the purview, at most universities, of the IT staff.

If the university administration can accomplish a meeting of the minds between IT and the library, then the library must sell the academic commons to the university faculty. The idea of a learning commons will be familiar to faculty in the hard sciences and most of the social sciences. As well, faculty in business and professional schools such as architecture, medicine, and law tend to be more open to the collaborative nature of a commons. The harder sell will be to faculty in the humanities, which, on most campuses, bear a heavy load of undergraduate student credit hours. In addition, all faculty members are generally very concerned when their libraries modify library spaces, such as removing current periodical areas, even if this is necessary to provide new open space. Faculty are equally concerned when a library proposes the replacement of paper journals with electronic archives, even when the shift can result in savings of funds and space.

With its own staff, university IT, and faculty behind the learning commons, the library is now ready to seek outside funding. Libraries must make a convincing argument that student outcomes will be improved at a minimal cost per student. Throughout this book, examples of how various universities established their academic or learning commons are presented. Included in these are how the universities found the funding and the barriers encountered at each.

In addition to these examples, the following is a list of the commons that have been established since 1990 and their URLs:

University of Tennessee's Studio, www.lib.utk.edu/studio/
University of Alabama's Sanford Media Resource and Design Center, www.lib.ua.edu/content/randd/podcast/index.html
University of Missouri–Kansas City's Information Commons, masterplan.umkc.edu/current-projects/miller-nichols-expansion.asp
Ohio State University's Knowledge Bank, kb.osu.edu/dspace/
George Mason University's Johnson Center, jcweb.gmu.edu/
McGill University, Walter Hitschfeld Geographic Information Centre, www.mcgill.ca/gic/
University of Arizona's Information Commons, www.ilc.arizona.edu/features/infocom.htm
Oregon State University's Information Commons, osulibrary.oregonstate.edu/computing/

University of North Carolina–Charlotte's Information Commons, library.uncc.edu/infocommons/
University of Texas–Austin's Flawn Academic Center, www.lib.utexas.edu/about/news/fac.html
University of Georgia's Zell B. Miller Learning Center, www.slc.uga.edu/
University of Michigan's Digital Media Union, www.dc.umich.edu/dmc/
University of Iowa's Information Arcade, www.lib.uiowa.edu/arcade/
University of Southern California's Leavey Library, www.usc.edu/libraries/locations/leavey/
Washington University's Arc Library Technology Center, library.wustl.edu/units/arc/

In many cases, published research has included learning centers that are more "vapor"—that is, resources that are strictly online—than actually established in physical areas within a library. Such attempts to set up a learning commons can run into a wide variety of barriers mentioned earlier in this chapter, as well as library faculty changes, replacement of deans, shifts in funding, and changes in priorities.

One constant within all libraries seeking to establish learning/academic/student commons is the need for flexibility and with that the willingness to adopt new technologies and solutions. When the University of Iowa established its Information Arcade in 1992, planners could not anticipate the rapid increase in processor speeds, the rapid drop in server space costs, or the rapid adoption of new technology by new university students and new university faculty. Mobile computing devices, thin laptops, and computer phones, along with online social network platforms like YouTube, Facebook, and Second Life, have shifted the manner in which students gather and process information. Yet, the demand for librarians has never been higher or more vital to future research. Libraries are a reflection of the trends in information creation and storage. The success of future researchers (our students) and current researchers (our colleagues) rests on the ability of libraries to track change, track research, store data, and present that research and data in a recognizable and searchable format.

THE LEARNING COMMONS: TEN MILESTONES

1. Learning the nation's education system is in crisis mode. More students are ill-prepared for university learning and more are dropping out after one or two semesters.
2. Undergraduate and graduate students are prone to use only the top level of the Web, what has been labeled the "surface Web" when conducting research.

3. The millennial library will offer a new cyberlibrary "face": a portal that guides students through the massive maze of databases and e-journals to the "deep" Web, as well as the stacks, and then shows them how to create the ideal search terms to find the best information.
4. The millennial library will brand its learning commons in the minds of its patrons, mainly students. It will convince these target consumers that the library is the one place where they can count on the support and resources that will help them be successful graduates.
5. The millennial library will find out the existing attitudes and beliefs of incoming students via an online survey targeting high school library usage, familiarity with online resources, and general feelings about the library.
6. The language of the resulting promotional campaign will be the "outside" language of students, not the "inside" language of librarians.
7. Roaming librarians will help students by being engaged librarians—perhaps wielding handheld online devices running Twitter, Facebook, and the library's databases.
8. Millennial librarians will teach students not only to find the best information, but also how to identify best sources of information on their own.
9. The learning commons will include group working areas equipped with multiscreen computers; an area specifically for students and designed to enhance the team effort, equipped with high-end audiovisual editors, for example, as well as other software identified as useful in the student surveys. Students will be provided their own space within the learning commons to store data and collaborate with fellow students.
10. The millennial library will offer courses on finding information, will provide mentors to help them in their learning, and will visit students in their respective departments and classrooms, reaching outside the brick and mortar of the traditional library.

SUMMARY

History of the Commons

"Commons" is open to a wide variety of definitions. Students' lack of access or prior experience require the university library to reach out, supply new tools, and reeducate potential users. Student needs include,

1. Opening up the library as an access point to the latest and best information
2. More on-site technology assistance that can address specific research and writing needs

3. Positioning the library as a campus-wide resource available to each department, and in some cases, physically in each department

Computers in a Big Room

Students may have preconceived ideas about what a library is. Yes, the commons should include computers. But it also needs to connect students to the best tools. And beyond just computers and software, libraries need to consider online storage schemes.

THE LEARNING COMMONS

Sometimes called a knowledge commons, a learning commons enhances the student's research activities, including access and use of databases, recognition of valid sources, writing skills, and proofing of work.

Libraries provide group working areas equipped with multiscreen computers that promote collaborative work among students. Of course learning commons may also have large, multiuser quiet rooms with individual workstations.

Expert assistance should be available either physically in the learning commons area within the library or available through chat or blogs via the help section of the library website.

THE MILLENNIAL LIBRARIAN

One trillion Web pages is not just a very large forest of information: This is an impossibly large forest of information. Sifting the good from the bad, the reliable from the suspect, the right paths from the wrong choices are not just difficult tasks, they are ones that escape even the best, most up-to-date researcher.

The millennial librarians are new state-of-the-art sifters, catalogers of information, sponsors of group learning activities, and teachers of the techniques that students need to conduct the best research. The millennial librarian has three tools (at the least) to assist in this journey:

Courses and Classes on Searching for Information

Finding information in the millennial library is a constant effort of searching, searching within results, and using what is found to search even deeper. The deeper the search—if properly defined—the richer the results, or so logic would suggest.

Library science is uniquely qualified to provide the broader picture with the best practices that lead to best results. A course in mining the Web would change from semester to semester, as the Web itself constantly changes.

The use of UGC as a guide to the best sources might bypass the sometimes unreliable, and often impenetrable, world of the peer-review academic journal. Tools, such as YouTube, might provide video resources as guides to the "where-it-is" and "how-to-use-it" challenges posed by students.

Mentoring Guides, Classes, and Sites

Student peers can literally float through the physical learning commons, providing instruction and encouragement to cohorts wrestling with an assignment. Training potential peer guides is key to the success of a commons.

The millennial library is a team sport, with students working with other students, and library faculty working with both student mentors and, if necessary, directly with students. Early introduction and bonding of freshmen and librarians is vital and can generate long-term relationships that can positively impact the overall learning experience of students in their university lives. Freshmen will benefit not only from such training in research tools, but have the necessary mind-set to actually use these tools in later classes.

The classes and courses in research methods should be backed up by a library website that reflects an "outside-in" approach to organization and presentation. Just as many faculty are using video posted on YouTube, so can libraries use video to capture the most important parts of research methods classes, especially those sections that discuss step-wise implementation of software installation and specific techniques, for example.

Support Sites: A Student Portal

A website portal that respects the user, avoids frames, and loads quickly with narrow, subject-defined pages will be used far more effectively than a site that attempts to treat the commons as a course or textbook. The portal site should also provide students with an opportunity to look at FAQs, help areas, and problems/solutions posed by cohorts. Any site created is a site that requires constant maintenance.

Outreach: Visiting Departments

Outreach includes the posting of new materials, typically by e-mail, to departments and in some cases directly to targeted student groups, such as majors or freshmen. Libraries use printed materials, such as posters, to announce special events, speakers, or classes. Visits by librarians to departments can include everything from social gatherings, such as student clubs, to attending faculty meetings, to actually setting up shop in an empty office or in a corner of a hall.

Equipped with a laptop, the visiting librarian can show students, one-on-one, how to find the right database or journal, how to use ILL, how to use various technologies at the library (e.g., scanner stations), how to refine search terms, and how to overcome many other barriers to academic success. Increasing the opportunity to interact with students also increases the opportunity to introduce students to their learning commons. The education of nonusers must start by visiting with librarians, showing students what they can accomplish with the tools available in the learning commons.

How Much Does the Commons Cost and What Are the Barriers?

Funding is almost always an issue. Budgets can run roughly $1 million at schools such as the University of Iowa, to $30 million at George Mason University.

The biggest barrier to any academic commons often comes from within the university. Power fiefdoms make the creation of a commons more a political challenge than a physical one. The territorial fault lines must be addressed by the library, the university, and the faculty. The bottom line here is that the most successful academic commons are likely to be a product of the university library and its staff, rather than a technology committee. As we have pointed out in this chapter and will repeat in other chapters, the academic commons is much more than computers and software. The best academic commons start with the best library professionals.

NOTES

1. Sara Hebel, "U.S. Falling Behind on Education and Lacks Data, Report Card Finds," *The Chronicle of Higher Education* 55, no. 6 (12 December 2008): A14–A15; Jean Marie Angelo, "United States Falling Behind in Higher Education," *University Business* (October 2006).
2. Channing Turner, "Film: America Falling Behind in Education," *Statepress.com* (12 September 2008).
3. David E. Henderson, "U.S. Falling Behind in Science, Most Graduate Students Are from Other Nations," *College News* (12 August 2010).
4. Besty O. Barefoot, "Higher Education's Revolving Door: Confronting the Problem of Student Drop Out in U.S. Colleges and Universities," *Open Learning* 19, no. 1 (February 2004): 9–18.

5. Jayant Madhaven, Loredana Afanasiev, Lyublena Antova, and Alon Halevy, *Harnessing the Deep Web: Present and Future,* in *4th Biennial Conference on Innovative Data Systems Research (CIDR)* (Asilomar, California, January 4–7, 2009); C. A. Wright, "The Academic Library as a Gateway to the Internet: An Analysis of the Extent and Nature of Search Engine Access from Academic Library Home Pages," *College & Research Libraries* 65, no. 4 (July 2004): 276–286; B. He, M. Patel, Z. Zhang, and K. C. C. Chang, "Accessing the Deep Web: A Survey," *Communications of the ACM* 50, no. 5 (2007): 95–101; D. Lewandowski and P. Mayr, "Exploring the Academic Invisible Web," *Library Hi Tech* 24, no. 4 (2006): 529–539.

6. Cathy De Rosa, Joanna Cantrell, Janet Hawk, and Alane Wilson, *College Students' Perceptions of Libraries and Information Resources* (Dublin, Ohio: Online Computer Library Center, 2006).

7. Steve Jones, *The Internet Goes to College: How Students Are Living in the Future with Today's Technology* (Washington, D.C.: Pew Internet & American Life Project, 2002).

8. Patricia A. Wood and James H. Walther, "The Future of Academic Libraries: Changing Formats and Delivery," *The Bottom Line: Managing Libraries Finances* 13, no. 4 (2000): 173–182.

9. Susan Gardner and Susanna Eng, "What Students Want: Generation Y and the Changing Function of the Academic Library," *Portal: Libraries and the Academy* 5, no. 3 (2005): 405.

10. Karin de Jager, "Navigators and Guides: The Value of Peer Assistance in Student Use of Electronic Library Facilities," *Vine: The Journal of Information and Knowledge Management Systems* 34, no. 3 (2004): 99–106.

11. De Rosa, Cantrell, Hawk, and Wilson, *College Students' Perceptions of Libraries and Information Resources.*

12. Jana Reeg-Steidinger, "Technology Student Assistants in Academic Libraries: We Can't Survive without 'Em!" *Technical Services Quarterly* 22, no. 4 (2005): 65–75.

13. Jana Reeg-Steidinger, "Technology Student Assistants in Academic Libraries: We Can't Survive without 'Em!" 65–75.

14. Rachel Applegate, "Built It and What? Measuring the Implementations and Outcomes of Information Commons" (29 March 2007); Gardner, "What Students Want: Generation Y and the Changing Function of the Academic Library," 405; Scott Bennett, *Libraries Designed for Learning* (Washington, D.C.: Council on Library and Information Resources, 2003); Kathleen Webb, "Measuring Library Space Use and Preferences: Charting a Path toward Increased Engagement," *Portal: Libraries and the Academy* 8, no. 4 (2008): 407.

15. Chris Ferguson, "Shaking the Conceptual Foundations, Too: Integrating Research and Technology Support for the Next Generation of Information Service," *College & Research Libraries* 61, no. 4 (2000): 300–311.

16. Neil L. Waters, "Why You Can't Cite Wikipedia in My Class," *Communications of the ACM* 50, no. 9 (2007): 15; S. Greenstein, "Wagging Wikipedia's Long Tail," *IEEE Micro* 27, no. 2 (2007): 6–7.

17. Kenneth R. Smith, "New Roles and Responsibilities for the University Library: Advancing Student Learning through Outcomes Assessment," *Journal of Library Administration* 35, no. 4 (July 2002): 29–36.

18. Jan Maxwell (associate dean of Ohio University Library), discussion of the library's commons areas with the author, Athens, Ohio, 2009.

19. Jesse Alpert and Nissan Hajaj, "We Knew the Web Was Big . . ." *Google Blog* (25 July 2008), googleblog.blogspot.com/2008/07/we-knew-web-was-big.html (11 July 2009).

20. Harvey Skinner, Sherry Biscope, and Blake Poland, "Quality of Internet Access: Barrier Behind Internet Use Statistics," *Social Science and Medicine* 57, no. 5 (2003): 875–880.

21. de Jager, "Navigators and Guides: The Value of Peer Assistance in Student Use of Electronic Library Facilities," 99–106.

22. Laurie MacWhinnie, "The Information Commons: The Academic Library of the Future," *Portal: Libraries and the Academy* 3, no. 2 (2003): 241.

23. MacWhinnie, "The Information Commons: The Academic Library of the Future," 241.

24. Andrew Copley, "Audio and Video Podcasts of Lectures for Campus-Based Students: Production and Evaluation of Student Use," *Innovations in Education and Teaching* 44, no. 4 (November 2007): 387–399; Abbie Brown, "Video Podcasting in Perspective: The History, Technology, Aesthetics, and Instructional Uses of a New Medium," *Journal of Educational Technology Systems* 36, no. 1 (2007): 3.

25. Barbara Dewey, "The Embedded Librarian: Strategic Campus Collaborations," *Resource Sharing Information Networks* 17, no. 1/2 (2004): 5; Larry Hardesty, "Successful Partnering to Transform the College Library: An Interview with Richard Ekman," *Portal: Libraries and the Academy* 4, no. 4 (2004): 455; Randall McClure, "How Do You Know That? An Investigation of Student Research Practices in the Digital Age," *Portal: Libraries and the Academy* 9, no. 1 (2009): 115; Tyler Walters, "Reinventing the Library—How Repositories Are Causing Librarians to Rethink Their Professional Roles," *Portal: Libraries and the Academy* 7, no. 2 (2007): 213.

26. Barbara Dewey, "The Embedded Librarian: Strategic Campus Collaborations," 5.

27. MacWhinnie, "The Information Commons: The Academic Library of the Future," 241.

28. Corydon Ireland, "Fair Shows Progress of Humanities in the Digital World," *Harvard Gazette* (28 December 2008).

29. Dan Cohen, "How Professors Use Technology," *Digital Humanities: Theory & Practice,* www.dancohen.org/blog/posts/data_on_how_professors_use_technology (22 February 2010).

30. In-person conversation with Brian Rossman, reference librarian and electronic information coordinator, Montana State University, July 28, 2009.

Chapter Two

The Teaching Commons

These are heady times for university pedagogy. While the university historically has been a place that values research above all other faculty activities, today it is responding to concerns that its graduates are not as sharp as they once were or should be. Modern educators are not only expected to produce stellar research, but to be equally as adroit in the classroom. Efforts are well underway at all areas of teaching administration to assess the outcomes of every student's classroom experiences. In addition, university educators are expected to teach more students, including those at a distance, a code phrase for online delivery of classes for every level of learning, whether undergraduate, graduate, or postgraduate. University educators must learn to create, share, and extend their pedagogy in ways impossible two decades ago, and that still remain inappropriate in the minds of many today.

It is not as if universities have not tried to track the in-class effectiveness of their faculty. Students have for some time provided the university with a grading of educators through the administration of end-of-course evaluations. While many university faculty handbooks suggest it is inappropriate to rely solely on these student-provided anonymous evaluation tools, the simplicity of such teacher-rating surveys is quite alluring for those looking for a quick, easy rating of classroom performance. For newly hired faculty, student evaluations can be brutal and demoralizing. Tossed into a classroom with little or no idea of how to teach—beyond their own experiences as a student—these new educators can face excoriation that can demoralize them so deeply they may develop a permanent animosity toward pedagogy, students, and teaching. Academic departments are ill-equipped to provide much more than solace to these newcomers. The millennial library can offer far more.

Yet, only a few years ago, the ability of libraries to have a significant impact on education was in doubt. As noted by Lesk in 2005,

> We don't yet know whether digital libraries will actually be effective in education. . . . Pedagogical techniques will have to be revised to deal with the wealth of online material, and this is a hard task in an educational establishment that has still not come to grips with the existence of pocket calculators.[1]

Clearly, hurdles remain. Yet the impetus to work cooperatively to create better teaching and learning outcomes seems irresistible in some quarters.

> The teaching commons in a networked environment seems an obvious solution—a way to share, modify and repurpose learning objects while reducing the costs to educational institutions of developing course materials totally in-house. It also provides a venue for sharing ideas, practices, and expertise in order to provide the best learning experience for students.[2]

Vellucci goes on to suggest that "educators face several problems that highlight the need for sharing resources." These include the very nature of the Internet as a "rapid and continuous change" agent. "This unremitting change and the scatter of literature make it difficult for educators to keep up with the increasing volume of new information and research in the field and incorporate it into course content."[3]

For starters, many of the educational tools used in the past were created to meet the special relationship within a face-to-face teaching environment. They may not migrate well to an online environment. In addition, university faculty are notoriously lone wolves when it comes to teaching. It is, literally, every man for himself. "Many educators are not accustomed to a more collaborative process for developing teaching materials."[4] And, as Hutchings and Huber noted in a Carnegie Foundation publication in 2005:

> Higher education has long fostered the robust academic commons created by scientific research and disciplinary scholarship, but until recently the same could not be said for teaching, which, for faculty in many settings, has been largely private work, guided by tradition, but uninformed by shared inquiry or understanding of what works.[5]

SHARING METHODS AND TOOLS

The sharing of teaching artifacts, such as syllabi and notes, is a more recent development, yet seems to be moving forward aggressively. The ultimate role of a university library in this area is to act as a key catalyst to draw together teaching collaborators from among other institutions to not only deliver education globally, but also provide an area where new teachers can learn from each other and from their mentors. These new teaching commons hold great promise of bearing fruit in the near term. Improving faculty performance and involvement in all three of these areas—teaching, sharing, and extending—require specific tools, techniques, and space that can and should reside within the teaching commons.

A New Focus: Improving the Teaching Methods of University Researchers

Even as more and more resources and attention are being funneled into teaching teachers to teach, the critical and, in many ways, clearer role of a professor at a major university is still to produce publishable research. While university educators are, more than ever in the past, encouraged to place more thought into their syllabi, track their efforts, and show measurable learning outcomes, the exact nature of how to accomplish these specific measurements has been vague and poorly defined. Putting out more effort to understand how to measure outcomes, for example, is additionally hard for many faculty, given that teaching has been treated historically as an ugly stepson by their institutions. Not surprisingly, classes and syllabi are seen by many faculty as a necessary evil, a part of the university contract that is a faint second to research (but, notably, often far more valuable than the service component). As noted by Agathocleous and Dean: "Until recently, teaching has played second fiddle to literary research as a mode of knowledge in academia, leaving new teachers with nowhere to turn for advice about teaching and no forum for discussion of the difficulties and opportunities they face in the classroom."[6] Scholarly research and the grant dollars that support it have held the highest ground within almost all major university departments for decades. As many have noted, while excellence in research is demanded within every university, excellence in teaching will not take place until such activity, and the effort it will take to attain it, is rewarded. Not until the university tradition holds in higher regard the scholarship of teaching, and not until it grants pedagogy higher standing and weight, will we see great strides in the wide canvas of higher education.

What Role for the Millennial Library?

As suggested by Agathocleous and Dean, the tide may be shifting on this research-centric approach within higher education. Recent emphasis at the federal and state levels on raising student learning outcomes and establishing measures of academic success, has resulted in more universities—at least at the leadership levels—seeking higher accountability and specific and measurable results in their classrooms.

Yet, this shift toward measurable results has left many faculty stranded, just as legislation like No Child Left Behind has left some university schools of education on a path approaching destruction.[7] And, just as high school educators are facing new and controversial standards for measuring performance, more and more boards of regents and accreditation committees are expecting specific learning outcomes from university classes. For many university educators, this is a wholly unknown and confusing territory. As the political conversation whirls around measured performance standards, the average university professor faces what seem to be vague demands: improve teaching, improve outcomes, improve student performance. While education training traditionally holds sway over subject expertise in the K–12 world, most doctoral programs spend scant time teaching their candidates the nature of the classroom and many others do not allow their graduate students to teach at all. While universities take great pains to train their graduate students how to conduct research and analyze the results, few—outside of schools of education—bother to teach teachers to teach. A brand new assistant professor is tossed into the classroom with no training, little guidance, and scant support. And, while programs might typically offer new faculty mentors to chart their progress toward a tenure defense, very few provide an in-the-flesh, in-the-classroom teaching guide.

In today's environment of increased stress on learning outcomes, the university must embrace the scholarship of teaching that calls faculty from all disciplines to examine and reexamine their own teaching abilities, as well as offering insight to the best practices of their colleagues. Such self- and cohort-examination must break through the isolation that is the typical university teaching experience. It must lead to a conversation among those expected to create tomorrow's scholars. Within the right environment and with the right compassionate support, this conversation can be enriching and enlightening—leading to a healthy exchange of ideas for improvements and a general sense that the work taken on is valued at the highest levels of the university. This inward study of teaching techniques and processes should also answer the irresistible movement within all universities toward online learning, distance education, and interinstitutional, collaborative degree awards, such as that offered by the Great Plains Interactive Distance Educational Alliance (www.gpidea.org) and others like it.

The millennial library will play a key role in this recent move toward improving teaching and learning standards. The library of the future will include within its four walls and within its online world a teaching commons that will provide a conceptual space "in which communities of educators committed to inquiry and innovation come together to exchange ideas about teaching and learning, and use them to meet the challenges of educating students for personal, professional, and civic life."[8]

We will look at three specific areas where the library will play a critical role in the coming decades: providing the online and offline tools to improve university educators, including student-directed tutorials covering basic learning topics; offering a place where educational tools can be shared, critiqued, and modified; and bridging the gap between classroom and distance education. We will also touch on the role of the millennial library in facilitating and improving educator mentoring. All of these activities will occur within the teaching commons, with faculty collaboration at every level, including mentorship. This last area, faculty mentoring, is a key component. The involvement of the library can ensure that this stage is more than simply creating lists of possible sources of help. Young faculty, often entering the classroom for the first time, need more than a titular nod of assistance. New educators need an interactive area where classroom veterans can step in virtually and address the issues faced on a daily basis in classrooms. Without mentor guidance, new educators will be subject to learning how to teach—if they do at all—through trial and error.

Online and Offline Tools to Assist University Educators

Barriers exist. As noted by Loertscher, "Experts say that the rank and file of any profession can't recreate itself because it's too enmeshed in the status quo."[9] Moving faculty away from teaching as a "private activity" that takes "place behind doors that are both metaphorically and physically closed to colleagues"[10] will require an interactive, carefully listening group of librarians.

This is precisely the role for the millennial librarians, for they are the caretakers of the teaching commons, and it is from their expertise in file sharing, cataloging, and collaboration that future teaching goals and standards will be met, updated, and met again. These new librarians are just as they have always been: neutral participants in the university experience, ready and willing to reach across the artificial barriers that separate classes, departments, schools, and colleges to enhance collaboration. Their new tools, gathered in the teaching commons, will reintroduce them as relevant to every professor on campus. The needs of students in this century will require all of the collaborative teaching skills the university faculty can muster, organized and facilitated by the catalytic millennial library's teaching commons. As noted by Brown and Adler:

> It is unlikely that sufficient resources will be available to build enough new campuses to meet the growing global demand for higher education—at least not

> the sort of campuses that we traditionally build for colleges and universities. Nor is it likely that the current methods of teaching and learning will suffice to prepare students for the lives that they will lead in the twenty-first century.[11]

The global call for higher teaching standards, more relevant student-teacher interaction, and measured learning outcomes places the educator both within his university and, simultaneously, in the world university of the teaching commons.

One of the most common barriers to teaching evaluation and improvement is actually being able to assess the educator's methods without presenting an added stress. Visiting a teacher in his classroom immediately changes the dynamics. No longer is it simply teacher and students, but also a third element that creates stress for the faculty member, as well as curiosity and distraction among the students. In addition, the presumption that a cohort within a department represents a neutral observer, as well as an expert observer, is often in error.

Within a millennial library's many tools will be ways in which teaching can be evaluated, critiqued, and improved with minimal disruption. The first step is to create a sense of trust with the teacher. The use of the information gathered will not be subject to department animosity or politics, but used by dispassionate evaluators who can provide positive, useful feedback. The use of a simple device, such as mini-laptop, to capture the actual class activities would be one way in which evaluators working within the millennial library's teaching commons could critique the techniques used by the professor and the reactions of the students. These evaluations could be provided through a secure area within the teaching commons that only specific experts—perhaps from a department of education, the subject area, or others both on and off campus—could view the video and provide meaningful feedback. Included might be suggestions on improving the student-teacher exchange, adding new activities to extend and enrich a particular teaching moment, and enhancing the actual style of the lecture delivery.

In addition, the teacher being evaluated could pose questions to the group, also within the secure teaching commons area, regarding particular issues or problems she encountered during the class time. The teacher must feel completely confident that the information shared by all participants will be private and used only to the betterment of the teaching methods. This sense of safety would enhance follow-up evaluations and facilitate improvements by assuring the teacher that the entire activity is a positive reinforcement and improvement activity. Lowering the sense of danger in opening up to an online teaching evaluation environment can lead to use of the teaching commons beyond the evaluation period.

Also within the teaching commons, a separate more open area—still secure to authorized users—could allow university educators to share experiences and ideas in a variety of areas. Accomplishments, failures, and approaching challenges could be addressed in a free exchange of ideas within a teaching commons blog area. This cannot be stressed enough: teachers, not only within a particular discipline but also across the university, will benefit from the knowledge and experience cohorts are willing to share. For example, a particular professor who uses an online technique, such as short videos to illustrate a topic, can share how to create these mini-movies. Rather than each professor being an island of information shut off from others, the teaching techniques of an entire university or an entire discipline can be shared with ease in a millennial library's teaching commons.

Offline, creating student-directed tutorials to improve classroom outcomes has risen to the top of many university agendas. Faced with limited budgets and increasing student enrollment, few institutions can afford to hire more faculty, as they have in the past, to meet increasing demand. Stretching the coverage of current faculty preserves financial resources for support staff, travel, and other funding needs.

The focus of these tutorials should address the most pressing needs for most university students: research techniques, writing skills, and exam preparation. Remarkably, at some universities, the research tools typically installed and made available online by the library are not well known among the faculty, much less students. Tools such as EndNote and RefWorks are accessible through the university library's website, in most cases, yet are not used as often as expected. Part of this is because the library staff is stretched beyond its limits in just making the tools available, much less providing in-person tutorials. Ensuring the tools are used is often not included in the goals of providing the software. Further, even if publicizing the research tools is part of the staff's goals, its ability to successfully do so is often hit or miss.

The millennial library must not just list the tools available on its website, but must ensure that students know of the presence of the applications, as well as how they can benefit from their use. For such tools as bibliographic software, including the previously mentioned RefWorks, EndNote, and dozens of others available online, faculty must be confident that their students are trained to effectively apply the technology. And, to follow up, assurance must be made that students are post-tested on their learning outcomes to assure they are ready to use the particular tools. These post-training tests can point out those students still in need of further preparation.

The teaching of technology, often in the form of software, is a source of great controversy within many universities. Such training is often seen as both inappropriate for a university and a waste of time given the rapid changes within the field of software. Even if a university were to think faculty should teach software, it must know that within two years, many of these tools will have become outmoded, out of date, or replaced by more efficient models. Hundreds of faculty hours spent teaching software is not only inefficient, it is discouraging.

In place of faculty individually teaching such courses, the task could be (and, frankly, should be) assigned to librarians. The modules could be created in concert with interested and qualified faculty, made available through the library's website, and modified on a regular basis by library staff. Included could be tools that would notify faculty when their students had completed each module. The most optimal format for theses modules would include video, much like the DVD software tools included in proprietary training packages.

SHARING TEACHING TOOLS AND IDEAS

As it is happening in the research commons, new technologies and software have made it possible for the sharing and exchange of instructional materials and ideas worldwide. This universal access could not come at a more important juncture in university education. As demand for education has increased globally, so has the demand that university education be measured and improved.

The lag cannot be placed at the feet of professors or any unwillingness on their part, in general, to share information. Educators have for many decades shared syllabi in their hallways and in academic conferences, offering new instructional materials and ideas to each other. Barriers that often have pushed away one researcher from another are much less present in the sharing of teaching methodology. Perhaps this is a perverse outcome of teaching being valued so lowly within academia for so many decades. Perhaps it is an acknowledgment on the part of faculty that few of them are experts and many are naive when it comes to teaching. Whatever the cause for this desire to share and to borrow from each other, the Web has opened it to the world. Methods and ideas flow back and forth through both faculty-created and institutional structures' sharing networks.

For example, the OpenCourseWare (OCW) initiative at the Massachusetts Institute of Technology—perhaps the first of its kind worldwide—provides free access to undergraduate- and graduate-level teaching materials and modules (ocw.mit.edu/index.htm). The syllabi and teaching support materials for the entire MIT catalog are offered free online. This constitutes more than two thousand courses, ranging from aeronautics to women's studies. Each online course area includes a syllabus, calendar, list of readings, and assignments. Educators outside of MIT are not only expected to freely use these materials, they are actively encouraged to do so. The program is supported by donations, both corporate and private. Other similar projects have sprung up, reinforcing that this need for educator-created and educator-shared material is vital to faculty (and students) globally.

This online sharing model comes with its own set of issues, including clearance on copyright and intellectual property rights, which is discussed in the next chapter. In addition, some faculty and university administrators are not convinced that all scholarly teaching tools should be available freely online, just as there exists resistance to open access to research and its accompanying data. Others worry that such open access to educational tools will favor those cultures with the highest technology adoption and fastest Web connections. As noted by Smith and Casserly, "That argument does not simply apply to the widening gap between the developing and developed world. We only have to compare the resources of the libraries and laboratories of the top twenty universities in the United States with the thousands of colleges and universities that are among them to see such inequities here at home."[12] The very competitive nature of higher education, with more and more universities competing for ever-decreasing outside funding sources, creates very real barriers to the idea of freely sharing what is created at one institution with other institutions, however noble the goal.

Finally, some faculty fear their work—whether it be their syllabi, their grading tool, or their lectures—will be stolen, and with that their credit for creating the materials. This is acted out online today with some faculty websites locked to all but students enrolled in a particular class. And for many universities and faculty members, that logic will continue, if only because the economic logic seems particularly strong to those involved.

The logic at other institutions, however, focuses more on the public good that arises from the free sharing of information, whether that is in the form of research or a class lecture. What separates projects such as MIT's from the casual individual faculty postings online of syllabi and notes is the cohesive format of the OCW site. Here, in one place, are all of the teaching tools and materials used by some of most esteemed professors in academia. These materials are easily accessible, easily searched, and easily shared globally by more than one hundred million visitors to the site (and its more than two hundred mirrored sites worldwide) each year (as of 2010).[13]

This is one pedagogical element that a teaching commons could address at any university library. All of a university's courses could be presented, along with coursework, learning modules, assignments, simulations, and testing materials. In addition, educators could improve their offerings via UGC, site visitors making cogent suggestions. This open peer-review model mirrors the model suggested in the previous chapter. Educators could receive feedback in the form of critiques and suggested additions. If a university's goal is to improve its teaching standards, adding such material to the teaching commons could provide the grist to accomplish significant advances on a global scale.

And, in fact, hundreds of other initiatives similar to MIT's OCW have been launched within a larger movement called open educational resources (OER). Included is Rice University's Connexions, a site for teaching modules that are critiqued by others.

> As a simple example of a lens, imagine a professional society independent of Connexions, such as the American Physical Society, that sets up a Web page containing a list of all physics Connexions modules and courses that it deems high quality. It can also post reviews of those modules and courses. The list would prove indispensable to students and instructors who trust the opinions of this society.[14]

By 2010, more than twelve thousand modules were made available by participating faculty in dozens of countries via Connexions. This, of course, only scratches the surface of what might be available in just a few years. It also raises the issue many departments feel they need to address: harmonizing of teaching tools and methods. Some academics are referring to this evening out of the differences in teaching methods as "blending." As described by McTighe, "The world of blended learning is a symphony of many genres of the educational sphere interconnecting to create an innovative, harmonious system of free thinking, high quality instruction, creativity and structure, all playing out at once for optimal outcome."[15]

This blending is especially enhanced by the teaching commons, where faculty not only within a single university, but also in institutions worldwide, can share style, content, and methods in an open, sharing approach to education. Over time, or so the thinking spins out, the differences between different educators in teaching expository writing, for example, would melt away. This can be an important outcome for educational units looking to track student assessment and learning. Without a single syllabi and course evaluation tools, varying learning outcomes could wreak havoc on assessment standards. In addition, in environments where prerequisites are required, the expectations of an educator in the higher level courses would be more likely met by a single syllabi than multiple and varying course plans.

This area of harmonization is not without controversy. As is sometimes the case in any university committee discussion, the driving goal is consensus rather than innovation. The result can be a plan that offends no one but accomplishes little. Rather than focusing on generating the best outcomes, the committee either fails to agree on anything or agrees on watered-down vague statements of intent that might include the setting of nebulous goals. All efforts should be made both within the participating faculty and the millennial library facilitators to ensure that the resulting course standards do not represent a dumbing down of expectations, but a robust effort to create a higher and more relevant outcome.

Also included in the teaching commons would be a place where educational tools could be shared, critiqued, and modified. Faculty could not only place their syllabi online (as mentioned previously), but also privately post in-progress courseware. Within an online room with selected faculty given access, educators with coinciding interests in a subject could offer the posting educator helpful comments based on their own experiences. The syllabus could be examined and reviewed by faculty worldwide or with the educator's university. Again, all efforts should be made to integrate the best practices ideas that can arise from robust online discussions.

The millennial librarian would play a key role here, connecting the educator seeking feedback with the most willing expert in the field. This ability to connect those needing information with those who have that information is at the core of any librarian's training. The difference in this situation is that the sought for information is in the form of a person, one who has posted in a similar area or who has published on the topic at hand. Finding a needle in a haystack is the special skill of all librarians, and one especially suited for the online environment of millennial librarians.

Bridging the Distance Education Gap

For some years, the Web has provided learners not located near an educational institution with the chance to take university courses at a distance. Starting perhaps with the University of Phoenix, academic educational institutions have looked for ways to integrate their product—learning—into a format that can be delivered online. Indeed, over the next few years, the demand for university education will skyrocket. Demand nearly quadrupled between 1980 and 2006, from 51 million to 140 million students in higher education. And all signs indicated an ever-increasing need, especially among older, nontraditional students, for access to university education.[16] As noted by Brown and Adler, "There are over 30 million people today qualified to enter a university who have no place to go. During the next decade, this 30 million will grow to 100 million. To meet this staggering demand, a major university needs to be created each week."[17] For most of these potential students, access will shift to online, as socioeconomic factors and advanced technology make it increasingly possible to learn at a university without physically attending the university. For example, one of the leading consortiums created almost a decade ago is the Great Plains Interactive Educational Alliance (gpidea.com). This agreement among more than a dozen universities—most located in the Midwestern region of the United States—allows masters-seeking students to enroll at any participating institution, take courses online at a variety of schools, and receive a degree or graduate certificate from any of the participating programs. Such cooperation among universities in their graduate programs is obviously unique. However, the success of this program makes it clear that it can be done and done well.

Yet, while distance education has raced forward in offering more and more classes via the Web, the online teaching methods necessary to deliver the best pedagogy has lagged. This is not to suggest that great strides have not been made. As all things seem to do online, the shape and character of distance education has evolved from a simple online syllabus to an online syllabus plus video to an online interactive platform that engages the faculty with students. Moving away from the "create a video and walk away" model of just a few years ago, faculty are now using the distance site to remain as in touch with students as they would be in a physical class environment. This requires some new thinking, plus some new software and dedicated server space.

The high interactive expectations of online users from their educational websites—including those within distance courses—can actually result in a richer educational experience. Educators responding to questions in chat sessions, in blogs, and through Twitter, all in real time, provide the student with the sense that the course is more than a canned presentation of mind-numbing slides. The teacher's interactive participation with students in a preset window (much like that of a class) is much closer to an actual classroom experience and much less like a packaged tutorial. With set online participation times, plus interactive chat sessions and message boards, interactive, online education can be a very demanding time challenge for educators. Careful planning of the who, what, when, and where of teachers and students is vital. Without strong time management, programs can face serious educator burnout and defections. Online education certainly needs to be available 24/7, but educators cannot be expected to be available every minute of every day.

The role of the library is to facilitate, as always, the professor's online class structure and schedule. At some universities, this distance education activity may have been split off into its own department, largely on the basis of the technology involved. Yet, much the same as special communication classes addressing the Internet and Web, such distance technology can be integrated back to the colleges and departments. That is, rather than distance education being seen as separate from the classroom experience, it can be a part of it. Faculty can engage not only traditional students in a classroom, but also those at a distance, all in real-time exchanges. With video support delivered by a variety of software packages—many open access—the classroom remains but is at the same time expanded globally.

The role of the millennial librarian is to train educators in this new delivery format, provide the necessary software and support, and archive the resulting classroom activities. This last step is critical for future examination and critiques of the educator's teaching practice. With each captured teaching moment, teachers can be mentored not only by on-campus and in-department cohorts, but also by colleagues worldwide. This is especially beneficial to those educators seeking the advice and guidance of experts in the curriculum. With post-lecture analysis and discussion, the teaching experience can be improved to a level not previously possible. The captured teaching lectures can be held in a secure area, under the control of the educators. That educator can allow mentors to log in and review the materials, offering improvements where necessary.

It is true that parts of this activity of enriching the distance education course could be handled by other entities on campus. Yet, the millennial library is uniquely positioned as the natural home for collaborative reviewing of education techniques, if only because of the, albeit recent, tradition of the teaching commons. The full value and impact of this commons is wrapped around the integrated and collaborative nature that teaching has never before experienced, and that educators have never enjoyed. Here, within the commons, the day-to-day teaching experience can be expanded globally, the day-to-day lecture can be evaluated and improved, and the resulting student experience can be improved daily.

By using tools, such as Skype, teachers can engage experts in real time via video from any other user similarly equipped. The back and forth of real-time video is, frankly, more common in K–12 classes, if only because of federal funding grants and private enterprise showcasing new technology. For example, Cisco's Human Network touts real-time video that connects classrooms around the globe.[18] The Cisco commercial portrays a young teacher visiting a wired classroom engaged in a field trip to a classroom in China, via an online connection.[19] This is more than just a gadget. It is a learning platform for both the students and the teacher. Imagine a professor being able to not just talk about Tim Berners-Lee and the creation of the World Wide Web, but to present a live connection to the inventor of HTML himself, via a real-time video connection. Imagine then being able to not only share the conversation with those in the room, but other students, logged on and watching the proceedings using the same video tools. Imagine then being able to save the entire lecture and videos in one secure or open place for later review and comment. The possibilities are endless and bound only by our imaginations. For example, how much more enriching would it have been watching Carl

Sagan's now famous Cosmos series with the chance to actually engage the author in a discussion. A very few students had that chance.[20] But, with the passing of that great author, this chance is now gone for the rest of us. Using the connections available via the Web, such small sessions of one teacher and a couple of dozen students can be expanded to thousands, possibly millions. Via an interactive online teaching environment, similar opportunities await the global teacher in a global classroom with global possibilities.

Sponsoring Teaching Mentorships

Universities traditionally have paired new professors with sage cohorts. The resulting mentorship is intended to provide the young researcher with direction and focus. This mentorship could also provide some direction on teaching, but this has been far more hit or miss. Typically, universities have relied upon student evaluations, even though the tool is unreliable and—in some institutions—noted as not the best measure of a teacher's performance.[21] But, it is the easiest. It is an evaluation provided by students, typically surveyed at the end or near the end of a semester. The troubles with such a survey are numerous and need not be repeated here. Suffice to say, reliance on such a simple survey alone is not a reliable measure of a teacher's performance, any more than simply looking at resulting grades in any one class is a measurement of learning outcomes.

Nor does either of these practices provide what all new (and many seasoned) professors really need: improvement. Seminars, workbooks, and other intensive tools can help. But another, more interactive tool is a mentor who can provide a floundering educator seasoned advice and guidance. So long as the mentor-educator match is based on mutual respect and professionalism, the gains that can be attained can outstrip any other measurement: it is, after all, a "teaching moment" that can clarify, correct, and affirm an educator's teaching techniques.

But how can a library facilitate mentoring?

Traditionally, the science of mentoring and the training of mentors has been the purview of schools of education.[22] The pattern of older-more-experienced teachers working with new educators in "inductive" relationships has evolved over the past thirty years, in reaction to the unsustainable autonomy of the teacher in the face of rising complexity within school systems. Teachers have been forced look past their own experiences as educators to seek guidance in dealing with a far more diversified student base and dissolving barriers between classrooms and between institutions.

The danger, as noted by Hargreaves and Fullan, is whether "this age [will] see positive new partnerships being created with groups and institutions beyond the school and teachers learning to work openly and authoritatively with those partners. . . . Or will it witness the deprofessionalization of teaching as teachers crumble under multiple pressures, intensified work demands, and reduced opportunities to learn from colleagues? Mentoring is embedded and embroiled in these developments."[23] And, the millennial library is the catalyst necessary to coordinate and implement the university-wide and discipline-wide mentoring among the various groups and institutions.

Typically, the research literature addressing mentoring has focused on the K–12 educators. Even Hargreaves and Fullan felt the biggest challenges for teachers were in grade schools, not universities. Indeed, it is ironic that they noted a change-over in primary education from the older teachers who came up in an age of the autonomous professional to the new age of young educators now expected to work within a far more complicated and shared environment.

Yet, new university scholars have always worked alone, in their research and their teaching. Instances when collaboration has gone further than the minimum required by the tenure review formula are odd enough to stand out. Part of this is because educators at the university level are isolated not only for their research interests, but also by their approach to the subjects they teach. Getting teachers into meaningful exchanges regarding techniques with a cohort in their department is far less likely than recruiting a cohort within that same department to collaborate on a research project. Indeed, the participation of researchers at conferences has long been justified as an opportunity to network with others interested in their areas of research, an interest apparently lacking within their home departments.

Thus, to be of maximum effectiveness, mentoring must be expanded past the walls of a particular department or university. The mentoring activities within the millennial library must provide educators opportunities to exchange ideas, challenges, and solutions to the day-to-day challenges of teaching students and teaching students to learn. And, rather than connecting teachers with a single mentor, the library's teaching commons can connect one with many and many with many, spurring the kinds of frank, open conversations rare in education. Gone will be the past artificial strictures of age, geography, and rank. A mentor exchange within a library blog or Second Life Web area will allow multiple teacher-to-teacher exchanges never before experienced.

The millennial library is the most appropriate area on every campus for this to take place. For here we have the technology know-how, as well as the cross-disciplinarians that can foster the widest possible exchanges and learning opportunities. Rather than this being left to individual departments or schools, or being seen as the purview of just schools of education, the activity would take place on, literally, common ground, a discipline-free territory where the teaching styles and approaches within a hard science, such as biology, might be of interest to those in the humanities, such as history.

This mentoring could extend far past building syllabi or creating exams. For example, a librarian might sponsor a course on creating rough videos of the sort often presented on platforms such as YouTube. From that learning experience, the librarian could then work with multiple educators to create their own videos, including minor editing and posting skills. And, from that, those who have learned and are using this new video tool to teach, could mentor others on new ideas and be enriched by the exchange. The wide-open nature of this exchange is far more likely within the university's library than in any other department on campus and, in many ways, far more efficient. Rather than having dozens of slightly different methods used with varying software and hardware, a more uniform approach would engender more interdisciplinary sharing and support.

ONE-ON-ONE COUNSELING AND ASSISTANCE

Finally, the millennial library should include within its mission, a physical place where educators can find professionals to work with directly on syllabi, course planning, and other educational tools. The library should also offer space set aside for on-site and distance collaboration. Collected within the teaching commons of a library might be offices of academic technology, class structure, and special projects, such as a writing and assessment center. Professionals who are familiar with the university's special goals, such as student outcomes, would be available to work individually with teachers or with groups.

The office of academic technology would provide teachers with the information and training on the latest tools to track and measure student learning, as well as suggest new ways to integrate technology into the syllabus. Such a teaching commons would also provide access to cross-institutional collaboration, as well as act as a conduit between on-campus educators and private, off-campus experts willing to visit with students.

THE TEACHING COMMONS: TEN MILESTONES

1. A university library will act as a catalyst to draw together teaching collaborators at other institutions to share and improve instruction methods and outcomes.
2. The teaching commons will provide the tools for an effective and dynamic mentoring system, matching seasoned veterans with new professors.

3. Within the millennial library will be collaboration rooms, where faculty and pedagogy experts can meet in person to discuss ways to improve student learning outcomes.
4. Online tools, including file sharing, online whiteboards, and Skype, housed with the teaching commons and maintained by librarians will enhance learning outcomes.
5. The teaching commons will facilitate tutorial sharing not only between departments and colleges, but also among outside institutions, government centers, and private nonprofit organizations dedicated to improving higher education.
6. Installation of tools, such as OCW, will provide open access to undergraduate and graduate teaching materials, notes, test outlines, and modules at institutions worldwide, such as those at MIT.
7. Teaching evaluation activities within the library's commons will include more robust and useful tools, such as video critiques of lectures, class note reviews, and presentation training.
8. The teaching commons will be a gateway to distance learning, opening up every university to students worldwide and, by doing so, attempting to satisfy the global demand for higher education.
9. The university library's role within the teaching commons will include one-on-one teaching counseling facilitated through the teaching commons via tools such as Second Life.
10. The teaching commons will provide a bank of additional data and resources, including multimedia lecture assistance.

SUMMARY

These are times of change within university teaching. Often seen as a necessary evil, part of the contract that every new researcher must deal with expeditiously, teaching is rising to a new level of importance. The expectations of K–12 education, especially in the areas of student outcomes and assessment, have moved up to the university. Teachers hired as researchers are also expected to perform their best in the classroom.

The millennial library and its teaching commons can be a catalyst by helping faculty create student-directed tutorials to improve classroom outcomes, as well as offering a place where educational tools can be shared, critiqued, and modified. The desired result will be better teaching, and by extension, better prepared students. The teaching commons offers a unique setting where a specified set of cohorts, whether local to the university or global, can share their thoughts on a teacher's teaching style and technique. The use of unobtrusive video captures will provide newly hired faculty with the rare chance to not only see their missteps, but to receive ideas on improving and enriching their methods from experts in their field and the field of education. This will require that faculty step out of the privacy of their classrooms and embrace open reviews of their teaching methods. The millennial librarian can facilitate this exchange through areas of the teaching commons set aside to support pedagogical discussions, either limited to a set of cohorts or to all faculty within an institution.

In addition, offline tools, such as tutorial videos created in cooperation with millennial librarians can bring students up to speed in areas a faculty member feels will best enhance her classroom or online educational experience. These need not be high-production videos, but must cover a topic sufficiently to ensure student understanding. Outcome surveying cannot only measure uptake rates, but also help those students who have failed to understand a particular topic, by directing them to another video or direct one-on-one tutoring with a faculty member.

By providing a physical space within the library to counsel and train educators from across the university, the library can also promote interdepartmental and interdisciplinary cooperation. Further it can provide the physical place for larger groups to work together both locally and at a distance.

The teaching commons can also house the teaching materials of its university faculty, including syllabi, tests, and notes. Such a move to make this universal within all universities is afoot, with MIT's OCW at the lead. As part of OCW, MIT has made the materials for all of its courses, more than two thousand, available free online.

To make such a movement more universal, institutions will have to both shift their attitudes toward the value of teaching compared to research and encourage their faculty to participate. This may not be as easy as it seems. Some faculty consider their teaching materials as private intellectual property, much as they might feel the same toward their research data. The highly competitive environment within universities only heightens the barriers to open sharing of teaching materials. The university might argue that such open sharing of pedagogic materials produces a societal benefit. Yet, it should also make a point of rewarding the teaching efforts of its faculty at least as much as it values that faculty's research.

This effort toward "blended" learning can lead to a higher degree of free thinking, free speech, and higher learning. Within a teaching commons, such sharing of methods, evaluating of techniques, and enriching of student class experience will be enhanced. The millennial librarian will be a catalyst, connecting educators with questions to cohorts with answers. The days of working "alone in the vineyards" will fade, as more and more collaboration is encouraged and enhanced with the teaching commons.

At the same time, the millennial library will play a key role in enhancing distance education. Counted on to meet much of the rising demand for education globally, distance education will connect students to educators online. The creation of online courses, as well as their delivery online, will be enhanced by the modern library. For example, the GPIdea project that serves more than a dozen universities in the Midwest allows masters students to enroll at any of the participating schools, take courses at any of these, and graduate with a degree from any of the institutions delivering the courses. Add to these courses a real-time online video experience, and you have what may be the best possible alternative to a classroom environment. The live nature of the video interaction is what separates these types of courses from shorter, goal-specific tutorials.

Linking new faculty to sage mentors via blogs is best handled through the university's teaching commons. The library connects those in specific areas with others of similar experience and interest. Such connections not only will result in better teaching, but joint involvement in other areas, such as research. A teaching commons might also consider providing a physical location where faculty can work face to face with professionals to improve their techniques.

As more and more emphasis is placed on raising the standards of university teaching and the expectations of student outcomes, the millennial library will be looked to more and more as a catalyst for change in teaching and learning.

NOTES

1. Michael Lesk, *Understanding Digital Libraries,* 2nd ed. (San Francisco: Morgan Kaufmann Publishers, 2005).
2. Sherry Vellucci, "The Metadata Education and Research Information Commons (MERIC): A Collaborative Teaching and Research Initiative," *Education for Information* 25, no. 3–4 (2007), 169.
3. Vellucci, "The Metadata Education and Research Information Commons (MERIC)," 171.
4. Vellucci, "The Metadata Education and Research Information Commons (MERIC)," 171.
5. Pat Hutchings and Mary Taylor Huber, "Building the Teaching Commons," Carnegie Foundation for the Advancement of Teaching, www.carnegiefoundation.org/perspectives/sub.asp?key=245&subkey=800 (accessed 17 June 2009).
6. Tanya Agathocleous and Ann C. Dean, eds., *Teaching Literature: A Companion* (New York: Palgrave MacMillan, 2003).

7. Ken Zeichner, "Reflections of a University-Based Teacher Educator on the Future of College- and University-Based Teacher Education," *Journal of Teacher Education* 57, no. 3 (2006): 326.

8. Hutchings and Huber, "Building the Teaching Commons," 1.

9. David Loertscher, "Flip This Library: School Libraries Need a Revolution, Not Evolution," *School Library Journal* 54, no. 11 (November 2008): 46–48.

10. Hutchings and Huber, "Building the Teaching Commons," 1.

11. John Seely Brown and Richard P. Adler, "Minds of Fire: Open Education, the Long Tail, and Learning 2.0," *EDUCAUSE Review* 43, no. 1 (January–February 2008): 1–19.

12. Marshall S. Smith and Catherine M. Casserly, "The Promise of Open Educational Resource," *Change: The Magazine of Higher Learning* 38, no. 5 (September–October 2006): 8–17.

13. ocw.mit.edu/about/our-history/

14. Connexions, "Connexions," Rice University, cnx.org/aboutus/history (accessed 2 November 2009).

15. Teaching and learning centre, 2006.

16. Karen MacGregor, "GLOBAL: Higher Education in the Future," *University World News: The Global Window on Higher Education*, no. 0083 (July 5, 2009).

17. Brown and Adler, "Minds of Fire: Open Education, the Long Tail, and Learning 2.0," 1–19.

18. Cisco, "Human Network," Cisco, www.cisco.com/web/about/humannetwork/video/index.html?POSITION=3rdPartyBanner&COUNTRY_SITE=us&CAMPAIGN=HN-Video&CREATIVE=instant_show&REFERRING_SITE=Washington+Post&DC_CID=34137782&DC_PID=42200369&DC_AID=219549324 (accessed 12 November 2009).

19. www.youtube.com/watch?v=vHFUwFgu5w4

20. Carl Sagan, Ann Druyan, and Steven Soter, *Cosmos: The Backbone of the Night*, Chapter 7, produced by Adrian Malone, David Kennard, Geoffrey Haines-Stiles, and Gregory Andorfer, directed by the producers and David Oyster, Richard Wells, Tom Weidlinger, et al. (www.youtube.com/watch?v=-OhweQWrltQ).

21. Mark Shevlin, Philip Banyard, Mark Davies, and Mark Griffiths, "The Validity of Student Evaluation in Higher Education: Love Me, Love My Lectures," *Assessment and Evaluation in Higher Education* 25, no. 4 (2000): 397–405.

22. Andy Hargreaves and Michael Fullan, "Mentoring in the New Millennium," *Theory into Practice* 39, no. 1 (Winter 2000): 50–56.

23. Hargreaves and Fullan, "Mentoring in the New Millennium," 52.

Chapter Three

The Research Commons

MAKING THE WEB WORK

One of the great promises of the World Wide Web was the ability to share—if not always quickly or easily—research ideas and results. The promise to faculty was a seamless environment with on- and off-campus colleagues that would speed up collaborative work on research data. In fact, the creator of the World Wide Web, Tim Berners-Lee, has suggested that at least one of his rationales for creating this online environment was so that he could share his physics research with cohorts worldwide. Prior to the Web, the most common online file transfer programs did not support the on-screen presentations of images. Yet, for physicists (and others in the hard sciences, as well as those in art, architecture, and many other academic fields) the ability to show a fellow researcher an actual image was often key to a productive collaborative experience. Lacking the image support, the paperwork required to secure grants and research publication would be shared via file transfer protocol (FTP), facsimile machines, or mail. Yet, even today, driven by the large size of some documents—especially grant applications—researchers at some universities are forced to rely upon traditional postal services. This can slow down a project and add complications to the editing process. And, perhaps more importantly, it also inhibits the free flow of ideas available via electronic messaging and data sharing.

The Web provides a unique platform for researchers to swap ideas, comment on grant proposals, share works in progress, run collaborative analysis, and review methods and policies, within their own departments and colleges and throughout their disciplines. Yet, even here however, the narrow bandwidth and high storage costs common in the 1990s resulted in institutional restrictions on large file transfers, either because the regional network itself could not accomplish the task, or because such activity slowed an entire university network to a crawl. In fact, the existence of a plethora of mostly free software in the 1990s—specifically designed to compress large files and thus enhance online transfers—reflected the dire need of researchers to successfully share data and other large files through a network clearly not ready for such demands.

It would take the quantum leap in bandwidth, computer clock speeds, and online storage in the early years of the new century (as referenced in the introduction) to make a university research commons even possible. Today, fiber optic networks carry far more information, computer clock speeds are far faster, and online storage is far more feasible than any of these were in the 1990s. These advancements have not only made a university research commons possible, but also have symbolically thrown down the gauntlet: If a university wishes to remain competitive with its research peers and to maintain its ranking among all educational institutions, it had best attend to its bandwidth. It is not too far a stretch to suggest that rather than counting volumes and monographs in the university library to measure the weightiness of a university, it might be more accurate to count how fast bits and bytes fly through its internal and external networks. What are often referred to as fat connections represent a commitment by the university to research, teaching, and learning. Without such a commitment at the start, any commons, but especially a research commons with its large file sharing requirements will be hampered, resulting in minimal scholarly success.

A research commons enhances information transfer among university faculty via a website that provides connections to the newest services and applications—as well as soon-to-be released tools—created by third-party open access providers. For example, cloud computing models can move all research data and other products out to a massively redundant and secure network of tens of thousands of computers. Gone is the need to store data on a researcher's computer, and with that, gone are also the limitations of hard drive space and the risks of data loss. Of course, as with any technology, use of cloud computing comes with its own issues. The same issues might arise among researchers considering using Skype or Second Life platforms to communicate visually in real time and with fellow researchers, or using the dozens of other similar tools that are available. Many faculty members know of these advances. Somewhat fewer use them. But even the limited adoption is more haphazard than planned, and the necessary training and troubleshooting that is part and parcel of any new technology are largely out of the reach of most researchers who might benefit from these new tools. For example, Skype is very easy to use, and yet can generate blank expressions when mentioned to faculty cohorts. It may be the name, or it may be the idea of actually communicating in real time with live video and audio that causes an almost perceptive backing away by some (usually older) faculty members.

Overcoming Barriers to Software or Hardware Adoption

This adoption barrier is one of the areas where a central administering unit, such as the university library, can overcome this technophobia that often freezes out faculty participation. By marketing the advantages and providing answers regarding potential and imagined hazards, a library-sponsored campaign can lower resistance among younger and older faculty. In a way, the library represents neutral ground, not belonging to any one college or any one discipline.

This neutral ground makes it possible for a research commons to bridge the artificial barriers that often separate departments and colleges, resulting in the sharing of new ideas and platforms. The university library is the logical central point through which research experts can reach out to help faculty, regardless of their disciplines, departments, or colleges. Each faculty-defined and faculty-driven project can be crafted to meet the specific needs requested by the participating researchers. This can be especially critical for new faculty members, who have received the traditional training in research methods and even new media resources available through libraries, but may be ignorant of the collaborative tools available within a research commons. The millennial librarian's role would be to craft not only an array of on-site and online tools to assist researchers, but to identify and introduce these faculty members to the resources available outside the university's network. For example, the library may provide a simple, point-and-click method for faculty to collaborate with cohorts at a distance in a safe, easy-to-use online environment. In addition, the millennial librarian might be expected to provide information and access to the latest learning and research tools online to encourage and enhance graduate student scholarly success.

These are new roles for a library, to be certain. Many libraries already offer training sessions for students and faculty to learn how to use tools, such as RefWorks or Write-N-Cite. Millennial librarians will take another step, providing newly hired faculty and newly tenured associates (often the two most productive researchers on a campus) the enhanced academic support and collaboration opportunities necessary to elevate the university's national and international status. However, none of this is quite as simple as it may sound.

Beyond providing software to improve the university's faculty research output, the library's research commons must also enhance the collaborative nature of academic work. This requires opening up portions of an area within the university network to off-campus collaborators working within a still secure site. These off-campus collaborators are often involved in grant writing or research planning—activities that would be greatly enhanced and completed more rapidly if those involved worked in real time in one online place. The research commons would provide such a place, where large files can be placed via FTP, rather than squeezed through narrow e-mail systems. Past issues within many university e-mail systems related to bandwidth abuse with users attaching large image and music files resulted in severe restrictions. The uploading of large files put tremendous stress on the networks and often resulted in failed transfers, partial transfers, or unreadable transfers of data. Some universities limit the attachment sizes to one megabyte (MB), or less. Recently, these restrictions have lessened at many universities, with limits now at 20–40 MB fairly routine. Yet, even these attachment limits are far too small for the transferring of grant applications, research files, and other types of data. At times, such types can be as large or larger than one gigabyte (GB). Not even the generous attachment limits—40 MB—of Google and other Internet browsers can accommodate the large files associated with faculty research.

The Role of the Millennial Library in Adoption

If this all feels very "techie," perhaps it is because it is very "techie." Part of the complexity here is that convergence of library science with new technology in the latter part of the last century not only opened up new possibilities for SILS students, but also created new expectations among university researchers of what a library could be. For this to happen, the technology of online file sharing and storage would have to become a key element in library science pedagogy. As noted by Hardesty in 2004, the university library changed rapidly in the latter years of the last century, largely because of these new technological expectations placed on librarians. No longer were librarians seen as merely collectors and maintainers of books and journals. They were increasingly looked to for leadership in the university's information systems, including e-mail and other tools—an activity that just a decade ago would have seemed foreign to the profession.[1] Not just locators of information, the new librarians, these millennial librarians are now expected to adopt and maintain the software that will support faculty communications and research. And, while some universities may look to off-campus software tools that will mesh within existing and new software packages on campus, such as Zimbra or Google e-mail, the actual implementation and control over these services fall generally within the purview of librarians or information scientists. The emergence of SILS on university campuses goes back only to the middle of the twentieth century. Schools of information science were added to many schools of library science, marking the rise of technology that would dramatically change both of these academic areas and foretold the ultimate online convergence of these two crafts.

The role of these new techno-librarians—these millennial librarians—revolves around trust. With the new research commons and its dedicated storage and bandwidth, researchers must be assured that the information they are presented is timely, accurate, and current. Those involved in the project would then be able to examine the files and make comments, all in real time. The advantages here are profound. No more mailing files to each participant via a postal service. No more passing comments and edits to the next participant. And, no need for another repetition of the entire process to attain a second, third, or fourth round of approvals. Many faculty researchers have related to this author that passing grant applications, for example, from one participant to another was highly inefficient, as weeks would drag into months. Often impending deadlines would force last minute changes made by the project prime investigator with little or no consultation with other team members. The result would be a less robust grant proposal or research article.

Having an area for each faculty member to place online data and works in progress also allows more collaboration both within and between disciplines. This also assures the secure capture of data and its long-term preservation. In addition, the research commons research platform would encourage more interdisciplinary, interinstitutional, and interdepartmental conversations, using such tools as online "chatting." And, perhaps most significantly would be the efficiencies in time, as researchers conduct meetings and discussion in real time, and generate decisions and consensus far easier and faster.

Managers of such a research commons area would anticipate future changes within academic software and provide an enhanced environment to introduce new technological advances to the university's increasingly diverse society. Information and support would be provided for the wide variety of tools available online, such as file sharing, blogs, video posting, on-network data manipulation, and other new systems vital to research in the new millennium. Such a project would be appropriately timed to take advantage of the vast numbers of open source software (essentially free software) and network systems available online. These include deep web search engines: Zippy (search.yippy.com/); SurfWax (www.surfwax.com/); The Internet Archive (www.archive.org/); Scirus (www.scirus.com/srsapp/); USA (www.usa.gov/); and massive support sites such as Library Spot (www.libraryspot.com/) and InfoPlease (www.infoplease.com/). In the area of academic publishing, Open Journal Systems (OJS, pkp.sfu.ca/?q=ojs) has emerged as a potential leader among at least nine free online journal-publishing solutions available as of early 2010.

Given this fairly recent explosion in open source software and open access support sites, especially those specifically intended to support faculty research and teaching, it is literally impossible (and inefficient) for any single faculty person to track down all the changes and new releases. The research commons must provide not only best practices for each supported software within the network, but also advice on new software packages as they are released. Weekly updates of all new software and off-campus research support tools should be posted to faculty. But more than just posting notes of upgrades, video tutorials on how to appropriately use these additional resources should be available, also within the commons. Robust use of video pedagogic tools extends a library's staff effectiveness with little budget impact, while offering faculty and graduate students a way of learning on their schedule. Ironically, while many universities offer some form of distance education that employ such video lectures and tutorials, some fail to extend that same practice to other areas of the university. These videos need not be produced with costly high-end production values. Simple, short videos using whiteboards and online examples, testing, and summaries can provide faculty and graduate students with the necessary information regarding new technologies upgrades. The videos can provide the opportunity for self-learning, on a flexible schedule, a key component necessary for successful training. The fact that these can be used over and over by new faculty and graduate students provides the library with an extended and growing resource.

The Components of a Research Commons

The three basic online tools of a research commons are software tools, storage, and access, the last of which we have previously discussed. Connections to some of the online tools already being used on a campus can be integrated immediately into the research commons site. However, it should not be assumed by the university library staff that these tools are widely known or understood. Each existing tool should be given the same amount of highlighting and tutorials that all new software packages and outside resources require. Identifying which tools are being used and the extent of that use can be assessed via the survey of faculty and graduate student researchers mentioned previously in chapter 1, as well as online traffic tracking available within almost all server software platforms.

The research commons itself should include resident software that faculty can use through open access, as part of the library's subscription, or for a small fee. These software packs could include a variety of well-known clients, including FTP, a variety of browsers, and other online tools. The research commons could also provide connections to outside software packages, again available either as open access or for a fee. These software assistants could include such platforms as Twitter and Skype. Instructions on how to make devices such as Google Blogs private should be included on the research commons site, rather than expecting patrons to wade through the software provider's sometimes vague website for answers.

As previously mentioned, the research commons should include online areas where research team members, both within and outside the university, could make available large files for sharing and modification. Finally, the research commons might include a physical area with support services, such as technology support and meeting rooms wired to support online, streaming video conferencing. The key here is that not all university libraries need to have every available device and software package. These libraries should focus on those that can meet the specific demands of researchers, as well as those that the millennial librarian already has identified as meeting a known faculty need. The key is that faculty certainly have some idea of the software solutions they believe they need for a project. They also can communicate problems, but may not be equipped to specify the software or hardware solutions required to resolve the need. Furthermore, it is unlikely they have the time or skills to keep up with the latest innovations or have the technical expertise to evaluate the potential impact of new tools on their research.

The Ohio University's research commons provides such a physical solution within its library. As noted in Appendix C, the research commons area within the Alden Library provides technology-ready conference rooms, as well as special offices of the library's Center for Academic Technology and Center for Teaching and Learning. Several other services are literally clustered on this third-floor commons area, all associated with faculty services.

THE RESEARCH COMMONS FACULTY ADVISORY BOARD

The placement of special support services, such as that at Ohio University, should be based on the specific needs of the patrons served. To help identify these needs, a research commons faculty advisory board should be formed, pulling together a handful of interested faculty from every college on campus. The simplest solution to this might be adding these duties to the university's faculty library advisory committee. These committees act as advisory to both the library administration, as well as report to the university's faculty senate. However, at many universities, library committee membership and attendance is foisted on disinterested or even hostile faculty members. Rather than being a committee of the willing, the committee becomes a flash point between faculty and the library administration. This must not be allowed to happen with the research commons faculty advisory board.

This new role for the faculty library committee is critical not only to the short-term relevancy of the research commons to patrons, but also to the long-term health and use of the new resource. The board would play a key role in proposing relevant new software additions by evaluating the new tools and consulting online resource sites such as:

The American Evaluation Association, www.eval.org/resources.asp
New Mexico State University Library's Evaluation Criteria Check List, lib.nmsu.edu/instruction/evalcrit.html
Online Evaluation Resource Library, oerl.sri.com/
Medical Library Association's User's Guide to Finding and Evaluating Health Information on the Web, www.mlanet.org/resources/userguide.html
Center for History and New Media has a collection of tools, including The Web Scrapbook, chnm.gmu.edu/tools/scrapbook/

These tools can assist the university library staff responsible for maintaining the site and would help build bridges with the patrons of the research commons area, leading to higher use of the resources. The faculty advisory board also would play a key role in advocating for the research commons, which would generate positive benefits to the library itself. An active board can augment a strong relationship between the university—both administration and faculty—and the library. By working closely with their university faculty, millennial librarians can target the resources needed most, work to ensure adoption and use of the newest appropriate software to meet faculty-specified needs, and track the requirements of researchers both in terms of immediate technological support and near- and long-term updates. It is critical to note here that researchers may not have any idea of new support technology solutions. Librarians plugged into the network should act as the experts—but hopefully not with an attitude of superiority—on new technology that can improve their patrons' efficiencies and, ultimately, research products. A library's academic commons is only as strong as the relationship with those it serves. Patrons expect the library to be responsive and actively seek new tools relevant to the needs of the research being conducted. As new research software packages become available, the millennial librarian must not only consult with the research commons faculty committee as to their usefulness, but also ensure that the potential users of the new tools are made aware of their availability and are trained to use the new tools.

Software Loaded and Available Locally

New software, both open access and proprietary, is released on a constant basis. The nature of some software is quite familiar to library patrons: programs designed to operate on a local desktop computer. They require maintenance on the part of the computer owner, whether by fixing bugs with patches from the manufacturer or installing regular updates. The owner also must be vigilant in avoiding viruses, data hacking, and other outside attacks, such as phishing, trojan horses, and spyware. The task of pushing back these often random attacks may be a nuisance for an individual computer user. However, to keep this in perspective, it can be far more challenging for a library technology manager with, for example, 500 computer stations.

The software required by an individual user obviously varies based on this person's field of research. Some will require software programs specific to a particular area of research, often corresponding to a college or department on campus, such as geography and global positioning systems, sociology and global information systems, or art and Photoshop. Others are broader in scope, addressing areas such as math, science, engineering, humanities, social sciences, business, law, and medicine. And, some are more general to the function of research itself, such as reference tools, office support applications, and utilities (e.g., image scanning, CD/DVD burning, browsers, and website construction). Researchers are increasingly using exotic tools such as wikis and bloggers for otherwise mundane communication.

These "local" programs often generate conflicts with other, older generations of the same software. For example, older versions of Microsoft Word cannot directly open documents created by the Word on newer computer operating platforms. Workarounds exist with manufacturer patches and other "app" solutions. Of course, the fear remains for some that such conflicts can result in lost information as well as damaged or inappropriately modified data. Options, such as saving files in a generic format, such as text or rich text format (rtf), can be an unsatisfying compromise, as some information may not retain formatting as initially intended. Finally, the routine, and at times endless, software updates pushed to users by manufacturers can grow to be a nuisance. And, if a user has several software programs installed locally, the updates can seem to be constant. For a library filled with five hundred to two thousand desktop computers, updates are most efficiently managed through an overarching network managing each unit. This efficient arrangement of computers networked to run off a main server or bundle of servers is far more functional at the desktop level than the older "dumb terminals" of the 1960s and 1970s: The network handles all calls to software from one secure area.

On the other hand, for researchers who tend not to work within groups, or who are likely to work in areas lacking a sufficiently robust access to the Web, local software is the best option. For these researchers, support in the form of technical experts, especially those available by telephone, is invaluable. Curing local desktop ills at a distance using a remote log-in from a tech center is not only efficient, it is also seen by the computer owner as a prompt, effective solution. Faculty are also keen to know when newer, at times superior, software options are available. Providing a physical help center within the research commons for local software users may seem redundant, given the dozens of support sites available at both software manufacturers and online review sites. However, for offline users such centers can provide two benefits currently unavailable at traditional online help sites:

- Confidence that the information provided is not being influenced by a proprietary interest
- Ability to talk one-on-one to a service tech who is local and available in person, if necessary

CLOUD COMPUTING

The latest "new" new media wave just washing over private enterprise is a "parallel and distributed system consisting of a collection of inter-connected and virtualized computers that are dynamically provisioned and presented as one or more unified computing resource."[2] This is the "cloud" that is referenced in many conversations regarding enterprises such as Google. Many metaphors spring to mind: Imagine a public utility, such as a city water system, that allows users to connect at will to this resource,

- without specifying from which source the water comes
- with the ability to cease the flow at any time
- without lessening the availability of water to other users

Clouds have some similarities to the old mainframe/dead terminals model mentioned earlier: one central computer serving out information on demand to "dead" terminals with no software beyond what is necessary to connect to the file server. As Wess notes, Seti@home and Folding@home are two excellent and more recent examples of an early cloud, wherein private individuals were asked to allow their computers, when at "rest," to run analyses on massive data sets collected by the projects.[3]

The efforts to make more services available to users include creating proprietary clouds that consumers and researchers use on a daily basis. A leader in establishing such a commercial cloud, Amazon launched Elastic Compute Cloud (EC2) in October 2007. Essentially, Amazon's model presents users with what appears to be a dedicated server, complete with specifications on space and access speeds. And, as noted by Weiss, "The real magic in EC2 is that customers can create and destroy machine instances at will. As a result, software can scale itself to exactly the amount of computing power it requires."[4] When the traffic to the site slows, the related supporting software actually scales down, reducing the chance of a "crash" that invariably results in lost data. This results in maximum efficiency, security, and low costs—certainly three terms that would appeal to any university research project. By relying on thousands of servers, the cloud provides the optimal research-sharing environment that is both local in appearance (much like any traditional PC) and also global in accessibility. It may represent the perfect collaboration machine.

In 2008, Google and IBM announced a joint effort to provide cloud computing to computer science schools. The offer was somewhat self-serving: Both need the work-ready graduates to help expand their cloud business plans. In the case of Google, the need could not be more pressing: With half a million servers scattered across several locations, the current Google cloud is "a network that is spread thin and wide rather than narrow and deep . . . a new kind of concentrated power—derived more from scale of the whole than any one constitute part."[5]

As noted, cloud computing remains largely the auspice of private enterprise, for now. And the players include leaders in the industry: Microsoft with its Azure and Sun with its Grid. Yet, as proposed by Delic and Walker in 2008, "academic computing clouds might appear soon, supporting the emergence of Science 2.0 activities."[6] This shift from local hard drives to born online, saved online, retrieved online, and edited online storage areas may seem unconnected to the day-to-day concerns of the millennial library. It is not. The formulation of how libraries will work together to provide far more services to the world of research will rely upon how well they interconnect with each other. And that connection will be in a cloud. As predicted by some leading futurists, by 2015 to 2020, the vast amount, perhaps as much as 90 percent, of computing worldwide, as well as data storage will be within the cloud.[7]

Several advantages of cloud computing make this at least a realistic consideration for libraries of all sizes. Clouds provide an alternative to software updates, code conflicts, and other nuisances relating to running programs locally on local hard drives. The simplicity of tapping into one program running concurrently across hundreds of thousands of servers allows data and analysis to move place to place, from researcher to researcher with little or no "hiccups" of incompatibility. Rather than software running locally on the researcher's hard drive, the application operates completely online. This includes the storage of data analyses, research articles, and other information, such as grant proposals and project information. All that is required from the user is to connect, log in, and open files that have been saved to online servers. Other advantages include:

- Limitless flexibility and scalability: the network responds to demand, opening up more space and more bandwidth as users need it
- Elimination of issues connected to local hard drive failures
- Elimination of the fear of theft of hardware containing research data
- Enhancement of collaboration among cohorts
- Accessibility enhancements: data and software tools available from any machine the researcher uses
- Reduction in the costs of hardware devices[8]

The cloud also eliminates the need to upgrade software at multiple locations (computer stations), as well as run time-consuming hard drive servicing such as defragmentation. The simplicity of the system would allow a university library to convert all computer stations (or almost all) to a firewall-protected wireless connection to its own "mini-cloud." This millennial library cloud—a fundamental feature of a low-cost academic commons—could provide not just the data storage and access to outside software platforms, but also unique and local packages developed to meet specific identified needs of faculty within the university network. It would also eliminate the often bizarre, impenetrable maze of separate servers that operate in various departments, schools, and colleges within the university. Such a fragmented, decentralized network is an authentication nightmare.

As mentioned, a cloud may seem to be beyond the purview—both in staff training and technical expertise—of the average library. It must not be so, however, if libraries are to remain leaders in their own field of expertise and in academic research. So long as librarians enhance their abilities and develop strong working relationships with service providers outside their brick-and-mortar enclosures, they will be able to tap into this technology as new entry points open and new facilitating software is created. To be part of the academic cloud computing (AC2), library administration also must look to participate across institutional boundaries, rather than relying solely on homegrown solutions. At the same time, libraries must realize their participation in the cloud cannot be restricted only to their own university users. The nature of the cloud is universal, not provincial. In some ways a global AC2.0 might be a natural offshoot of the global university, an institution of the future that would connect educators worldwide, either within a multi-university structure or through a loosely connected online cooperative.

However, issues persist regarding security, property rights, control, and local customization. As noted by University of Alberta librarian Truitt in 2009, "We are responsible for the service we provide and for the content we have been entrusted. We cannot shrug off this duty by simply consigning our services and our stuff to the cloud. To do so leaves us vulnerable to an irreparable loss of creditability with our users; eventually some among us would rightly ask, 'So what *is* it that you folks *do* anyway?'"[9]

In the meantime, as we await AC2.0 to (possibly) blossom, other infrastructure as a service (IaaS) models are already available to support file exchange and modification.

Wikis

The online movement of large files for the purpose of viewing and comment by cohorts can be accomplished today using programs such as a wiki. A wiki—easy, efficient, and intuitive to use—can manage much larger file transfers than traditional e-mail. And, wikis can work seamlessly with other software applications, enhancing research sharing and updating among a group within a secure online "place." And, given they are entirely online-only platforms running on their own software, they work seamlessly across and among institutions and a variety of computers and operating systems. Originally intended as a database manipulation software option, wikis are now a simplified method for users to add, modify, and delete information within an open, yet moderated and somewhat secure environment. They present research teams the transparency of a what-you-see-is-what-you-get (WYSIWYG) information entry, along with the ability to revert to a previous version of the document being modified. This archiving function is a wiki default and extremely valuable to any research team wanting to compare newer and older versions of articles or grant applications. It also provides ways to identify updates as valid through "patrolled revisions." Wikis are an excellent example of software that was designed for one purpose, but has evolved into a newer, much more expansive tool for academic research. Second Life is another tool, as is Skype. A comprehensive list of online research support programs such as wikis, Skype, and Second Life is detailed in Appendix B.

OVERCOMING FEARS OF DATA LOSS

A drawback for some researchers is a general sense of anxiety—"where is my data being stored and how secure is it?" Millennial librarians can expect to encounter this valid anxiety in many areas of concern about the research commons. Assurances must be made early in the "conversation," including precise details of how the information is protected. Clear, straightforward procedures must be communicated to each researcher who is considering using the research commons for research activities. Losing years of data can cripple any project. But it also represents a failure on the part of the library, even though the cause of the loss may be peripheral. The millennial library must ensure that all data is more than simply secure: it must include offline, locked-down, redundant data storage.

Part of the reticence within the faculty community is the new interface that often comes along with the cloud. Asking researchers to store information in a manner which they are not familiar with can hike this apprehension and slow adoption. The eyeOS platform (eyeos.org), for example, attempts to ease concerns by reproducing "the familiar desktop metaphor—with icons for files, folders, and applications—all living in the browser window."[10] Other applications are also being tested, such as Open-Laszlo (www.openlaszlo.org), to assist cloud site developers to create these user-friendly interfaces.

The bottom line is that with hundreds of thousands of servers, all acting in concert with each other, and under careful management, massive amounts of data can be stored as easily as a user making a request of her own computer's hard drive. In fact, the experience would be the same, except the size of the files could be much larger, and accessed by collaborators much, much faster. Examples of this are many, including Google Docs, Adobe Buzzword, and Amazon Web Services (AWS). The last of these provides data storage, as well as transfer in and out of the cloud, at a very low fee. For example, a faculty project with 50 GB of data uploaded to and downloaded from the cloud twenty times would cost $120 a month, as of August 2010.

However, the issue of data loss hardly scratches the surface of the potential troubles that might arise from cloud data storage and transfer. As Hayes notes, "If you move to a competing service provider, can you take your data with you? Could you lose access to your documents if you fail to pay your bill? Do you have the power to expunge documents that are no longer wanted?"[11] In addition, who controls access in the case of a civil action or government subpoena? Would you be notified if the government under a legal path, such as the Patriot Act, demanded access to your data?

Until such issues are resolved, a full flight to the cloud is unlikely. Yet, cloud computing will run the course of Twitter and Facebook, with answers to the issues presented following long after significant numbers of researchers avail themselves of such services. As noted by Nicolas Carr, the idea will become as common as using a wall socket for electricity.

> The arrival of cloud computing—which transforms computer processing, data storage, and software applications into utilities served up by central plants—marks a fundamental change in the economics of computing. It pushes down the price and expands the availability of computing in a way that effectively removes, or at least radically diminishes, capacity constraints on users. A PC suddenly becomes a terminal through which you can access and manipulate a mammoth computer that literally expands to meet your needs. What used to be hard or even impossible suddenly becomes easy.[12]

SERVER SPACE WITHIN THE COMMONS

Creating an online area for faculty research is at the core of an academic commons. The area—typically a very large capacity server or series of servers, but not necessarily a cloud—must be secure, easy to access, support a variety of operating systems, and work with a vast assortment of software programs, both resident and online. A major upside to some of these online applications is the ability of researchers to collaborate with cohorts in real time within a secure area. Working live with other researchers on a project not only saves time but, especially in times of financial stress, reduces the impact of travel on budgets (and researchers) and lessens the necessity for faculty university-to-university exchanges.

The research space should provide generous storage capacities and guarantee researchers that the backing up of data will occur offsite, preferably in a distant geographic locale to avoid loss of data resulting from a natural disaster. Off-site data storage might be arranged via a cooperative with another library. You store theirs, they store yours. The arrangement would include an automatic "crawler" that would compare all the files in the library's research commons and back up all those newer than what is already archived. The arrangement is especially efficient because neither library would be expending much in funds, the activity could be automated to occur every twenty-four hours at off-peak bandwidth times (e.g., 2 A.M.), and little staff management would be necessary.

The computers used to connect to AC2 need not be expensive or even recent models. Further, libraries on tight budgets might consider repurposing computers made available in public areas for use in the faculty/graduate student research commons. This provides in-library access for researchers working within the AC2 on site, without large budget outlays.

THE PHYSICAL SUPPORT SPACE AND SERVICES

In addition to online support, the millennial library is, of course, a physical place. Like most organizations, growth revolves around the interior administrative structure. Adding features such as a help desk or ILL services might often be based upon the convenience of those working in the library. This approach misses the point. As many forward-thinking libraries are finding, services should be clustered to serve the needs of those served, not those actually providing the service. This includes support for research, grant-writing, and other academic faculty needs. While all manner of research material can be placed online, some should be delivered face-to-face. And, while a wide variety of support services can be accessed online, some are better delivered in person. As libraries retool themselves to deliver support services, collecting into one physical area those features the library can offer is a great convenience for researchers. The library should serve as a single-stop resource that eliminates the frustration for faculty having to first penetrate what is often a vague bureaucratic hierarchy of departments and offices, then identify which university personnel can actually provide the necessary support. I liken it to a university website—often structured with nomenclature that makes sense to those within the website team, but not to those who actually need to use the site. After all, how many people outside the university actually understand what the provost of a university does?

Making sure the way in which offices are named within a research commons area can make the difference between usage and bewilderment. For example, a contact link for reserving conference rooms would be far easier to find and understand for a faculty person if it was listed online as "Conference Rooms—Reserving," rather than "Space Management."

Ideas on what might be within a faculty research commons are presented in the case studies included throughout this book.

Conference Rooms

It may be the most pressing need addressed by all faculty engaged in collaborative research: a room to talk with others about the project. Space for group meetings is a limited commodity at any university. Establishing group space as a priority is imperative. The university library should not only provide a meeting room for up to twelve persons but also the tools to allow the meeting to extend beyond the library's walls. Computer workstations designed to allow several collaborators to talk online in real time would assist faculty needing to get immediate feedback and suggestions. This can be accomplished through a variety of software tools listed in Appendix B. Ensuring that the research team leader and others working within the project are familiar with how the software operates is also highly advantageous. The online ability to share ideas and images is as old as the online environment itself and resides at the core of Berners-Lee's initial outline of the World Wide Web. Equipping these rooms with video capacity would attract researchers from virtually every college and department on campus. Adding other group synergy features, such as walls that allow for the posting of notes, would further enhance the discussions during meetings.

Grant-writing Assistance

The ability to put packages together that will attract funding support is not an innate human ability. We are not born grant writers. Often the ability of a researcher to make the best arguments, to follow the appropriate procedures, and include all the relevant data separates those who win grants from those who do not. Many universities have such grant-writing support, but usually located elsewhere on campus than at the library. Yet, logically, the library is where researchers go—in person or online—to gather the necessary research to support a grant. Why not post and house the grant-writing services where the researches are likely to visit in person? The millennial library should be the source of support in this area. The grant advisors would be positioned to work within the project proposal as it evolves online. Working with the primary investigator—who, of course, is working with cohorts online—the grant advisor can assist in real time to create the strongest package, which would increase its chance of success. Of course, as noted, grant writers can get assistance online. This does not replace the need for an on-site professional who can move the project down avenues unknown to most academicians, especially those vying for first-time funding. Again, grant writing is not a skill any of us are blessed with at birth: A trained grant writer can make the sometimes small differences that result in proposals being funded.

PROJECT DEVELOPMENT OFFICE

Many professors, especially first and second year, are unfamiliar with how to create and maintain a project. Professionals within the millennial library can produce generic guidelines, as well as specific one-on-one support. In addition, the library—in its continuing efforts to extend its reach—should consider adding videos on subjects like grant writing. These can be reasonable lengths, should be informative, and easy to follow. Pointing interested faculty to resources found online and within the library can have the substantial impact that makes research partners into research primary investigators. Such offices must be placed in the same area as all of the faculty resources—the research commons.

TECHNOLOGY ASSISTANCE AND DEVELOPMENT OFFICE

One of the biggest challenges for all libraries is making certain university faculty are aware of the services available within its university commons. This gap in communication is especially important in the area of technology. Too often the addition of new software options—available online or through the research commons—is left to the hit-or-miss policy or word of mouth publicity. Such a method of promoting new technical assistance may tend to favor those most networked within the university, rather than those who can immediately and most profitably benefit from service. The millennial library will prominently feature the latest most-valued software and support packages, as well as create faculty-targeted classes in the new software. Over time, the library will be considered to be the first place to go for the latest information on new technology. This "clearinghouse" approach fits well within the academic commons.

For projects of sufficient size and funding, the library may wish to set aside a special meeting and support staff area. This type of project involvement by the library would further accentuate its role as more than just a support unit, but as an integral part of all academic activities within a university. The library's support, as exhibited by this dedicated space, would also ensure that the university itself is seen as a leader in research among its cohort institutions, offering up itself as the millennial research model. Full-throated involvement is improved by such acts of deep involvement in a project's success that extend far beyond mere funding support.

THE RESEARCH COMMONS TEN MILESTONES

1. The research commons will be a global platform for research presentation, critiques, and sharing.
2. The commons will provide a way station for large file transfers between research collaborators and evaluations with secure, restricted access.
3. Millennial librarians will provide newly hired faculty and newly tenured associates the enhanced academic support and collaboration opportunities necessary to elevate the university's national and international status.

4. The research commons must provide not only best practices for each supported software within the network, but also advice on new software packages as they are released.
5. The commons could also provide connections to outside software packages, again available either as open access or for a fee. These software assistants could include such platforms as Twitter, wikis, and Skype.
6. Instructions on how to make devices such as Google Blogs private should be included on the commons site, rather than expecting patrons to wade through the software provider's sometimes vague website for answers.
7. As the research commons area within the Ohio University's Alden Library is doing, the research commons must provide technology-ready conference rooms, as well as special offices of such centers as academic technology and teaching and learning.
8. A research commons committee will facilitate evaluation of new software packages, advising on the adoption and elimination of online research tools.
9. The millennial library must act as a clearinghouse for new ideas, such as cloud computing as it relates to the efficiency and success of university researchers.
10. The millennial library will prominently feature the latest and greatest software and support packages and will create faculty-targeted classes in the new software, both online and in class.

SUMMARY

At its core, a university library is a reflection of a deep human desire for efficient access to information. That is, rather than having a duplicative set of journals and monographs in every department on campus, all would be located in a single place, with access available to all quickly and easily. Some limitations are placed on the physical resources available within the library, such as reference material and time limits on how long users can check out material. And while some of these restrictions are eliminated or lessened by online library resources, no library should assume that this is the end of its duty to the university community. As access has become easier, more questions have arisen, questions that can be answered one at a time or can be used to create a more supportive, self-sustaining conversation: a research commons.

The research commons within a millennial library must be more than a series of software packages and hard drives—though that is a good place to start. For a university in this new century to be successful, it must have a library that is active at all phases of a faculty person's research. From concept development, to grant writing, to project implementation and follow-up, a millennial library will inject itself into the progression, supporting faculty with new software platforms, like Skype and virtual world collaborations, to new media meeting rooms and on-site professionals.

Using the web as a research commons area, academics will be able to share their ideas with others on and off campus, receiving immediate feedback. Rather than having to cut corners to make a grant deadline, for example, research team members will be able to collaborate in real time on various issues as they arise. It is the collaborative nature that is at the heart of the research commons. Enhancing that collaboration with appropriate software and staff support will reap major benefits to the project, and to the university and its library.

It is within the research commons that the SILS-trained faculty will play a vital role. They will not only make available the tools of collaboration, but will provide faculty with the training and support to enhance outcomes. Nothing creates more success than success itself. The millennial library, with its trained staff and its new mission, will be a key element in all research, facilitating and improving the finished products.

The library will be the expert on collaborative software, providing not only access, but also training to faculty and graduate students. Some of this will be accomplished using simple video tutorials.

The actual physical place for a research commons could include specialized support, such as that offered at the Ohio University's Alden Library. Technology-ready conference rooms, along with professionals in academic technology and pedagogy, will provide faculty a source for the answers that often either go unanswered or poorly resolved by researchers working in isolation. The library could, in such a dedicated area, offer in-person training for some more complex software platforms not used by enough faculty to warrant a training video, or software that requires one-on-one interactivity.

The millennial library will also be a source of data storage and data security. Collaborating with another library such information could be backed up at minimal costs. Providing assurance that data is safe and available only to the researchers involved in the project is a key element in building the trust necessary to make the research commons successful. This trust is also very important should the library be asked to support a researcher's use of cloud computing. AC2 should be an option for all researchers. AC2 reduces hardware and software costs to researchers and the library, and provides for more collaborative opportunities with project cohorts. Along with AC2, use of wikis is fast becoming a choice for collaborative researchers working with large files.

Server space within the library itself should be generous enough to support very large files often associated with grants and projects. Physical space at the library should also include specialized conference rooms to enhance project collaboration. And, finally, technological assistance must be provided around the clock. Having such technology experts available 24/7 will improve research outcomes and build within researchers a sense of confidence.

Please refer to the appendixes for information on local, online, and collaborative software.

NOTES

1. Larry Hardesty, "Successful Partnering to Transform the College Library: An Interview with Richard Ekman," *Portal: Libraries and the Academy* 4, no. 4 (2004): 455.
2. Rajkumar Buyya, Chee Shin Yeo, Srikumar Venugopal, James Broberg, and Ivona Br, "Cloud Computing and Emerging IT Platforms: Vision, Hype, and Reality for Delivering Computing as the 5th Utility," *Future Generation Computer Systems* 25, no. 6 (December 11, 2008): 599–616.
3. Lindsey Wess, Joan Beam, and Allison Cowgill, "Implementing an Information Commons in a University Library," *Journal of Academic Librarianship* 27, no. 6 (2001): 432.
4. Aaron Weiss, "Computing in the Clouds," *ACM Networker* 11, no. 4 (December 2007): 16–25.
5. Wess, Beam, and Cowgill, "Implementing an Information Commons in a University Library," 432.
6. Kemal A. Delic and Martin Anthony Walker, "Emergence of the Academic Computing Clouds," *ACM Ubiquity* 9, no. 31 (August 5–11, 2008): 1–4.
7. Michael R. Nelson, "The Cloud, the Crowd, and Public Policy: A New Age of More Flexible, Less Expensive, and More Secure Computing Will Emerge if Governments Act Wisely," *Computing* 25, no. 4 (Summer 2009): 71–78.
8. Nelson, "The Cloud, the Crowd, and Public Policy," 71–78.
9. Marc Truitt, "Computing in the Clouds: Silver Lining or Stormy Weather Ahead?" *Information Technologies and Libraries* (September 2009): 107–108.
10. Brian Hayes, "Cloud Computing: As Software Migrates from Local PCS to Distant Internet Servers, Users and Developers Alike Go Along for the Ride," *Communications of the Association for Computing Machinery* 51, no. 7 (July 2008): 9–11.
11. Hayes, "Cloud Computing: As Software Migrates," 9–11.
12. Nicholas Carr, "The New Economics of Computing: Are We Missing the Point about Cloud Computing?" www.roughtype.com/archives/2008/11/the_new_economi.php (accessed 25 June 2010).

Part Two

THE SUPPORTING ELEMENTS OF AN ACADEMIC COMMONS

We have discussed the needs for learning, teaching, and research commons, located within the university's library. And we have discussed some of the unique elements that might make up each. In this section we will deal with the long-term implications of some traditional activities within most libraries, such as ILL, as well as the more recent effects of new models, such as e-reserves, electronic books, and an emerging new role for libraries: publishing. The more traditional activities will be cast anew, within the overarching role of the millennial library as collector, keeper, and sharer of information. The newer roles are themselves matters of great debate and certainly should not be taken lightly. All millennial libraries should heed the old wisdom that simply because they can do something means they should do that something.

However, just as all universities are—and have been for a very long time—the promoters of education and research excellence, so they will continue to become more deeply involved in all phases of student and faculty development via the various areas of the academic commons. What may change is the public image of the library as created by the commons. Whatever the outcomes, the continued shift toward a very central role within all learning, teaching, and research activities will require a reassessment of old library activities. For example, in terms of research objects, whether they are journal articles, books, notes, or any other element associated with faculty and grad student activity, the libraries through the centuries have not only acted as repositories, but also as active organizers or sharers for otherwise hard-to-find materials. This role as organizer and keeper of information traditionally might be considered that of an archivist and thus not classically seen as central to the role of a librarian. While libraries are rapidly changing to become the holders of all knowledge created within a host university or college, the ongoing task of ranking the value of the materials has resided for at least a millennium elsewhere. And, in many cases, libraries are entering an area historically left to private entities—storing data in a form that comes close to publishing. So, while libraries and publishing are today loosely linked, it would be a mistake to suggest that, by posting online e-reserves, the library is now a publisher. The act of publishing is driven by needs not present (but certainly open to addition) in libraries: curiosity, artistry, and even vanity. But it also involves various other activities also not present in most libraries, millennial or not: reviewing, editing, layout, and promoting, to name a few.

As we discuss the role of the millennial library in the areas of e-reserves, books, and online journals, it is key that we keep in mind that to enter these areas, far more must be present to qualify any entity as a "publisher." Simply providing access to materials via ILL, for example, has never been seen as an act of publishing. However, millennial libraries will be involved in more and more activities, including electronic books, hosting online journals, and other research presentations that may appear to some to qualify as publishing. In some cases, it may—especially if a university press is moved online and under the auspices of the library, as happened at Utah State in 2009.[1] This adds a function to a library as not only a gatherer, but also as an active player in the creation of information.

At the same time, at the other end of creation, libraries are clearing out areas to provide a more open research room, filled with computers:

> Box by box, decades of past scholarship are being packed up and emptied from two old libraries, Physics and Engineering, to make way for the future: a smaller but more efficient and largely electronic library that can accommodate the vast, expanding and interrelated literature of Physics, Computer Science and Engineering. "The role of this new library is less to do with shelving and checking out books—and much more about research and discovery," said Andrew Herkovic, director of communications and development at Stanford Libraries.[2]

But, as noted by Kuny in 1997, as more and more data is lost because of outdated formats and software, "it falls to librarians and archivists to hold the tradition which reveres history and the published heritage of our times."[3] And with the coming increased flow of information from retiring Baby Boom researchers handing off their life works to libraries, a system of storage is not just a matter of convenience: it is vital to preservation of data that once lost, can never be retrieved, re-created, or restored.

It is within these concerns that old activities will continue and new ones will be added. And, in the next four chapters we will examine the common elements that would be used in such an academic commons—whether learning, teaching, or research—starting with the collection and preservation of information in electronic form.

NOTES

1. Norman Oder, "Utah State University Press Merges into Library: Move a Reaction to Budget Pressure and Effort to Pursue Digital, OA Publishing," *Library Journal* (5 November 2009).
2. Lisa M. Krieger, "Stanford University Prepares for Bookless Library," *San Jose Mercury* (18 May 2010).
3. Terry Kuny, "A Digital Dark Ages? Challenges to the Preservation of Electronic Information," *63rd IFLA Council and General Conference* (1997).

Chapter Four

The Components of an Academic Commons Archiving Scheme

Archiving, Institutional Repositories, and e-Reserves

LIBRARIES AND ARCHIVES

A study published in 2008 found that few universities only offering master's and baccalaureate degrees had established an online repository for e-reserves. At the same time, larger, doctorate-granting universities were either well on the way to opening their e-reserves or had plans underway to do so. In fact, the study found that of those that had implemented or were planning to open what the researchers described as institutional repositories, almost two-thirds were doctoral universities. Among all universities with no plans in place to create research repositories (but with some interest to do so), almost 90 percent were masters' and baccalaureate schools. Overall, of the schools participating in the study, more than half reported no plans to implement an institutional repository. The authors of the study describe the lack of these e-reserves as a "sleeping beast of demand," likely to generate the creation of more repositories in more universities in the coming years.[1]

Coincidentally, as the demand for access to online material has risen in the past few years, the cost of hard drives and online storage devices has fallen. The result has been a shift in the discussion about the storing of information from "what is important enough to save" to "why not save everything?" This is especially ironic, given that one of the annual activities at most libraries is devising a strategy to add more materials to a finite space, while at the same time strategically using limited budget resources to support the greater good. This usually involves making decisions about what particular monograph or journal will be switched from paper to digital, as well as what publications will be eliminated, moved to storage, shifted to other areas within the library, or simply given away. The task is not as simple as it sounds. It requires library administrators to make value judgments based on a variety of possible criteria: cost, use, perceived value, size, and availability. The first two of these, cost and use, are perhaps the most controversial. When combined, cost and use represent the value of a collection to a library's patron. If the item is used a great deal, then its associated higher cost can be justified. Low use and high cost generally result in the library not purchasing the item or supporting continued subscriptions, in the case of a journal. In breaking down the rationales for purchase, librarians are driven by a number of factors, including the simplicity of the item versus its complexity, its relevance to course offerings versus its innate intellectualism, or even its short-term popularity versus a presumed long-term value. Add to this the average number of monographs published annually within the United States of 300,000 (and roughly a million worldwide), and it is easy to see why the paper volumes within any library are in a constant state of change.

This need to add and subtract still continues. Libraries are fixed in place and only a few have the luxury of expanding in size. Thus whatever new item comes into the library in a physical form requires that something already present must leave. The same spatial pressure requires libraries seeking to provide a physical place for a learning commons, such as that discussed in chapter 1, to move existing holdings to free up the necessary room for such a service feature. However, this need to find space only involves items like print journals and books, and other offline collections.

Are Millennial Librarians Really Archivists?

The online storage space of a library server, which might be considered infinite or close to infinite, faces an entirely unique set of challenges that has little to do with physical space. Judgments must be made, but not in regard to how often a particular article is used nor on its physical size or any other traditional attributes that would guide the decisions of librarians. Rather than dealing with the size of a new collection, libraries face only the issue of use and cost. That is, the value of the work to the patrons of the library. These library patrons can be generally described as students, teachers, and researchers. The millennial librarian administration must make value judgments as to which collections will best serve its patrons. These value judgments can be made in concert with the target patrons, or wholly independently by library administration. It may be driven more by cost than use. It may be related more to the library server capacity or to the level of expertise among its library technicians. Whatever the measure, the library's administration must now be considered a judge in a more powerful way than ever seen in the history of universities.

So have we entered a new era? Is the librarian now an archivist? Not if the definition of an archivist is limited to those who keep records, usually of business and government activities. Not if the role of a librarian is to shelf and loan books, or as Casserly said it: "the systemic efficient and economic stewardship of [one library's] resources."[2] If we broaden the meaning of the archivist term "record" to include any data—content neutral and located within many different areas—then it is not a stretch to suggest that the role of the librarian in the new century is more of that of an archivist, though it is doubtful that many librarians or archivists would feel comfortable with this conclusion. Archivists usually consider themselves as separate from their library cohorts, both in purpose and practice. And, the history of archivists described in the Dutch work *Manual for the Arrangement and Description of Archives*[3] is that of a professional concerned with the source of the work that creates the collection, rather than making possible connections of that work with others or in making any value judgments regarding the work itself. Temporal, geographic, and thematic arrangements (shelving and organizing, for short) are the purviews of the librarian, according to the *Manual.*

So, why should we be concerned with whatever description the *Manual* may have set forth for archivists and librarians? Because, in many ways, librarians are becoming more like archivists, just as archivists, some argue, acted in the past more like librarians. And, the reason why this distinction between these two old professions is so important is that new technology, in the form of e-reserves, requires that librarians take a new look at their roles in information gathering, sorting, and delivering, and, in many ways, think more like archivists than their predecessors: similar to information managers than information keepers. But, how are today's librarians like archivists?

The answer lays in a shift or perhaps better described as competing definitions of archivists and their archives that arose in the twentieth century. The Dutch model, *The Manual*, for archiving that had been carried forward the early part of the past century by individuals such as Jenkinson,[4] prohibited any act on the part of the archivist to evaluate a work. As noted by Cook and Schwartz, any activity by an archivist to apply "personal judgment" or to consider the need of the materials by researchers would "tarnish the impartiality of archives as evidence" of past work. "The archivist's role was to keep, not select archives."[5] If a work was corrected, this model of archiving would leave it up to the creator of the work. This has its own set of issues, of course, addressed by Cook and Schwartz and others. Specifically, allowing authors to change their works "would allow the archival legacy to be perverted by administration whim or state ideology, as in the former Soviet Union, where provenance was undermined by the establishment of one state fonds [collections] and archival records attained value solely by the degree to which they reflected the 'official' view of history."[6] The archivist's duty was to ensure that differing works were kept separate from each other, while tracking those works that were created by the same institutional body that created the first work. Archives were not collected and stored based on when they were created, where they were created, or even the subject they addressed. The entire structure was driven without regard for the nature of the work itself.

This might be a workable system, setting aside issues of accuracy and ethics, if the amount of information remained reasonably constant or, at the least, grew at a constant pace. Yet, by the middle of the twentieth century, the amount of material available to be archived was growing so rapidly that circumstances engendered a new standard: "The emphasis of archives work has shifted from preservation of records to the selection of records for preservation."[7] The amount of information pouring into archives spiked significantly during World War II to the point where archivists were faced with more material to manage than they had time or space to devote to the task. Thus, the task changed: Materials were evaluated as to importance, relevance, and long-term value. This represents a significant break from Jenkinson's standards, and, in many ways, pushed archivists toward a reviewer function more than merely that of cataloger. This is significant as we track the approaching changes in librarianship and, ironically, has more to do with issues not as significant today: limitations on space and time versus cost and use.

In the midst of the last century the stated goals of librarians and archivists seem to come so close to each other that the differences lack distinction. Indeed, Schellenberg, perhaps the strongest advocate for the modern "appraising" archivist, suggests that—given the need for archivists to be concerned with the secondary use of materials for such activities as research—the commonalities between the two professionals should be strengthened and broadened.[8] Still other voices, such as Bradsher, advocate for a clear line of distinction between the two professions, a distinction of powerful relevance when considering the millennial library's e-reserves goals. "Although libraries often maintain archival materials and manuscript collections, their primary function is to house and make available collections of books and other printed materials."[9] The archivist's "function is to maintain accumulations of the records or papers of organic entities and individuals, including printed archival materials, such as manuals produced by an agency, organization or institution." The distinction between libraries and archives is primarily in the "way these holdings are created, acquired, maintained and administered."[10]

Three of these standards—acquisition, maintenance, and administration—are rendered less significant by the emergence of digital transport, sharing, and storage. It should be noted here that Casserly defined the activities of "library practice" as ownership (acquired), place (maintained), and control (administered).[11] She also added the role of permanence (sustainability), which we will address later in this book.

Setting aside the nature of special holdings, such as the personal letters of Edgar Allan Poe or the original handwritten scripts of Shakespeare, the manner in which information is acquired, maintained, and administered online is not distinguished by the type of information contained in the file. This is a truth shared by the Internet itself. Files are, literally, just packets of bytes, whether they contain images of the aforementioned letters and scripts or if they are movies, sound recordings, or any other form of information.

Thus, the collection and storage of information might not only serve as a workable definition of an archive, it is as well at least part of what could be a fair description of a library's card catalog—minus a retrieval function. Libraries are historically associated with public information gathered from individual works and stored without any relational methodology. Today, the library's method of storage and the mechanisms necessary to retrieve the information are systematically not that different from the industrial practices of archivists. Even to the point of access authorization, the storage practices now used by university libraries are remarkably similar to those used by archivists within the government and private industry. They differ, in many cases, as to the types of information preserved. But they differ much less than they have in the past as to the physical format of the files to be preserved.

The key difference between archives and libraries may be that the information storage scheme for libraries must provide for accessibility. Users must be able to find desired information—whether originally a monograph, draft papers, or a conference presentation—quickly and with some degree of confidence as to the authenticity of the information contain therein. Additionally, users must be able to see how these collections are related to other collections via this search function. This may provide the best distinction between a library acting as an archive and a library acting as an information commons. In some ways, librarians are returning to the ethos of Jenkinson: All information must be stored because all information can be stored. The role of the millennial librarian will not be that of an appraiser but of an expert in information storage and retrieval. And the latter of these two functions—retrieval—will require the best skills. For finding the right tree in a forest of more than a trillion trees will be no small feat. Yet, simply making information accessible does not qualify the library as a publisher, as we will discuss later.

Whether archivists follow a similar path that is facing librarians is not the purview of this book, except to note that at least in regard to the nature of the information preserved, collections in this century will reflect the same expansive nature of Jenkinson, if not his maintenance ethos. That is, more and more information can be preserved without the necessity of Norton's culling techniques (unless the archive itself is a work of publishing artistry). However, it is unlikely that owners of information should expect archivists to revert to the Jenkinson standard of "updating and modification," a passive role that was so heartily criticized in the past century. One major difference between archivists and librarians remains crystal clear, regardless of the role either plays in information storage. Librarians are unlikely to ever be defined by the archivist standard suggested by Cook and Schwartz: "Archives and management by archivists, will always reflect power relationships. Archives . . . are not passive storehouses of old stuff, but active sites where social power is negotiated, contested, confirmed."[12]

This does not suggest a passive state for librarians. Rather, the tools used by librarians and archivists will deal more with how information is stored so as to enhance its retrieval. Yet, even within this context, how data are labeled reflects power. For what is called one thing and not another will have as much control over what types of researchers will actually be capable of accessing that information.

Finding the (Right) Information

First and foremost, librarians are professional guides to finding information. They are also engaged in preserving data, which again is traditionally the role of an archivist. In some cases, librarians and their libraries have been defined in terms of the nature of the collections with which they work and protect. Librarians and libraries also have been defined by what their collections support in terms of research and teaching. And, they often have been defined by the professional nature of the patrons they serve. The role of a library as a keeper of monographs, magazines, journals, films, and other materials undeniably defined—until recently—their purpose. As libraries have grown in holdings, the role of the librarian within this complex system of collections that is maintained in a logical, searchable schematic also grew. Universities once boasted of library holdings as a measure of the institution's academic standing. Some still do. University libraries were (and still are) segmented into strata that reflect their position as upper tier, middle, or public. At the top are the one hundred or so research libraries. Yet, few if any libraries are measured higher for how effective they are in facilitating access to information over the size of the holdings they provide locally. And, until recently, all libraries provided roughly the same method of access to their holdings: a card catalog.

For centuries, information was produced, usually in book form, and a librarian either considered the publication necessary as a general work, or particularly appropriate because of a specific topic of importance to that library. The systems of cataloging and their histories are familiar to any graduating library science student. What may not be so familiar is the almost invisible nature of the cataloging that reflected, at times, as much of a political function of the librarian in an information "management" role. Where in the library the newly acquired book appeared on the shelf and on what floor of the stacks that particular book appeared defined in its own way the nature of the information inherent in that publication. This was no small matter. Until the creation of electronic catalogs, researchers generally restricted their searches to a set of "cards" within a distinct section of a box and to a specific shelf of information products (typically books) defined as related to one another. Any first-year graduate student knows the practice of finding one book of note on a shelf, and then scanning the surrounding books for possible volumes of similar and relevant data. Academic communities frowned on researchers who wandered into "inappropriate" areas of the libraries, no matter how similar the information may appear. Political science, for example, has its agenda building theory; mass communications, its agenda setting theory. And nary the twain shall meet, even though they have much in common. In fact, journal peer reviewers might frown on as inappropriate the citing of research from the "other side of the fence," no matter how illuminating that research may be.

The role of the librarian was to gather the information, separate it, and send it to its own "community," sometimes at the insistence of a particular academic faculty, but often by the tradition associated with the research itself or the authors who produced it. Huge rifts exist between the artificial islands (departments and colleges) within universities. Humanities remain distinct from life science, business from journalism, agriculture from human ecology. Yet, because of this, research in one area, such as the works of Weber in economics, might be completely unknown to an undergraduate or graduate student in journalism studying the long-term demise of newspapers. These artificial and ephemeral lines between regimens, to some extent, disappear almost at the very moment when research queries are posed to databases.

Yet, the databases themselves reflect an artificial demarcation of information, often defined by the journals they contain. For example, ProCite may catalog articles in economics, while JSTOR gathers articles dealing with journalism. Thus, a journalism researcher probing the cases of the death of newspapers would likely miss the works of Weber that might touch on and illuminate the nature of the subject. The same biases and strictures that kept some economic theory away from mass communication theory in card catalogs continue within electronic databases.

With the emergence of metadatabases—especially those user-created, such as Google's Custom Search (google.com/coop), Clusty (clusty.com), Dogpile (www.dogpile.com), SurfWax (www.surfwax.com), Copernic Agent (www.copernic.com), and others mentioned in chapter 3—researchers will be able to search multiple sources for information, but still not proprietary databases. These metasearch engines do not provide actual access to subscription databases. However, in the future, they could generate a citation that could then be used by the patron to retrieve the article in question by logging into the library's database site. This technology may require additional fine-tuning before it could be used reliably. Yet, it holds the promise that at some point, searching multiple subscription databases will be possible. As noted by UC-Berkeley: "Few meta-searchers allow you to delve into the largest, most useful search engine databases. They tend to return results from smaller and/or free search engines and miscellaneous free directories, often small and highly commercial."[13] The university went on to note that individual databases available through library subscriptions may still hold more promise for researchers than metasearch engines: "Although we respect the potential of textual analysis and clustering technologies, we recommend directly searching individual search engines [databases] to get the most precise results, and using meta-searchers if you want to explore more broadly." Again, this may be a reflection of an academic bias that mistrusts any research not generated by like-trained, like-educated, and like-institutionalized researchers.

Yet, because information—often the best information—exists within proprietary databases, undergraduate and some graduate students use what is easiest to find, what we discussed earlier as "the surface Web." As long as there are multiple databases, library experts will be vital in helping in the search process. With the emergence of one, massive search engine capable to peering into every database, the need for a professional searcher—that is, a millennial librarian—will only be heightened more. In fact, so much more, that the past suggested role of a librarian as political arbitrator of what constitutes the appropriate inclusions or "clumping" of research into specific categories is rendered moot by the nature of electronic research in the millennial era. In the past few decades, the expected role of the librarian has shifted from a cataloger of information, or even definer of collections, to a scientist of search methods. That is, we now have millions of records of all types, from novels to movies to chat sessions to blogs. Search within the millennial library is not reliant on computer-trained experts with some knowledge of a specific field or a specific database, though the latter does reflect the vestiges of research "specialties." Rather, research going forward will rely heavily on librarians especially adept within a field, but also familiar with many other related fields, all backed by a familiarity with the tools of technology that each day are made easier to use. It is a point-and-click universe.

The millennial librarian might be best described as a wielder of magnets, each specifically well suited to draw from the vast collection of artifacts appropriate for a specific task from what can be described as a hybrid collection of print and online reserves. Different magnets would draw different results. The defining of the nature of the magnet, rather than a specific subject collection or database, would be the driving force, the defining tool for searches. In an academic environment that remains largely balkanized, the ability of the librarian to cross these artificial barriers is a key to a search's success. Thus, a skilled librarian, fostering the best practices, could minimize the bias held by schools of academics for only that research conducted by "their own herd" as opposed to that from other disciplines.

How well a university library accomplishes this cross-disciplinary activity takes them far from the past role as mere acquirers and keepers of print materials. Indeed, as noted by Casserly, "In order to collect [digital resources], libraries must lease rather than purchase, access rather than house, and develop ways of evaluating, describing, and maintaining the accessibility of dynamic content."[14] Recently, university libraries have turned to a neutral measure of their effectiveness: LibQUAL, a measuring device created and maintained by the Association of Research Libraries. As noted on its website, the roles of LibQUAL are to,

- Foster a culture of excellence in providing library service
- Help libraries better understand user perceptions of library service quality
- Collect and interpret library user feedback systematically over time
- Provide libraries with comparable assessment information from peer institutions
- Identify best practices in library service
- Enhance library staff members' analytical skills for interpreting and acting on data[15]

Perhaps the last of these is most salient for our discussion: "interpreting and acting on data." The millennial librarian must be trained to determine how to define the magnet itself. That is, the kind of research drawn from the information commons of the Web will be defined and constricted by the search terms used. The success of any search is based largely on the terms used and the pattern of the search statement. With the infinite nature of the Web's well of information, choosing the right approach to finding the right sources of data is not just critical, it defines the very nature of the resulting research that will be based on these sources. How those bits of data are tagged and stored is critical to the long-term health of research and, by extension, progress of civilization.

Early in the era of Web building, search engines relied heavily on metadata contained within the code of the Web page. This code was intended to alert "spiders" as to the nature of the page and the content searchers could expect to find. The resulting practices often led to abuse by Web builders, each striving to appear at the top—or at least in the top ten—of every searcher's first page. This desire was not without reason: most searchers rarely delve much further than the first few pages of their results, no matter how many millions of hits they generate in their search. An entire cottage industry developed consisting of "experts" who could promise website owners that their sites would appear in the top ten. Over time, the practice of "gaming" the system pushed legitimate sites farther and farther down search results listings to the point that finding actual valid information had become almost impossible without carefully worded queries.

Search engine developers then started penalizing Web pages that clearly employed unfair tactics such as repeating certain words hundreds of times or using a meta statement that looked like a dictionary. While this change helped, it still rendered what was becoming a very large forest of information, impenetrable, except to the highly skilled or very lucky searchers.

Then came Google. And others like Google. The logic behind searches at Google is less about counting words in sites than about how Web users actually value the site. The more uses that refer to the site, put links to the site on their websites, or communicate with the site, the higher the ranking. This pattern of human interaction with a site is comparable to a librarian ranking journals by how much they are used. This strategy comes with its own set of issues, one of which is best exemplified by the now famous (infamous?) spoofing by a group that, in unison, tricked search engines into listing their political opposition site at the top of a search for a presidential candidate in 2004. Such spoofing can occur in commercial sites as businesses engage in similar efforts to hijack the search engine's tracking methods to affect the results. While this sort of manipulation is far less likely within an academic database, ranking data by usage allows for the segregation of popular research from that deemed unpopular, rather than most robust above the weak or questionable articles. And a system that relies upon the number of "pageviews" a research site receives ignores the intent of the visitor. Some researchers may want to look at published data in order to refute it. Their visit to a site should not be automatically presumed to be an endorsement of the data.

When using Google Scholar, one is more likely to see results based on highest citation rates first. In addition, no matter how the research article is ranked, whether by users or by librarians, the results will inherently favor one over another simply based on the listing bias of "top ten" links presented in all browser pages. Sometimes this ranking is a matter of personal bias that occurs when the metadata is attached to a file. That is, those who regulate information access need not overtly censor a particular work in order to effectively censor it.[16] More often than not, ranking in the top ten of a Google search has less to do with the quality of the associated site than the convenience and/or laxity of searchers. That is, the first source found is best because it is the first source found. This, obviously, renders the intelligence of the researcher moot and the content-oblivious matrix of the search engine supreme.

On the other hand, more devious activities can render a work "censored" merely by how the data in question is tagged. Given the enormity of the data field of the Web, what Ketelaar referred to as a "mode of power"[17] of censorship can be accomplished simply by ensuring the data in question is labeled in such a way that no general search will rank it in the top five thousand results. Finding such a deeply buried record might require the searcher to know exact and specific details of the file being sought. Knowing such precise details would be so unlikely as to raise doubts as to whether the record would ever be found. That is, with miscoding malfeasance or misfeasance, research or data could be buried so deep into the archive or e-reserve as to render it effectively lost and, thus, censored.

New versions of software can leave files created by older, unsupported computer programs literally "orphaned," thus generating the same result. Examples of this abound. Consider that some new software platforms cannot open files created by older versions of the same program. Such data is rendered lost by obsolescence. It remains available online, but not to anyone using the newer software. And, while many software manufacturers may pledge to always provide backward support for older file types, this is not always the case (e.g., Word 2007 versus Word 5.0). Preservation, therefore, is more than merely having a file that contains the data. It must also preserve the tools necessary to open such files.

The threat of information being forever lost puts a heavy burden on those charged with preserving access to the data. In the case of a book being improperly shelved in a library, staff can administer a shelf-by-shelf search which, while painstakingly slow, will eventually result in the volume being recovered. Attempting this within a database with one or two million records would be almost impossible. Attempting it within a web of one trillion pages—latest estimate by Google, as of July 2008[18]—is effectively futile.

Add to this the lack of a standard nomenclature shared by all those engaged in preserving records, including both those researchers in differing fields and those within the same disciplines, and the result is a dangerously fragile system. The ability to organize and label information online requires what is described as a *semantic* Web, one in which information preservers (as well as researchers themselves) come to agree what the word "tree," for instance, actually means.

THE SEMANTIC WEB

One of the goals Tim Berners-Lee, creator of the code that supports the World Wide Web, set for his creation would be the ability to share information regarding his physics research with his cohorts. The idea of sharing data and research has always been a driving force behind the Web. It requires, however, several elements to be in the right place, starting with standards and protocols and an agreement on images and other supporting material. One of the most challenging goals among various research groups and policy makers is getting existing datasets in formats that allow for combined searches. Given that this concept will radically change the way information is coded, stored, and retrieved, researchers embarking on new data-gathering projects should be aware of the implications.

Berners-Lee also envisioned the semantic Web to yield powerful searches for data, searches not possible with traditional tools, such as those provided by Web spiders or even the enhanced methods used by Google. The semantic Web, as defined by Berners-Lee, is "a web of data that can be processed directly and indirectly by machines."[19] That is, it is itself part of the Web and can provide access to information independent of a particular application, platform, or domain. It runs, in a sense, above the Web, acting as an intelligent agent with higher search abilities than anything used today. It has its own Web code language that is composed of objects defined and used in conjunction with other objects included within a dataset.

The semantic Web does not include artificial intelligence, something often associated with current discussions regarding "agents." It relies on rules of inference that create a pathway between different datasets. It does not think like a human, but has enough information and a relational language that makes it possible to find information with logical pathways, no matter the data's source. Rather than looking for specific metadata filled with specific words, the semantic Web uses objects to find specific data that itself includes the rules of inference—objects—that will make it possible for a researcher to find the precise document or dataset necessary for a project. It does require that the dataset include semantic metadata which, when appropriately defined, will allow computers to understand how the information is related to other data. The result is a web composed of one very large dataset intended to be accessible by all researchers, no matter what kind of platform or software they are using locally.

Many tools are associated with the semantic Web. And, many librarians have been at the forefront of the semantic Web movement. And, again, it is not the purpose here to suggest that all library technicians themselves become involved in the semantic coding of datasets though, notably, many SILSs offer courses touching directly on this subject. However, at a minimum, a library's staff should be familiar with the terms associated with the semantic Web, such as resource description framework (RDF); its corresponding data formats, such as RDF/XML, N3, Turtle, N-Triples; and its schemes, such as ontology web language (OWL).

If we are to believe the tenets of the semantic Web (and I personally have my doubts), the resulting knowledge base system would allow a researcher a few years from now to not only find a particularly relevant article, but then find the associated dataset, how it was created, what other datasets have been created based on it, and what other findings have been published. It enhances access to relevant information, faster and more accurately than is possible today. "Search quality," a term used by Google, is enhanced and made more accurate, which is the goal of any researcher using the Web to find information. It is as if the library's card catalog could provide a researcher not only the best reference card, but also all the relating cards associated with that single card. It must be noted that the copyright and intellectual property rights issues, which we will explore later in this book, are far from resolved. The ownership status of some databases, for example, is sufficiently vague to render any direct access to these files very unlikely in the near term.

E-RESERVES: WHAT IS PRESERVED?

Just as the lines between librarians and archivists have blurred in the last two decades, both roles moving away, as posited by Bantin, from mere custody of data to "good recordkeeping,"[20] so have the lines separating what should be saved from what should be destroyed. Data is a vague term, of course, and can be taken to include everything that occurs moment to moment. It requires no act of appraisal, no judgment as to whether the record, dataset, or research has some intrinsic value. If one takes this to its extreme, recordkeeping of what occurs in a classroom would include everything from notes on the blackboard to the gestures made by the professor in reaction to a student's sneeze. The ability to do just that and store essentially every point as a data point is fast upon us. The time is not far off that a single computer with a single hard drive will be capable of storing all the data created in the span of human history.

Thus, the choice for the millennial library is not really what to store for future use, but what not to preserve. The traditional contents for an archive of a worthy author might include such personal items as letters or other correspondence, personal notes, as well as other artifacts of a person's life. In today's more electronic village, these likely would be such items as e-mails, blogs, and other social media networks. But would a library's e-reserves need to include these? Beyond the simplistic "why not" is the issue of relevance. Are e-mails important? Such a judgment of the value of an item puts us back into Duranti's world of appraisal.[21] Who is to judge whether the musing of a researcher in e-mails to a colleague would not be something of value to future researchers? And, more importantly, upon whom would it fall to determine if the data in question is not of storage value? Notably, when a rookie player in baseball gets his first hit in the major leagues, the ball is preserved, not because the powers that be are convinced the player will be in the Hall of Fame, but because they cannot be certain he will not. The logic is that the personal letters of Einstein certainly are likely to be of interest to someone. Who can say for certain they will not be of any importance. Better to err on the side of saving than that of tossing. As noted by a developer engaged with the Google Book Project, making more information available is far more important than deciding what should and should not be saved at all.[22] Yet, does this mean we should preserve the grocery list of Einstein?

Setting aside the issue of personal communications, a library's e-reserves would, at a minimum, hold research papers and possibly the data collected supporting the publication. This is what is at the heart of the National Institutes of Health's (NIH) initiative to place into the public sphere all research and data funded by public institutions.[23] Thus all materials would be appraised by one existing organization, such as an academic journal using peer review, then at some later point made available and free to all. This later point is currently set at one year. It is likely that delay will become shorter. Then again, it could become longer, a creature of the same copyright pressures that have rendered the constitutional phrase "for a limited time" a mockery. But whatever the terms of the publishing of research and its accompanying data, the concept of a library saving an electronic copy of all publicly funded research moves the library into a new sphere: academic publishing. As noted by Simpson and Hey in 2006:

> Over the ensuing years, two complementary solutions have evolved:
>
> - Open Access Repositories where articles, conference papers, books, book sections, reports, theses, learning objects and multimedia are deposited in open electronic archives
> - Open Access Journals where publishers do not charge subscriptions or online access fees but instead look to other publishing models, including author pays for publication[24]

Many university libraries have already moved toward offering a form of publishing to support those interested in starting an online journal. For some, the offer is management software and individuals who can set up and maintain the server system. For other libraries, some editorial boards and staff are included. All of this interest in online publishing is driven by one supposed verity: Print academic research journals will at some point be supplanted by strictly online versions. That is, it is the print that will die and not, it is hoped, the journal. And, yet, this presumed print obituary ignores the current state and overstates its coming demise.

For the time being, this presumption is already believed among many of our younger academic colleagues. Online research publishing by university libraries appears to be a lifeboat to academic library acquisition staffs that struggle annually to meet the ever-rising academic database archive fees charged by large publishers. And, this imagined lifeboat might be feared by some of these very same academic publishers, most of whom share the same worries (and readership data) that haunt owners of traditional journalism outlets such as newspapers and magazines. We are in the midst of a paradigm shift from print to digital in all phases of our research, from collection of data to its analysis and sharing, to the final published product. But, as already mentioned earlier, this shift comes with its own set of troubles (lost data, lost journals, lost research). It is not suggested that the millennial library should ignore this shift. It is suggested that a wise library administration would carefully manage and assess the move toward these models. We will discuss this in chapters nine and ten. For now, let us consider the actual form of the research and data stored within the library's e-reserves.

IN WHAT FORMAT?

Mention online academic publishing to a crowd of academics and you are sure to find some who find the entire idea of eliminating the tangible printed works for "electrons" very disturbing. Part of their distress may be well founded. Visit the World Wide Web Consortium's website (www.w3.org) and spend any time wandering through the site, and it is possible to encounter three forms of hypertext markup language (HTML) coding for a simple em dash. With the changes in the "accepted" HTML standards by the consortium itself, rendering something as innocuous as a long dash symbol poses a real challenge for browsers. Of course, other characters present challenges, such as quotation marks, exclamation points, and special characters such as copyright symbols. Ultimately, the question of readability over time can generate a real uneasiness among online journal publishers and researchers, online or not. As each generation of HTML is born, modifications to the underlying coding, as was the case for the em dash, can render prior coding obsolete. The em dash, as was pointed out by research in 2006, was once simply "emdash," then coded as "151," then "8212"—each upgrade rendering the previous coding as an error, not an em dash.[25] Anyone who has converted a Microsoft Word document into HTML will likely have noticed that "smart quotes" do not render as quotes at all but as unreadable special characters.

However, while the most common formatting option, other than HTML, is the popular PDF file, owned by Adobe, even here new online journal publishers face issues. Two of the most obvious issues are the storing of any research within a proprietary software format and the larger, potentially browser-freezing file sizes. Some commercial Web reviewers, such as those at UseIt .com and pass4press.com, list far more issues, such as image resolution, font embedding, page sizing, compression, as well as browser crashes.[26] But just focusing on the ownership and file size, it is of note that the International Organization for Standardization (ISO) has adopted a form of PDF (PDF/A) that it believes represents the best choice for long-term electronic archiving.

> The feature-rich nature of PDF can create difficulties in preserving information over the long-term, and some useful features of the PDF file format are incompatible with the demands of long-term preservation. For example, PDF documents are not necessarily self-contained, drawing on system fonts and other content stored external to the original file. As time passes, and especially as technology changes, these external connections can be broken, and the dependencies cause information to be lost. Additionally, because of the lack of standardization among the many PDF development tools on the market, there is inconsistency in the implementation of the file format. This lack of standardization could be chaotic for the information managers of the future, especially as it would be difficult (if not impossible) for them to "get under the hood" of the PDF files unless a format specification were put in place that specifically addressed long-term preservation needs.[27]

The ISO does not address the issue of using proprietary software. Storing research long term within a proprietary software environment raises issues of long-term access, software availability, and a host of other potential challenges. What if the very basis of Adobe's PDF software changes or is significantly modified in such a way that accessing past journal research is only possible with forms of the software no long supported by upgraded computer system software? What if some online virus is spread that acts on only the software "readers," but by doing so, threatens access to archived research? What if a virus uses a browser's access of a research article to insidiously modify that PDF? Possibly even reversing the download to a phantom upload?

We have not had enough experience in the field to know with certainty what the outcomes might be to any of these questions. What is certain is that independent approaches to the issue will not bear the sort of outcomes we need most: a single, open access software package to create and sustain access to research and its data. PDF/A—a relatively new version of the Adobe Acrobat program that creates a self-contained file—may offer the best option to date for the actual articles ready to be published. Then again, HTML5, a significant upgrade strongly supported by Apple, poses a very real challenge to PDF/A. Datasets present a much larger and more immediate challenge, as mentioned in the previous semantic Web section. Attaching the appropriate semantic labels to individual files may not be an option, but a requirement attached to familiar incentives, such as federal grants. Millennial libraries should be aware of at least the minimum requirements and activities already in place.[28]

E-RESERVE HOSTING

The decision of where data will be hosted—on which server the files will reside—can be driven by network capacity, cost, or prestige. On-campus storage costs may not be the barrier: hard drive costs have been falling precipitously in recent years, with a multiple-terabyte server now within most library budgets. What is a barrier is the bandwidth available and its fluctuations based on campus use.

Many universities, having seen their e-reserves evolve in fits and starts over the past fifteen years, may be reticent or simply unable to provide a secure on-campus, online storage area. With hundreds, possibly thousands of subnetwork servers operating within a university domain, the ability to provide authentication—authorization via passwords to incoming visitors to the site and its contents—is a massive challenge. For instance, editorial boards for new journals may encounter significant resistance from university technology professionals to server hosting within a university because of the stress visitors will put on the bandwidth. The overtaxed bandwidth within some universities may provide only slow downloads of even moderately large articles. As noted by Fritz in a discussion regarding video files, "some university network administrators see it [these files] as a potential network 'killer'."[29] Additionally, many universities already face challenges of users sending large files or in other ways overtaxing the network, especially at certain times of the day, such as 8:00–9:00 a.m. and 4:00–5:00 p.m.

The storage issue of data could be resolved by storing journal files at off-campus providers such as Box.net, FlipDrive, Storegate, and IDrive. Charges for storage space through these providers as of August 2009 ran roughly from $20 to $40 per 100 GB per month. Notably, these fees are 90 percent less than they were in 2007. Services provided include

Remote Access
Mobile Access
Private File Sharing
Public File Sharing
Scheduled Backup
File Search
Drag-and-Drop

The "front-end" of the e-reserves might be within a university, foundation, or nonprofit, with the actual location of the academic articles at one of these secure off-campus providers.

Finally, the need for a university to present itself as a leader in a particular area of research, such as oceanography, may create a sense of mission dedicated to solving the network and cost issues presented in the publishing of an online journal. If the journal is seen as part of the mission of the university to excel in biosciences, for example, the funds to support that online publication can be built into the grants for other funding vehicles. This treads on areas of university politics which, while the mastering of it is vital to any publication trying to survive the turf battles within any university, is outside the scope of this book. This is not to minimize in any way the importance that publishing boards address the political issues of territorialism that are de facto a part of all universities, in one form or another. We will visit these and other issues involving the millennial library as a publisher in chapter 6.

OPPORTUNITIES AND CHALLENGES FOR E-RESERVES

Libraries must go further than creating database links to online resources. As noted by Herrera and Aldana, the preferred practices will be to ensure that "all electronic resources are catalogued and made accessible in ways that parallels other library materials."[30] Specifically, merely placing a list of links to databases with little or no guidance is not as useful to patrons as a more descriptive guide. As more and more databases come online and as more and more home-generated content is placed into a library's institutional reserve, the need will increase for robust and dynamic descriptions of that data. "Those who prefer web-based lists and require in-depth descriptions depend upon the [library] subject specialists to provide them."[31]

Librarians must use their positions within the e-reserves to accomplish much more than cataloging research and its accompanying data. They must play a role as researchers and as cross-discipline catalysts among disparate researchers. As noted by Manoff, while librarians have been concerned with their ability to support research, "they have been less actively engaged in pursuing such scholarship themselves."[32] Librarians would benefit from "more interdisciplinary conversations with fields like sociology, media studies, cultural studies, history, history of the book, and even literary studies where scholars are confronting similar issues and harnessing theory in a way to make connections and transcend the limits of constituted disciplines."[33] In turn, these fields, and others, such as mass communications, would be "enriched by the perspective of librarians and archivists working inside the archive who occupy a privileged terrain."[34] As Garber notes, the task of the millennial librarian "is to re-imagine the boundaries of what we have come to see are disciplines and have the courage to re-think them."[35]

Finally, and perhaps most importantly, as universities undertake the creation of these repositories, they must take care not to do so without a full appreciation of the long-term commitment they are making. If the failure of a single academic journal can be deemed a tragedy, the failure of a university's institutional repository, e-reserve, dSpace, or whatever it chooses to call its online archive, would be a calamity. As the years pass, more and more research will reside in these archives. And, as the decades continue, researchers—both on and off campus—will come to rely on these reserves to support and validate their own works. The ability of researchers in the future to cite data preserved within a university's archives is not just a matter of convenience, it is the backbone of progress.

The loss of an archive, as noted by Lynch, can arise from a variety of sources: loss of funding, management malfeasance, or technical failures. "As we think about institutional repositories today, there is much less redundancy than we have had in our systems of print publication and libraries, so any one single institutional failure can cause more damage."[36] Such losses, Lynch continues "may greatly set back scholarly acceptance of authorship of digital works; they may have a corrosive effect on the trust that underpins campus communities; they may undermine broad support for higher education."[37]

Lynch concludes that such failures are almost certain. That need not be the case if every university considering establishing an online archive considers the need for permanence, the need for a protection of these works no matter what other budgetary challenges exist. A university may lose its student commons and visit far less harm on its own head than allowing its electronic archive to fail.

Having said this, the value of these repositories is indisputable. They can support academic progress and change forever the way that research is conducted. They foster an outpouring of cross-disciplinary work. They can alter permanently the manner in which information is preserved for the common good. With careful planning, a university's e-reserve can become as valuable a measure of an institution's place in the academic world as library holdings once provided, and perhaps far more.

E-RESERVES: TEN MILESTONES

1. While only a few universities have created e-reserves, there are signs more will in the coming years.

2. Librarians must decide what to save. The obvious are research papers. But what about research data, e-mails between researchers, blogs, and other digital information?
3. Librarians in this century should reexamine their role in terms of storage of materials. Because of the abundance of online storage capacity, they may become more like archivists than the more traditional librarian role of the past few centuries.
4. Librarians must prepare themselves to answer the question of what they will preserve locally (on the library's servers) versus rely upon outside sources for retrieval. The citing of issues of acquisition and storage in the new media era cannot push these questions back. Other standards must be developed, and developed soon.
5. Librarians must publicize their expertise in the use of effectiveness of meta-search engines.
6. Beyond the use of LibQUAL, millennial librarians must be trained in the creation and application of meta-statements used to tag articles within their e-reserves. This must be done professionally, with not even a hint of academic bias.
7. While hardly a standard (or even an emerging standard), the semantic Web is worthy of some attention in the coming years. Some of the tools available in this objects-orienting tagging system are RDFOWL.
8. The shift from paper to bytes is moving rapidly in some areas, such as academic journals, and much more slowly in other areas, such as books. The millennial library must determine if it is to be an open access repository, or a login (as is done to gain access to online databases housed at the university library), or subscription based. It could be a combination of all of these, and might consider a fee based in "depth."
9. The millennial library should adopt the PDF/A format for its electronic reserves and should consider using off-campus backup services to protect its archives.
10. Careful planning, budgeting, and the institution of best practices procedures must be in place *prior* to the institution of an e-reserve, if only for the sake of those who have entrusted the library to provide access to information.

SUMMARY

The demand for access to online resources has risen in the past few years, just as the cost of hard drives and other online storage devices has fallen. The result has been a shift in the concept of storing information from "what is important enough to store" to "why not store everything?"

This shift suggests that, in many ways, librarians are becoming more like archivists, just as archivists, some argue, acted more like librarians once. New technology, in the form of e-reserves, requires that librarians take a new look at their roles in information gathering, sorting, and serving, and, in many ways think more like archivists than their predecessors, more like information managers than information keepers.

The distinction between libraries and archives is primarily in the "way these holdings are created, acquired, maintained and administered." Three of these standards—acquisition, maintenance, and administration—are rendered less significant by the emergence of digital storage.

The collection and storage of information not only might serve as a workable definition of an archive, it is also at least part of what might be a fair description of a library's card catalog—minus a retrieval function. Librarians are historically seen as associated with public information gathered from individual works and stored without any relational methodology. Today, the library's method of storage and the mechanisms necessary to retrieve the information are systematically not that different from the industrial practices of archivists.

First and foremost, librarians are professional guides to finding information. They are also engaged in preserving data, which again is traditionally the role of an archivist. In some cases, librarians and their libraries have been defined in terms of the nature of the collections with which they work and protect. Librarians and libraries also have been defined by what their collections support in terms of research and teaching. Few if any libraries are measured higher for how effective they are in facilitating access to information over the size of the holdings they provide locally. And, until recently, all libraries provided roughly the same method of access to their holdings: a card catalog.

The historical role of the librarian was to gather information, separate it, and send it to its own "community," sometimes at the insistence of the academic community, but often by the tradition associated with the research itself or the authors who produced it. The role of a librarian as political arbitrator of what constitutes the appropriate inclusions or "clumping" of research into specific categories is rendered unnecessary by the nature of electronic research in the millennial era. Research going forward will rely heavily on librarians especially adept within a field, backed by a familiarity with the tools of technology that each day are made easier to use. It is a point-and-click universe.

The millennial librarian might be best described as a wielder of magnets, each specifically well-suited to draw from the vast collection of artifacts appropriate for a specific task out of what can be called a hybrid collection of print and online reserves. A university library's ability to foster cross-disciplinary research takes them far from the past role as mere acquirers and keepers of print materials.

Recently, university libraries have turned to a neutral measure of their effectiveness: LibQUAL, a measuring device created and maintained by ARL. The millennial librarian must be trained to determine how to refine research searches of the information commons defined and constricted by the search terms used.

Finding a deeply "buried" record might require the searcher to know exact and specific details of the file being sought. Knowing such precise details would be so unlikely as to raise the doubt as to whether the record could ever be found. The threat of information being forever lost puts a heavy burden on those in charge of saving the data. Attempting a search blindly within a Web of one trillion pages is effectively futile.

The ability to organize and label information online requires what is described as a semantic Web, one in which information preservers (as well as researchers themselves) come to agree what the word "tree," for instance, actually means. Tim Berners-Lee envisioned the semantic Web to make very powerful searches for data possible, searches not possible with traditional tools, such as provided by Web spiders or even the enhanced methods used by Google. The semantic Web, as defined by Berners-Lee, is "a web of data that can be processed directly and indirectly by machines." It relies on rules of inference that create a pathway between different datasets. Rather than looking for specific metadata filled with specific words, the semantic Web uses objects to find specific data that it itself includes in the rules of inference—objects—that will make it possible for a researcher to find the precise document or dataset necessary for a project.

"Search quality," a term used by Google, can be enhanced and made more accurate, which is the goal of any researcher using the Web to find information. It is as if the library's card catalog could provide a researcher not only the best reference card, but also all the related cards associated with that single card.

The ability to do just that and store essentially every point as a data point is fast upon us. The time is not far off that a single computer with a single hard drive will be capable of storing all the accumulated data of human history. Thus, the choice for the millennial library is not really what to store for future use, but what not to accumulate. Are e-mails important? The personal letters of Einstein certainly would be of interest to someone. Setting aside the issue of personal communication, a library's e-reserves would, at a minimum, hold research papers and possibly the data collected supporting the publication. This is at the heart of the National Institutes of Health's initiative to place into the public sphere all research and data funded by public funds. Thus all materials would be "appraised" by one existing organization, such as an academic journal using peer review, then at some later point made available and free to all. Many university libraries have already moved toward offering publishing houses to serve those interested in starting an online journal.

Mention online academic publishing to a crowd of academics and you are sure to find some who find the entire idea of eliminating the tangible printed works for "electrons" very disturbing. The question of readability over time can generate a very real uneasiness among online journal publishers and researchers, online or not.

The most common formatting option, other than HTML, is the popular PDF file, owned by Adobe. This poses potential problems for new online journal publishers. Two of the most obvious are the storing of any research within a proprietary software format and the larger, potentially browser-freezing file sizes. It is of note that the ISO has adopted a form of PDF (PDF/A) that it believes represents the best choice for long-term electronic archiving.

We have not had enough experience in the field to know with certainty what the outcomes might be to any of these questions. What is certain is that independent approaches to the issue will not bear the sort of outcomes we need most: a single, open access software package to create and sustain access to research and its data. PDF/A may offer the best option to date for the actual articles ready to be published.

The decision of where data will be hosted can be driven by network capacity, cost, or prestige. On-campus storage costs may not be the barrier: Hard drive costs have fallen precipitously in recent years, with a multiple-terabyte server now within most library budgets. What is a barrier is the bandwidth available and its fluctuations based on campus use.

The need for a university to present itself as a leader in a particular area of research, such as oceanography, may create a sense of mission dedicated to solving the network and cost issues presented in the publishing of an online journal. If the journal is seen as part of the mission of the university to excel in biosciences, for example, the funds to support that online publication can be built into the grants for other funding vehicles.

Libraries must go further than creating database links to online resources. As more and more databases come online, and as more and more home-generated content is placed into a library's institutional reserve, the need will increase for robust and dynamic descriptions of that data. Librarians must play a role as researchers and as cross-discipline catalysts among disparate researchers.

Finally librarians must take care not to create repositories without a full appreciation of the long-term commitment they are making. If the failure of a single academic journal can be deemed a tragedy, the failure of a university's institutional repository, e-reserve, dSpace, or whatever it chooses to call its online archive, would be a calamity. Some suggest that such failures are almost certain. That need not be the case if every university considering establishing an online archive considers the need for permanence, the need for a protection of these works no matter what other budgetary challenges exist.

The value of these repositories is indisputable. They can support academic progress and change forever the way that research is conducted. They foster an outpouring of cross-disciplinary work. They can alter permanently the manner in which information is preserved for the common good. With careful planning, a university's e-reserve can become as valuable a measure of an institution's place in the academic world as library holdings once provided, and perhaps far more.

NOTES

1. Karen Markey, "Institutional Repositories: The Experience of Master's and Baccalaureate Institutions," *Portal: Libraries and the Academy* 8, no. 2 (2008): 157.
2. Mary Casserly, "Developing a Concept of Collection for the Digital Age," *Portal: Libraries and the Academy* 2, no. 4 (2002): 577.
3. S. Muller, J. A. Feith, and R. Fruin, *Manual for the Arrangement and Description of Archives* (Dutch Association of Archivists, 1898).
4. Hilary Jenkinson, *Manual of Archive Administration* (London: Percy Lund, Humphries and Co., 1922); Oliver W. Holmes, "Sir Hilary Jenkinson, 1882–1961," *The American Archivist* 24, no. 3 (July 1961): 345–347.
5. Terry Cook and Joan M. Schwartz, "Archives, Records, and Power: From (Postmodern) Theory to (Archival) Performance," *Archival Science* 2 (2002): 171–185.
6. Cook, "Archives, Records, and Power: From (Postmodern) Theory to (Archival) Performance"; Jennifer Howard, "Anti-Open Access by Publishing Group Loses Another University Press," *The Chronicles of Higher Education* (4 October 2007).
7. Margaret Cross Norton, "Records Disposal," in *Norton on Archives: The Writings of Margaret Cross Norton on Archives and Records Management*, ed. Thornton W. Mitchell (Carbondale: Southern Illinois University Press, 1975): 1–288, as cited in Cook, "Archives, Records, and Power: From (Postmodern) Theory to (Archival) Performance," 171.
8. Arthur Schellenberg, *Modern Archives: Principles and Techniques* (Chicago: University of Chicago Press, 1956).
9. James Gregory Bradsher, "Introduction," in *Managing Archives and Archival Institutions*, ed. James Gregory Bradsher (Chicago: University of Chicago Press, 1988): 1–18.

10. Bradsher, "Introduction," 1–18.
11. Casserly, "Developing a Concept of Collection for the Digital Age," 577.
12. Cook and Schwartz, 172.
13. www.lib.berkeley.edu/TeachingLib/Guides/Internet//MetaSearch.html
14. Casserly, "Developing a Concept of Collection for the Digital Age," 577.
15. "LibQUAL+TM: Defining and Promoting Library Service Quality," Association of Research Libraries, www.libqual.org/About/Information/index.cfm (5 August 2009).
16. Google, "We Knew the Web Was Big . . ." Google, googleblog.blogspot.com/2008/07/we-knew-web-was-big.html (25 February 2010).
17. Eric Ketelaar, "Archival Temples, Archival Prisons: Modes of Power and Protection," *Archival Science* 2 (2002): 221–228.
18. Google, "We Knew the Web Was Big . . . "
19. Tim Berners-Lee and Mark Fischetti, *Weaving the Web: The Original Design and Ultimate Destiny of the World Wide Web* (New York: HarperCollins, 2000); Marion Stubbs and Geoff Gibbons, "Hans Adolf Krebs (1900–1981): His Life and Times," *International Union of Biochemistry and Molecular Biology* 50, no. 3 (2008): 163–166.
20. Phillip Bantin, "Strategies for the Development of Partnerships in the Management of Electronic Records," Indiana University Electronic Records Project, Phase II (2000–2002).
21. Luciana Duranti, "The Concept of Appraisal and Archival Theory," *The American Archivist* 57, no. 2 (1994): 328–344.
22. Jennie Johnson, telephone interview with the author, discussing Google Books (5 August 2009).
23. *The National Institutes of Health Public Access Policy,* Sec. 218, Public Law (May 22, 2008) (accessed 8 June 2008).
24. Pauline Simpson and Jessie Hey, "Repositories for Research: Southampton's Evolving Role in the Knowledge Cycle," *Program* (August 2006): 1–6.
25. Thomas H. P. Gould, "Dash It All: The Secret War for the Heart of HTML," *The Vocabula Review* 8, no. 12 (2006): www.vocabula.com/2006/VRDEC06Gould.asp.
26. Jakob Nielsen, "PDF: Unfit for Human Consumption," useIt.com, www.useit.com/alertbox/20030714.html (3 June 2008); Pass4Press, "Top 10 Problems with PDFs," pass4press.com, www.pass4press.com/cgi-bin/wms.pl/970 (3 June 2008); Gould, "Dash It All."
27. "Frequently Asked Questions about ISO SCIT Activities and Related Technologies on Digital Imaging," International Organization for Standardization, isotc.iso.org/livelink/livelink/fetch/2000/2489/Ittf_Home/Scit/faq.html#WhyPDFA (3 June 2008).
28. Brian McBride, *RDF Semantics,* World Wide Web Consortium (2004).
29. Jeffrey Fritz, "Taming IP Video: Understanding How to Implement Bandwidth-Chewing Video Over an IP Network Can Help Domesticate a Potential Network Hog into a Well-Mannered Ally," *EdTech: Focus on Higher Education,* May–June 2008 (29 May 2008).
30. Gail Herrera, "Integrating Electronic Resources into the Library Catalog: A Collaborative Approach," *Portal: Libraries and the Academy* 1, no. 3 (2001): 241.

31. Herrera, "Integrating Electronic Resources."

32. Marlene Manoff, "Theories of the Archive from Across the Disciplines," *Portal: Libraries and the Academy* 4, no. 1 (2004): 9–23.

33. Manoff, "Theories of the Archive from Across the Disciplines," 22.

34. Manoff, "Theories of the Archive from Across the Disciplines," 22.

35. Marjorie B. Garber, *Academic Instincts* (Princeton, N.J.: Princeton University Press, 2001): 200; as cited in Manoff, "Theories of the Archive from Across the Disciplines," 9.

36. Clifford A. Lynch, "Institutional Repositories: Essential Infrastructure for Scholarship in the Digital Age," *Portal: Libraries and the Academy* 3, no. 2 (2003): 327–336.

37. Lynch, "Institutional Repositories," 334.

Chapter Five

The Electronic Book

REACHING THE DIGITAL PATRON

Today's university students were born digital: they read digitally, they listen digitally, and they watch digitally.[1] They may even think digitally. But even more importantly, they communicate digitally, share ideas digitally, and are as comfortable with digital devices as their parents are with a television remote control. Maybe even more so. According to the 2006 Pew Internet and American Life Project, of American children twelve to seventeen years old:

- About half reported sending or receiving a text message over their phone in the past twenty-four hours. That's roughly double the proportion of their older siblings (aged 26-40).
- A majority have used a social networking site and more than 40 percent have created a personal profile.
- Eighty-seven percent used the Internet in 2004, up from 73 percent in 2000. The frequency of teens' online usage was up 51 percent over the same period.
- Ninety-three percent of American teens ages twelve to seventeen use the Internet.
- Fifty-one percent of online teens go online daily, with 24 percent doing so several times a day.[2]

Yet, one barrier remains difficult for some students (and their parents) to cross: the e-book. College students may accept—even revel in—the searching for academic research online, but the printed book (and campus newspaper) remains a sacred ground of convenience, with an ease of use unmatched by electronic book readers. And the numbers bear this out: As noted by the

Association of American Publishers early in 2010, sales of print books were up 4 percent in 2009, despite the economic recession. Clearly the words on paper remain popular. That's not to say that e-books are doomed. In that same press release, AAP noted that sales for e-books were up 176 percent in 2009 from 2008.[3] Tracking back, e-book sales in 2007 increased 26.6 percent over 2006 (hitting $67.2 million) and almost tripled two years later, reaching $170 million in 2009.[4] While these numbers are miniscule compared to all book sales (almost $24 billion in 2009), the trend is obvious.[5] The popularity of new reading devices is clearly growing and rapidly, recession or not. As new devices are rolled out, such as the iPad, traditionalists may switch sides to take advantage of the convenience and options digital readers can provide.

In the meantime, while the demise of print has been the prediction of many academics (myself included), it is equally obvious that tomorrow's readers of books will switch back and forth between handheld readers and traditional paper for some time to come. The millennial library's future patrons will not only be the students that are seen in reading rooms today, but will also include their younger, more digitally acclimated siblings, who could likely still be reading about Winnie the Pooh in print. This is not a settled issue.

Table 5.1. Are Books Really Dying?

	*2002 ($)**	*2009 ($)**	*Growth Rate 2002–2009*
Trade (Total)	7,144,188	8,067,524	1.80%
Adult hardbound	2,371,553	2,604,159	1.30%
Adult paperbound	1,876,620	2,241,386	2.60%
Juvenile hardbound	1,636,248	1,704,475	0.60%
Juvenile paperbound	1,259,767	1,517,504	2.70%
Book clubs & mail order	852,384	588,461	–5.20%
Mass market paperback	1,216,710	1,042,143	–2.20%
Audiobooks	143,410	191,979	4.30%
Religious	556,799	658,724	2.40%
E-books	7,337	313,167	71.00%
Professional	3,155,191	3,357,022	0.90%
El-Hi (K–12 education)	5,795,044	5,237,976	–1.40%
Higher education	3,025,029	4,264,543	5.00%
All other	136,488	134,167	–0.20%
Total	22,032,580	23,855,706	1.10%

* in thousands of dollars

Source: Management Practice, Inc., 2010.

The spirited debate has centered on the pluses and minuses of print versus digital, as outlined by Hawkins back in 2000.[6] The pluses: e-books are available online; they are presented on a device that can provide additional capabilities; and they do not wear out with frequent use. The minuses: they present copyright and security issues; they are not collectable; they lack the feel of printed books; and they are not available in a global catalog, but rather in proprietary form. The last of these may be one of the more formidable barriers: Buying any book that can only be presented on one type of reader is primitive and harkens back to the days of early word processing. Yet, despite all the warnings of doom, we have far to go before the economics of book publishing is seriously in doubt.

While the threat to printed books is small (indeed, very small), to remain relevant, millennial libraries must be part of the e-books discussion now, if only to offer their professional view on issues such as uniform format standards, reading device specifications, copyright holder rights, and access technology. Just as libraries have entered the publishing field of academic journals (as will be discussed in chapter 6), they will play a major role in the storage, retrieval, and creation of e-books. The millennial library's academic commons will be able to provide to future e-book publishers what most readers have never been expected to find (except in critiques and annotated publications): the created work in context; the created text explained; and the created concepts enriched. Embraced fully, the world of e-books will be enhanced by the academic commons in an engaged millennial library, supporting and enriching publishing far past anything heretofore imagined.

WHY BOOKS IN PRINT MAY LAST LONGER THAN JOURNALS IN PRINT

The transition from print-only to print-and-bytes has touched almost all academic journals. In many ways, academic journal publishers have made the transition of including access to online research via subscription databases far more smoothly than that of newspapers. And while there are dire predictions of the death of books on paper, the latest AAP numbers cited above certainly don't suggest an immediate demise. This may be because the relationship of the researcher to journal article and the book reader to the printed page is very different. Researchers, even if they print out an online article, are reading only a few pages, compared to that of a book. The relationship of the book reader to the traditional format of the printed tome goes back much further, perhaps even to that of the Bible, versus the relatively more recently invented academic journal. Finally, whether it is dog-earing favorite pages, underlining favorite passages, or the purchasing of favorite editions, the object of a book reader's love is far different from that of the largely emotional indifference shown by journal researchers. To a degree, we are still in the very, very early stages of e-books, a stage similar to that of online newspapers in the 1990s. The format presented on readers, such as Kindle, is not so far distanced from the austere and primitive offering of the *New York Times* in its early online years. What the *Times* and almost all other online newspapers have learned is that simply being what they were before being online—that is, a newspaper—is not sufficient for a multitasking, multidistracted, multitracked readership. Those publications that have repackaged their information have thrived, adding interactivity and video, and beckoning readers to participate with blogs and message boards. We need some similar wider thinking when it comes to e-book readers. So, while the emergence of e-books is upon us, it is important to note that we still are splashing about in the shallow end of the pool.

Considering the various issues regarding journal articles being stored, indexed, and made available online, it is not hard to imagine future books taking the same path. Yet, the issues surrounding e-books are far more complex. We must consider devices, formats, presentation, and potentially the largest force within this movement: Google Books. Let us first look, however, at the brief (when compared to the millennia of all communications) but very rich history of not only books themselves, but also this more recent change of novels from atoms to bytes that may be the last major area of change in publishing provided to us by new media.

A SHORT HISTORY OF PRINT

In some ways, books have come full circle. Prior to Gutenberg's 1450 printing press, books were created one at a time, typically providing monasteries with substantial income in the production of illuminated Bibles, romances, histories, and other best sellers of the times. Some of these books were plain, handwritten, with little beyond the words. Others were far more expansive, veritable works of art with illustrative scenes and designs intended to portray various portions of the work. Typically, the more expensive works were Holy Bibles ordered by those with the means to pay for them.[7] Such works themselves were far more than just text. The experience of the reader was enhanced, certain impenetrable sections of the Bible, for example, were explained via the artwork in accordance with the approved Catechism, with the intent that each user was led to an appropriate (and sanctioned) conclusion. Of course, the cost for these illuminated texts was very high and varied from place to place and from year to year. And, as Schramm notes, the books themselves were symbolic of the great social divide between those who owned these artifacts and could actually read the text within them and those who could do neither. The collection of Chaucer, some sixty books purchased by the "keeper of the king's customs" centuries before Gutenberg, would have been valued at 100 times a trained scribe's annual wages. Such collections were rare, accessible only to royalty and the church. Even after Gutenberg's invention, the price of printed books remained high, and assuming that the average worker could even read, it was very unlikely he could purchase them, or would be even allowed to do so. Yet, it is not too much to suggest that the creation of a comparably printed (and thus cheaper) Bible had a profound effect on the rise of the Reformation and the resulting schisms later within the Protestant movement.

In the years following Gutenberg's invention, the manual transcribing of books decreased, as would be expected, and the average price for unadorned texts created by scribes dropped even more significantly. On the other hand, the increasingly expensive illuminated Bibles continued to be created, but were destined for only the richest of patrons. Access to the ideas within books, before and after the invention of moveable type, remained highly regulated for centuries. Not until well into the eighteenth century was the printed book available to common workers in places like Great Britain and the Netherlands, largely because of the rise in literacy combined with the falling cost of publication.[8]

Jumping forward to the twentieth century and the creation of the first e-book, the impulse to render a book in an electronic format is almost as old as the personal computer. Based on a design imagined by Alan Kay in 1968 and called the DynaBook, Xerox created in the early 1970s the Alto, a device now more comparable to a laptop computer. In some ways, Kay envisioned a device that would appeal mainly to youth, one that he called "A Personal Computer for Children of All Ages."[9] The motivation was to skip past the rendering of ink to paper, generate significant cost-savings, and widen the access to literature worldwide. Just as the emergence of large bookstores, such as Borders and Barnes and Noble, had led many to predict the death of many small independent bookstores, the ability to read electronically would lead to the next generation of vendors and readers. Or so it was thought.

As any regular user of Amazon.com is aware, however, the independent bookstores are still alive, though, invariably some have died and some new ones have risen. The connecting by Amazon of vast numbers of the small bookstores into one very large online shopping experience literally saved the independent operators. By plugging these small bookstores into one massive marketing network, Amazon, in effect, positioned itself as the independent's global marketing group. The independent bookstore provides the book after it is ordered at the Amazon site. Readers interested in an obscure volume found they were at least as likely to find it online at Amazon.com as they were at a Big Box bookstore, if not more so. The delivery scheme involved posting the book by mail to the buyer, but at least the reader could be assured of soon receiving the desired tome, at some point in time.

But what if the impatient reader were not willing to wait a few days for the prized book? What if the reader wanted it right now? Within this context, it seems that the e-book would do well in this get-it-now environment. After all, what is more important to the have-it-now boomer generation than immediate access? Just as academicians were clamoring for instant access to research sources—as we discussed previously—readers were likewise clamoring for their favorite novel. Indeed, immediate access to research books ought to follow the same paths as had their kin, academic journal articles, or so it was believed. However, this idea of instant access to a desired book, oddly, did not lead to the adoption of the e-book. Defenders of paper books noted issues of readability, the tactile feeling of a book in their hands, and the ability to earmark pages. This, and other factors, has slowed the progression of novel from picas to pixels. And, as rapidly as academic research has poured into online journals, the move to online books has been in fits and starts. Above all, the physical nature of an e-book is one factor, as mentioned. Until the device intended to display the e-book does more than simply display the book, it is unlikely to expand much beyond a very narrow following. Manufacturers of e-book readers are likely to see small numbers of early adopters compared to overall print readership as long as the potential of the electronic devices is restricted and hobbled.

DEVICES

Beginning in 2008, multiple manufacturers entered the e-book market with devices ranging from small handhelds to larger book-size formats. All, including Amazon's Kindle and Sony's e-Reader, attempted to display the book content as close to what a paperback would present, with a vertical rectangular 2:1 ratio of height versus width. These devices allow page-by-page reading (as with a print book), or entire volume searches (not possible with the print alternative outside of a limited index). Yet, the desire to present the book on the e-reader as close to the original format is not so distant from early newspapers that literally presented PDF copies of their front pages on websites. If we have learned anything from those early mistakes of newspaper, a reader's experience with an online book should be far different from that of a book online.

The e-reader advertising focuses on its electronic features, versus the benefits on which a consumer typically bases the purchase of a book. One particular model notes features within the context of print artifacts:

> Slim: Just over one-third of an inch, as thin as most magazines
> Lightweight: At 10.2 ounces, lighter than a typical paperback
> Wireless: 3G wireless lets you download books right from your Kindle, anytime, anywhere; no monthly fees, service plans, or hunting for Wi-Fi hotspots
> Books in Under Sixty Seconds: Get books delivered in less than sixty seconds; no PC required
> Paper-like Display: Reads like real paper; now boasts sixteen shades of gray for clear text and even crisper images
> Long Battery Life: Twenty-five percent longer battery life; read for days without recharging
> Carry Your Library: Holds over 1,500 books
> Read-to-Me: With the new text-to-speech feature, Kindle can read every newspaper, magazine, blog, and book aloud to you, unless the book's rights holder made the feature unavailable
> Free Book Samples: Download and read first chapters for free before you decide to buy
> Large Selection: Over 300,000 books plus U.S. and international newspapers, magazines, and blogs available[10]

While all these features would seem to be a strong inducement to switch from print (or even earlier models of e-readers), some drawbacks noted by one user raises the possibility that the e-book, as currently configured in its various iterations, may not be ready for the mass market.[11] This blogger raises the types of concerns expressed about e-books in general:

> Transfer of electronic books and materials in the swap to another reader;
> Loss of some features because of non-compatible publisher formatting;
> Changing text-to-speech standards and availability;
> Changing display options, such as text justification;
> Issues involving memory options;
> Issues regarding battery recharging;
> Elimination of content management features, such as particular folder naming function;
> A shift in software specifications;
> Hard to read type on screens sensitive to sunlight;
> Inability to manipulate the type sizes and fonts.[12]

These last two complaints are especially relevant for the market of older readers, already widely seen as not predisposed to the adoption of new media. Without the ability to easily read screens or change font sizes and types, these elderly readers—often with weaker vision than their children—may stick to their larger-print books. These and other limitations within the e-book arena suggest that the lack of standards that so often occurs in a new publishing field may be seriously slowing adoption. Each device has its own standards, not set by book publishers, but by manufacturers of the devices. This back-to-front arrangement puts the "printer" in charge of the format of the book, rather than the publisher's editorial and design teams. This is especially magnified with the presentation of books via handheld devices, like Kindles and iPods. Again, the publishers are not included in the process and the standards have been allowed to vary widely, much to the harm of readers and device adoption.

It is not suggested that book publishers were always in agreement about font size and type. No doubt evidence could be found of early differences not only between various publishers in, for example, various places in Britain, but also various publishers in various countries. Yet, those differences have been smoothed away over the intervening centuries. The pattern of a relative height versus width, along with considerations for line length and font size has led several generations of readers to expect their books to look and feel a certain predictable way. And while some books deviate from this, they usually fall into a particular genre, such as those intended for children. And, even here, some sense of standardization is present.

The resulting printing format standard is now being imposed on an electronic device that may not be suitable for the intended content. As Hawkins notes, one of the biggest hurdles in the adoption phase of e-books is the "quality of print portrayed on screens."[13] But Hawkins poses the issue confusingly to "e-book producers," a vague term. Does he mean publishers or manufacturers of the readers? This is no small matter of style. The issue of standards for devices is intrinsically wrapped up with the issue of format. Without a top-down standard set by publishers, we are left to a world not unlike one that would have evolved had manufacturers of CD players been led to create music discs that worked only on their machines. One has only to consider the ultimate resolution that occurred within the video tape industry (VHS versus BetaMax) or with the standards in high-definition digital video discs (HD-DVD versus Blu-Ray[14]) to appreciate the consequences and potential delays in consumer adoption. Until publishers engage in the actual setting of standards, the progression to an e-books world will be slow and haphazard. Consumers, concerned that they are not left stranded on the beach by a format no longer preferred or supported, may choose to "wait and see" what standard prevails.

However, even market-wide standards may not be sufficient to lure readers—even early adopters—away from print artifacts. Converting print readers to computer readers requires much more than a gray screen and exact replication of the original book. Because of the electronic format, readers expect the book online to be far more than just words. Leveraging the ability of the Web to interconnect readers to sources, additional materials, and other readers has worked well for those willing to toss out the previous standards, such as those online news websites based not only on the formats established by a printing press or television camera.

FORMAT

Once publishers (and librarians) step out from behind the device manufacturers and claim their prime role in not only the marketing of e-books, but also the creative packaging of these works, they will face some of the same challenges that newspapers which have moved online have struggled with in the past decade. Jonathan Dube, editor and publisher of CyberJournalist.net, noted in 2007 some of these challenges:

> Telling news stories online is exciting and challenging because of all the tools at our disposal. Online journalists must think on multiple levels at once: words, ideas, story structure, design, interactives, audio, video, photos, news judgment. It's easy for online journalists, most of whom have been trained in traditional media, to stick to broadcast and print storytelling forms. But that would be a waste. In online journalism you have many more elements to choose from—so use them. Combine the best of each world:
>
> - Use print to explain;
> - Use multimedia to show;
> - Use interactives to demonstrate and engage.[15]

And, as millennial libraries move into the role as presenters and re-presenters of written works, they will be forced to address many of these same issues. Is it really sufficient to merely place material in the public sphere and wait for users to access it? An affirmative response would suggest the only role that librarians have in this new century is to store information in such a way to ensure its easy retrieval. As we discussed in chapter 4, this may have been the expected role at some point in the past, but it is no longer true today.

Librarians are re-packagers of old content into a format accessible, meaningful, and valuable to readers. They have traditionally accomplished this with archives and other special collections and with special events surrounding a collection of books of a particular genre.

For academics, the nature of the sought-after research is not as important as it might be to a traditional reader. That is, while a reader picks a novel to spend time buried in the plot, the researcher is looking for information from (typically) nonfiction sources. Even those humanities professors doing work on Shakespeare, for example, would find a digital artifact easier to search and easier to cite. It is the access to the information that would drive the academic researcher to an e-book version of *Wuthering Heights*. The nonacademic is less interested in searching for the term "self-destruction" in *Anna Karenina* than simply encountering it within the pages of Tolstoy's work. This is all well and good. However, consider the number of academic readers compared to casual readers. The economics of printed books compared to printed journals is driven, clearly, more by the nature and behavior of the end users than by the cost of ink and paper.

The successful adoption of e-books written by academics might require someone, perhaps millennial librarians, to offer connections between the researcher and the publication, as well as providing additional information in the form of annotations. In the addition of annotations, we are not referring to those books already in the public sphere being converted into digital forms. We are addressing the creation of solely online books of the near future. Procedures for cataloging e-books (born in print and re-created digital) have already been created by university libraries, such as those at Yale.[16] But annotation techniques and standards are far from settled. At what point does the referencing within a book to information that may be relevant to understanding the author's writings become a nuisance, both visually and editorially? This chapter of the book could be presented online with every word linked to an outside source offering definitions and noteworthy information. I doubt the average reader, academic or not, would find it useful or comfortable attempting to slough through such a visual disaster. Lines must be drawn as to how much of a book requires annotation.

To some degree, this discussion of online versus print in regards to books versus journal articles is inappropriately placed within the context of the publication's production technique. Is a book simply a very long journal article? In point of fact, attempting to define the differences between the two when they are online becomes a bit of a challenge. Researchers seek information online not by the journal volume or issue, but by the individual journal article. Thus, at least one publishing style difference between books and journals—

the multiple articles that are bound into one volume or issue—may not remain significant in the future.

But researchers are not the only patrons of the millennial library. Students interested in a Shakespearean play would find for example, the enhancement of *King Lear* through appropriate hyperlinked annotations invaluable. Indeed, the average reader of an author such as Sir Arthur Conan Doyle would understand *A Study in Scarlet* far more if it included notes and links explaining the largely temporal references used by Doyle, as was offered in print by Baring-Gould.[17] The reading is enhanced, illuminated, and far more enjoyable than the sense of being left in the dark by contemporary allusions that have long-since lost their meaning. Explaining references and other relevant material referred to in a story is rare in print forms, but has long been the core of online publishing. Such "deep linking" made possible by hyperlinking provides readers the opportunity to pursue a particular path, tracking an idea or reference to other ideas that may exist several layers inside an outside website source. Add in links to video and other nonpaper references, and you have a new, richer creation not possible in print books.

For those millennial libraries not considering such involvement in the publishing of e-books, understanding the issues surrounding these publications is still very valuable. It should be clear here that the millennial librarian is not required to create new content as a function of being considered millennial. However, it is undeniable that it is a valuable function for a keeper of all information to not only be able to find that information, but also hold the knowledge of what data connects to what other data, what references might be illuminated by other references. In an ironic way, the millennial librarian will play the role similar to that of the medieval monk by adding content to existing text, as the monks did by illuminating Holy Bibles. The relevant content is found and linked where appropriate. Such connections may be to other works, but could just as easily be connected to a movie, a song, or a theater performance. It could be a video interview with the author. It could be a video of a roundtable discussion of the work. For example, rather than struggling through a Shakespearean play—a type of work many hold is best viewed, not read—what if the student or faculty member could access a video of a particular scene? What if the online text of the play included a written notation that suggests that a video of a scene is available? What if the student had the choice of watching the scene in an historical format or a postmodern setting? This evolves the learning and research experience from a static, linear model to a fully user-involved interaction where the reader is integrated into an evolving process of gathering, analysis, and feedback.

This type of content manipulation is likely to be outside the scope of a traditional print-bound publisher. This activity defines the core role of the millennial library, where content will be constantly enriched and interconnected. The librarian in this new environment moves away from merely counting and storage, and moves into the unique and vital position as the one player in this entire act of finding who literally knows where all the bodies are buried, and can act as a catalyst in assisting authors to enrich their works. In the helpful hands of a millennial librarian, an author becomes the creator of an e-book that opens doors to a world of concepts, sharing, and creativity by involving other authors and their works in a web of information.

This shared environment will likely provoke a large amount of UGC, with readers within an academic commons providing valuable reactions and suggestions to authors and librarians. With the revisions suggested by this UGC, each work becomes stronger, research becomes more valuable, and academic outcomes will lead to new ideas. The inclusion of a comments section at the end of chapters is certainly one method. But librarians may find that creating a locally hosted blog and/or message boards also a valuable addition, especially if the local university author or subject area expert can be engaged to moderate the conversations. For starters, the discussion within a message board would be constant, an evolving back-and-forth conversation, rather than the one-shot tradition of peer review. Authors will be able to respond, offering suggestions and questions to message posters (acts ironically similar to teaching). Sharing ideas freely would encourage more innovation, updating, and accuracy. This work itself would become much more valuable to academics, given that the updates and revisions would be an effort toward accuracy and precision. The act of authorship and research in isolation would be replaced by a rich conversation. Stand this in contrast to the many non-academic blogs posted now and it is easy to see the increased value of the serious, far more enlightening discourse that could evolve.

Of course, how to present these comments should be carefully considered. Each library should think about establishing a published policy clearly stating its procedures. Revisions and additions could be presented as new editions, with older editions left on the website to preserve citations of the previous work. This preservation of older "editions" is a controversial topic within online publishing itself. Some online journal managers and editors believe that once an article is published, it cannot be changed. Some believe corrections must be published separate from the original document. Others, including this author, believe the hypertext quality of PDF/A should be suited to provide readers with an immediate opportunity to see corrections and updates. Generally, decisions regarding the updating of publications should involve the author and, possibly, the copyright holder. If the previous version is to be saved, a link to this should be provided in the updated version, and vice versa. Some commentary can be added on both versions providing the rationale for the update.

The degree of change that would be required to justify a new edition is also vague. Corrections of minor details, such as typos, numerical transpositions, and dates would not necessitate an entirely new edition, but might be addressed by way of new "printings." Look at J. R. R. Tolkien and the many printings *Lord of the Rings* used to clean up irregularities found by readers and forwarded to the author. This does not suggest the changes be done literally in the dark of night. Rather, changes to minor errors should be recorded using footnotes, a form of annotation itself. The effort here is to provide as thorough a record of the research and any changes to the publication as is possible. As an online journal editor myself, it is our policy to offer articles that have major changes and updates as new editions, with a link back to the previous version. Had we the funding to support a larger editorial mission, footnotes might be included in the new edition referencing changes.

Presentation

In 2000, Hawkins succinctly outlined the advantages and disadvantages of print books and e-books. Books on paper are easy to use, easy to carry, and easy to add handwritten notes. They are reasonably priced and the printed words on paper are reliably legible, either in full sun, shade, or as Hawkins suggests, "the dim light of the full moon."[18] On the negative side, paper books are costly to print, ship, and store. They are resistant to corrections and updates, requiring an entirely new press run. Finding information within a printed book relies entirely on the indexing (if one exists) and the incentives to provide a thorough guide to contents is almost always counterbalanced by the associated high costs.

Online books—e-books—on the other hand are cheaper to produce, easier to ship and store, and far easier to search than conventional printed ones. They can be updated far more easily, and they can contain links to additional reference materials. Also, they can include colorful illustrations at little to no cost. So, why did e-books not supplant printed books by 2000, as some had predicted they would? And will the iPad become the change agent that many believe? Well, in addition to the format issue discussed earlier, the answer to both these questions may be related to the way the material is presented to readers.

As we found in the discussion regarding online journals, the type of code used to produce digital books can vary from PDFs to HTML to Flash, and many of the same concerns around these options have arisen. Specifically in regard to e-books, two areas of concern have risen: should the book be presented as a series of scanned images, or as real electronic text, either in HTML or some other format specifically designed for a particular reader device. Interestingly, the idea of format is rarely an issue for printed books. These books are vertical rectangles with a roughly 2:1 height to width ratio. They are—on the whole—black ink on white paper, and traditionally have been printed in a serif font, such as Times New Roman.

Serif fonts were long ago abandoned online as harder to read than fonts such as Arial and Verdana because of image pixilation. Yet, the presentation of an e-book, as suggested by the manufacturers of the various electronic readers created to date, is still expected to adhere to the 2:1 ratio. This is interesting because that ratio has everything to do with the format of the printing presses used to create a paperback or novel. Nothing suggests that there is some cosmic basis for the ratio other than its tradition.

Thus, it is entirely possible that at some point in the future, the necessity to present an e-book in the currently proposed vertical format (i.e., Kindle, Sony E-Reader, iPad) would fade and a more Web-like look would emerge. In part, this makes sense because the traditional lines that define what is an academic journal, a book, a movie, and an audio record have more to do with the production requirements for the distribution of each product. Presses are required for journals, specialized presses for books, and audiovisual equipment for CDs and movies. With one distribution channel—the Web—the necessity to differentiate between the forms of media is rendered moot. In fact, the Web itself sees no difference between them in terms of distribution: a packet is a packet. The tools currently at the edges of the Web, software such as browsers, are themselves fading into the Web, replaced by the cloud-centered applications mentioned earlier. The network, expanding to speeds unimagined even five years ago, is becoming more and more capable of providing everything from storage to file updating without engaging a hard drive on a local machine.

And so, perhaps, the change from paper to atoms for books may not be as far off as some might believe. Those of us in mass communication love to cite adoption patterns of media, such as the years it took for radio and television to reach full market saturation compared to the months it took the Web to do the same. Thus far, the increase in e-book sales has been impressive, to be sure, but miniscule compared to overall book sales globally. We have discussed many of the potential reasons for this. However, if any one device may shift the tide of adoption in this area, it might be the iPad. Aggressively designed to meet many of the shortcomings cited by users of other devices, Apple's new reader may push the e-book market past its tipping point. Much of the hype surrounding this device centers on the thousands of apps that are being devised to support all manner of reading, listening, and creativity. Notably in the fall of 2010, Google and Apple came to an agreement—a very unexpected agreement—to allow support of Google Docs on iPads. Add to this the full-throated support of HTML5 versus Flash by Apple, the podcasts of all classes by the University of Minnesota,[19] and the addition of many new features that synchronize an iPad to a user's laptop and smartphone and it becomes clear that technological advances are moving rapidly in this field of education and books. As publishers of e-books become more involved in the editorial form in which these works are created (as described earlier in this chapter), readers may find that the combination of a swift, sleek, feature-loaded device, such as the iPad, and the redefined physical appearance of the book itself may be the catalyst for rapid adoption.

THE E-BOOKS COMMONS: AUTHOR AS PUBLISHER

For those millennial libraries interested (or thrust by others) into the enterprise of online book publishing, we are nearing an important tipping point: author as scholar versus author as publisher. Those authors unable to attract the attention of or pass the standards of review at publishing houses—either because of the quality of the book or the minimal market size—have for decades used vanity presses to present their works to the public. Costly to publish more than a few to give to friends and associates, these works have rarely been taken seriously. They are considered a reflection of an author's desire to be known and the associated willingness to pay substantial funds to do so, versus the unwillingness of a respected publisher to be involved in the process. Yet, as we move more and more toward the ease of directly publishing to the Web, the cost of publishing these books falls out of the equation, while, at the same time, the distribution soars.

The publishing of "vanity" works of fiction has increased dramatically in recent years, and, generally speaking, this is not an issue for librarians. However, the line between "vanity" and "scientific" is not so clear for some. And, each year, as we move more and more toward direct online publishing, the calls will increase for some standards of evaluation, some method to identify the worthy.

Universities are already involved in this. It is their faculty, largely, that produce the works in question. Evaluating whether the works should be "certified" or "peer reviewed" by a university or multi-university panel might be the best next step. And within most universities, this is likely to fall on the shoulders of those who will be asked to put the work online: the millennial librarians managing the academic commons. This management or oversight function might follow the UGC path suggested earlier in regards to academic journal publishing. It might require the creation of a panel to evaluate proposed books—something similar to today's peer review.

Clearly, this is a sensitive issue. Universities and their libraries would be subject to significant pressure on the part of their faculty members to publish all proposed works. At the same time, standards of quality—or lack thereof—will evolve over time. In some ways, this is not very different than what we see today among the publishing houses: some have a higher standing than others, often related to the quality and importance of the works they publish. It may be that the same will occur within libraries: some will be seen as applying higher standards. Some will be seen as not as strict. Either way, the reputation of a university library will, over time, become an imprint on their works. This reasonably could lead an author to seek to publish elsewhere, so as not to be associated with a less-than-best publishing operation.

In the background, however, is another initiative of which every millennial librarian must be fully aware, the Google Books project: The procedures and best practices used by Google may become a standard for rapid digitizing of books and monographs.

GOOGLE BOOKS: MAKING ALL INFORMATION AVAILABLE

As of August 2009, Google Books had put some form of 10 million books online, most searchable over the course of five years. The goal, according to a spokesperson for Google, is to make the world's information universally accessible. The status of the Google Books project was, as of mid-2010, still in legal limbo regarding copyright and property rights. Yet the plan by the Google Books staff to put all non-copyrighted works online continues. The task is monumental given that the total number of book titles alone is somewhere between 65 million and 100 million (estimates vary, obviously). And, while the total number of Web pages estimated by Google in 2008 has surpassed 1 trillion, the company's Google Books team believes that the vast amount of information in the world is still not accessible online, and that most of this information is in books. Thus, scanning that information and making it as accessible and searchable as a website by anyone anywhere will take some time.[20]

Declared on the Google website to be a project in existence since the beginning of the company itself in 1996, the book project is one of many that have been started in the past twenty years. The American Memory project, for example, was started as a pilot project in 1990. Its goal is to provide

> Free and open access through the Internet to written and spoken words, sound recordings, still and moving images, prints, maps, and sheet music that docu-

> ment the American experience. It is a digital record of American history and creativity. These materials, from the collections of the Library of Congress and other institutions, chronicle historical events, people, places, and ideas that continue to shape America, serving the public as a resource for education and lifelong learning.[21]

Project Gutenberg was started much earlier, in the 1970s: "The Project Gutenberg Philosophy is to make information, books and other materials available to the general public in forms a vast majority of the computers, programs and people can easily read, use, quote, and search."[22] Many similar projects have been underway since the mid-1990s, such as iBiblio.org and the Internet Archive's Million Book Project.

The rationale and stated purpose for all of these sites is to provide universal access online to what was largely restricted by geography (and to a lesser extent in recent years, class). An example cited on the Google history site is that of the Bodleian library at Oxford University and its centuries-old "uncut" books that have never been accessed since they were placed, sealed in a, presumably, remote area of storage. Google started working with the library in 2004 and by 2009 announced that, "For the first time a large proportion of Oxford's 19th century out-of-copyright holdings will be made easily accessible to a new generation of readers around the globe."[23]

Pause for a moment and consider what has happened here. Works that lay dormant and presumed forgotten are found, in a way, and not just made available to the denizens surrounding Oxford, but the entire planet. The other works made available include the first English translation (1729) of Newton's *Mathematical Principles of Natural Philosophy*; the first edition of Jane Austen's *Emma* (1815); John Cassell's *Illustrated History of England* (1857); and Charles Darwin's first edition of *On the Origin of Species* (1859). The impact of the project was summarized by Ben Bunnell, manager of Google's Book Search Library Partnerships team: "With most of Oxford's 19th century public domain works now digitized and available to users online, we look forward to continuing our partnership with Oxford to digitize more content as it becomes available and to working together to bring more books to more people in more languages around the world."[24] It is as if, rather than scholars traveling at great personal cost and danger thousands of miles to a library in Alexandria to view a text only available there, digital texts are brought to them. This facile transformation and instant transportation of rare volumes underlines what was noted by a good friend some fifteen years ago regarding the Web, "there is no there, there."

To date, more than forty libraries are working with Google to digitize special collections and books that in the past would have required the reader to travel thousands of miles to access. In some ways, the efforts of Google and others to digitize all information eliminates the reliance of researchers upon the "happy accident" of literally stumbling upon a collection. One cannot be expected to look for a relevant book without first knowing the book exists, and then knowing its relevance. It is not unheard of for a collection to remain untouched for decades by anyone, much less potentially interested researchers. As related by Google spokesperson Jennie Johnson, an academic researcher in 2007 was looking for information for her dissertation regarding roads built in nineteenth-century England. In particular, she sought information about a particular engineer involved in the project. She had visited Oxford's library in person and had used typical research tools such as ILL with no success. It wasn't until she searched within Google Books that she found twelve volumes that mentioned the engineer by name. These were books she not only had not found before, but did not even know existed. Indeed, as also related by Johnson, some researchers are finding books in dark corners of libraries that have never been touched by anyone since they were shelved. For the Google Books project, the goal is a simple one: Make all information available online, whether it is an actual book, magazine, newspaper, or any other print format, and then make it accessible. "So as long as the information can be found online, we think that is the goal, not whether it is the form of a book."[25]

In the case of the Google Books project, material is presented in one of three physical forms: full, partial, or snippet views. The determination of which of these is appropriate is based upon an interpretation by the legal advisors at Google of the U.S. Copyright Act of 1976 (as amended).[26] We will discuss in greater detail the issues surrounding copyright later in chapter 8.

For now, let us consider—briefly—the process that Google uses in determining what portions of a book or document are made available online. The procedure should be of interest to librarians considering the potential generation of future e-books on issues of particular interest to its patrons. Google Books provides full text access to all works published before 1923. Prior to October 2009, the amount posted online of a work published after 1923 was based on negotiations with the copyright holder. In general, Google started by making 20 percent of the book viewable. This 20 percent rule is an interesting contrast to the 10 percent "minimum rule" misapplied to the Copyright Act, to be discussed in chapter 8.

More than 20 percent can be posted if the copyright holder agrees. For works published after 1923 made available by one of the forty participating libraries, Google places online snippets of text corresponding to the search terms used by the researcher. It also provides a link to a library that has the book in its holdings, as well as links to online bookstores where the work can be purchased.

In October 2009, an agreement was finalized between Google Books and the Authors Guild and the American Association of Publishers. Now put back into doubt by a court decision some weeks after, this agreement allows Google to expand the amount of information viewable within boundaries established in 2008 by the relevant parties. Contained within the agreement are stipulations that allow Google to provide groups of books, what it calls "bundles" to libraries, as well as apply a tiered fee structure based on the size and nature of a library (public school versus private higher education institution).

Some parts of books are copyrighted, even if the main text is not copyrightable. For example, a recently published version of Homer's fourth century B.C.E. work, *The Iliad,* might be still in copyright based on certain unique features within the work, such as the foreword, annotation, and translation. For publications such as this, only snippets were available prior to the October 2009 agreement. Researchers looking for a full-access online copy would be provided links to those editions of the work published prior to 1923.

According to Johnson, more and more publishers have found that providing access to more than 20 percent of a book actually results in higher sales of these works. "Those interested in a book and who can actually access more than the 20 percent see the work as more valuable," Johnson notes.

Google Books is working on ways the search experience can be enhanced. For example, many researchers have found that by locating one book of interest on a shelf, other relevant books can be found nearby. Millennial librarians should note that what the Google Books project suggests is that the ability of the researcher to scan online will supersede the traditional use of a list of call numbers. That is, sampling books in and around a found book on a shelf will be replaced by the ability to search the full text of books.

One of the unique features of the Google Books project—and one that could be emulated by all millennial libraries—is its partner program. Google is working with more than forty libraries to put online special collections, such as the Nettie Lee Benson Latin American Collection at the University of Texas. Included in this collection will be such works as the "BiblioNoticias" series of subject bibliographies (1990–present), as well as a digitization of the microfilm set of nineteenth-century Independent Mexico in Newspapers and those of the 1900–1920 Revolutionary Mexico in Newspapers. Several other similar projects are underway.

At the University of Wisconsin–Madison Libraries, Google Books has collaborated to digitize more than 200,000 works since 2006.

> The combined library holdings of UW–Madison and the Wisconsin Historical Society make up one of the largest collections of documents and historical materials in the United States. In 2006, UW–Madison and Google announced a

> partnership to digitize these collections and make them available far beyond the university's boundaries.[27]

Agreements with other libraries include more standards regarding the general digitizing of holdings that are unavailable elsewhere. The objective is to scan the world's books, not just the most popular. For example, at Oxford libraries, Google is scanning books that have little or no patron interest. "Why bother with these books? Well, if the books are good enough to be in a library, they are good enough to be scanned," Johnson notes.[28] In addition, rather than limited by space, the millennial library can provide access to all information regardless of how many patrons "check out" the document online. The method adopted by Google eliminates the need to create special metadata to track a particular book. The metadata attached is via an automated system. The resulting user access is straightforward, with no special codes or search terms necessary, eliminating the need to have the exact search term.

Johnson notes that the actual technology used to scan the books is proprietary to Google and is based on trial and error practices. The intent is to scan even the most fragile books without causing any damage to the book or its binding. The book is scanned, and the resulting image is then converted to text by an optical character reader. At the same time, an HTML version of the text is created for use in handheld mobile devices. "It involves multiple steps—scan, OCR, and then a check of the quality of page," Johnson notes. Google also built technology used to check the accuracy of the scan. The system does have its imperfections, such as the handwritten note that appears in *Alice in Wonderland*. "It will take a while to solve issues like that," Johnson notes.[29]

But the vision itself is one that all libraries can embrace: Put every book online so every person can read every book. In a way, the ultimate end of Gutenberg's invention extends from the ability to create a new thing—a book—and then the elimination of the physical nature of the work. Even with inexpensive books, an expense remains. Online books are free from the ink, paper, and water (all with environmental impacts) involved in the physical creation of the predecessor. "You shouldn't have to know that you are looking for a book. You are looking for information," Johnson adds. That the information comes in a form we have called a book (or monograph) is irrelevant.

While the 2009 agreement, still in limbo at the time of this publication, with publishers only covers books, Google is actively pursuing agreements with companies, such as Time Life, to scan images. It is also engaged in the digitization of all microforms at public and university libraries.

CONCLUSIONS

E-books are both books online and they are online books. That is, e-books are not only the scanning and posting of existing books in HTML and PDF, they are also books that were never ink on paper. For the once-print-now-online books, the issue is one of access. Online resources are accessible anywhere in the world, and so long as the method to make the product is standardized, any reading device will work. Yet, we are only at the beginning of this shift to online reading. It will take some time, but e-books will eventually minimize the nature of the reading device compared to the habits and preferences of readers as a potential barrier.

That may not be enough. For e-books to be accepted by the mass of readers, they must be repackaged to take full advantage of the electronic, networked nature of the medium. If the e-book is only the book as it appeared on paper moved digitally to an e-reader, adoption and usage will be slow and driven by economics, not demand. If, however, the story is presented as text wrapped around images and video and commentary and reading groups, then we have an interactive experience that rivals all that readers have come to expect from their other Web information sites. The value-added, interactive, content will offer readers an enriching reading experience. This is not the end of the book, but a re-creation (evolution?) of the e-book as something far more than it has ever been: the center of a total commitment to the reader.

Today's music groups are finding that to make money in an increasingly digital sharing environment they must revert to the model of the 1950s: tours. Releases of music, whether vinyl or on CDs, are not long for this world, not with instant digital sharing. Book publishers don't have that option of putting authors on the road, so to speak. This is a delicate issue. On the one hand, some bands—notably the Beatles in the 1970s—may find the idea of touring to be incompatible with their musical style. The Beatles had evolved into a studio group by the time of *Abbey Road*. The question that stands before publishers, researchers, and millennial librarians is, perhaps put plainly, "How do we sustain the research milieu already created and deeply in place?" The traditional pattern cannot be sustained, at least not beyond the short term, perhaps ten to fifteen years. Something must give. But what? And how?

In the rush into an "it is all out there" age, we have delved into the issues surrounding how the role of millennial librarians has changed radically from cataloger to deliverer of information. With e-books this shift will be far more exaggerated. For what has been discussed only minimally is the radical change e-books will bring to the reading experience and what readers will expect (demand?) from those creating and publishing these works.

What remains is how and, perhaps if, libraries will fund such endeavors. Google uses advertising and search word auctions to underwrite its work. It is unlikely that university libraries will take this approach. Yet, without some involvement, many potentially great works that lack the Amazon defined market value will go unpublished and, therefore, unknown. University libraries, specifically millennial libraries, will either address this challenge, or fall victim to the traditions that have held back academic progress for centuries: tradition, fiefdoms, fear.

SUMMARY

Students are digital: they read digitally, they listen digitally, and they watch digitally. They also communicate digitally, share ideas digitally, and are as comfortable with digital devices as their parents are with a television remote control. Embraced fully, the world of e-books must digitize all aspects to publishing works. But it must also expand the publishing to a full experience of video, UGC, and other interactive opportunities.

We have come full circle. From single copies of books transcribed, to Gutenberg's 1450 mass market printing press, back to online text. Based on a design imagined by Alan Kay in 1968 as the DynaBook, Xerox created in the early 1970s the Alto, a reader device now more comparable to a laptop computer. And, just as large box book sellers were predicted to kill small independent bookstores, so was the ability to read electronically predicted to kill printing presses. Yet, the independent bookstores are still alive. And, despite the significant advantages of e-books over their paper cousins, the book as three hundred pages of ink on paper persists.

Part of the issue with adoption of the e-book may be the device on which it is read. Rather than designing the device as a carrier of the online book, we remain in the age of the device defining the e-book. Even market-wide standards may not be sufficient to lure readers—even early adopters—away from print artifacts.

Publishers and librarians must claim their prime role in not only the marketing of e-books, but also the creative packaging of these works. This is the same challenge that newspapers have faced in the past decade. Librarians are repackagers of old content into a format accessible, meaningful, and valuable to readers. The successful adoption of e-books by readers will require librarians to find connections between publications of similar subjects, or to provide additional information in the form of annotations.

Explaining references and other material alluded to in text is hard to do in print forms, but has long been the core of online publishing. Such linking provides readers the opportunity to pursue a particular path, tracking an idea or reference to other ideas. This is at the heart of creativity and critical thinking. It explodes the notion of the passive reader, dutifully following the track of words presented by an author or researcher.

The millennial librarian is not only the keeper of all information, the one able to find information, but also has the knowledge of what data connects to other data. Thus, the relevant content is found and linked where appropriate. Such connections may be to other works, but could just as easily be connected to a movie, a song, or a theater performance. It could be a video interview with the author. It could be a video of a discussion of the work.

This type of content manipulation is likely to be outside the scope of a traditional print-bound publisher. This activity defines the core role of the millennial library, where content will be constantly enriched and interconnected.

Book authors will find the enriching UGC posted with their work far more valuable than a handful of comments provided through peer review. For starters, the discussion within a message board would be constant, an evolving back-and-forth conversation, rather than the one-shot tradition of peer review.

We are creatures of habit. Books are in the physical format that they are in because of tradition. It is entirely possible that at some point in the future, the necessity to present an e-book in the currently proposed vertical format (e.g., Kindle, Sony E-Reader) will fade and a more Web-like look would emerge (e.g., iPad). In part this makes sense because the traditional lines that define what is an academic journal, a book, a movie, and a audio record have more to do with the production requirements for the distribution of each product.

We are nearing an important tipping point: author as scholar, author as publisher. The vanity publishing of works of fiction has increased dramatically in recent years and, generally speaking, this is not an issue for librarians. However, the line between "vanity" and "scientific" is not so clear. Universities are already involved in this. It is their faculty that produce the work. Evaluating whether the work should be "certified" or "peer reviewed" by a university or multi-university panel might be the best next step. And within most universities, this is likely to fall on the shoulders of those who will be asked to put the work online: the librarians managing the university commons.

As of August 2009, Google Books had put some form of 10 million books online, most searchable over the course of five years. The goal, according a spokesperson for Google, is to make the world's information universally accessible. The task is monumental given the total number of book titles alone is somewhere between 65 million and 100 million (estimates vary, obviously). Millennial librarians should note that what the Google Books project suggests is that the ability of the researcher to scan online will supercede the traditional use of a list of call numbers. That is, sampling books in and around a found book on a shelf will be replaced by the ability to search the full text of books.

One of the most unique features of the Google Books project—and one that could be emulated by all millennium libraries—is its partner program. Google is working with more than forty libraries to put online special collections, such as the Nettie Lee Benson Latin American Collection at the University of Texas.

E-BOOK TEN MILESTONES

1. Our new students may have been born digitally and may seek information strictly online; but, if so, they will miss out on a wealth of information that exists both in the deeper areas of the Web and in traditional book forms (print). Millennial librarians must establish regimens to guide these students back to what might be seen as old-fashioned research objects: books.
2. If the millennial library chooses to be involved in e-books, it should commit itself to doing more than simply placing digital monographs on its server: (a) It should create digital collections, bundled with links to helpful videos archives, as well as other artifacts, such as author blogs and e-mails; (b) It should do as much as it can to provide annotation of specific passages of books that would enhance the reading; and, (c) It should provide feedback, perhaps in the form of a blog, giving electronic readers some sense of what users are saying about their reading experience. Rather than simply shoving the e-book experience on readers, developers should find out how they can enhance the experience. An academic commons can be a good source for student and faculty feedback (as well as administrators).
3. The readership experience with books is very different than the researcher's experience with journals. The form is different, the length different, and the interaction different.
4. While watching the evolution of e-book reading devices, it would be wise for the millennial library to remain on the sideline for the near term. The devices are not fully developed to provide the kind of reading experience necessary to warrant a library providing devices to patrons. As long as the creators of reading devices are not the publishers of books, this gap will not close for some years to come.
5. It is likely that a device such as the iPad will tip the scales toward rapid increases in e-book readership, so long as publishers become more engaged in the manner in which the book appears on the screen. A book on an iPad must be much more than just the book itself and must include annotation, including video, to illuminate text (much as monks illuminated Bibles five centuries ago).

6. Any publisher of an e-book must be fully aware that the reader expects print to provide explanation, multimedia to enhance the experience, and interactivity to demonstrate and engage the reader.
7. If the millennial library enters into the creation of books written by its faculty, it must provide the same rigorous editorial team that is available with larger print book publishers. It also must apply some sort of review system to assure readers that what has been created has passed some measure of scholastic standards.
8. The Google Books project, perhaps the largest of its kind to date, intends to place millions of digital copies of open access books online within the next few years. The millennial librarian must keep this and other similar projects in context. Even with the robust efforts of Google, millions of other books will remain only in print for decades to come.
9. Millennial libraries will not only look for ways to collaborate with private enterprise efforts, such as that of Google, but will look for willing partners within academia. This is especially the case with rare books and manuscripts. Providing the rare holdings of a library online, as is being done at Oxford, not only makes these holdings available worldwide, it can also publicize the existence of materials that have fallen into the dustiest areas of a library.
10. Millennial libraries should embrace partnerships with private efforts, such as the Google project, to extend the reach and availability of digitized academic works.

NOTES

1. John Palfrey and Urs Gasser, *Born Digital: Understanding the First Generation of Digital Natives* (New York: Basic Books, 2008), 365.

2. Amanda Lenhart, *A Timeline of Teens and Technology* (San Francisco: Pew Internet & American Life Project, 2007).

3. Tina Jordan, "AAP Reports Publishing Sales Up 4.1% in 2009, Year End E-Book Sales Reach $169.5 Million," Association of American Publishers, www.publishers.org/main/PressCenter/Archicves/2010_February/SalesUp4.1in2009Release.htm (19 February 2010).

4. Byron Anderson, "Electronic Roundup: E-Book Growth," *Behavioral & Social Sciences Librarian* 28, no. 17 (17 August 2009): 74–76.

5. Jordan, "AAP Reports."

6. Donald T. Hawkins, "Books: A Major Publishing Revolution," *Online* 24, no. 4 (July–August 2000): 15–28.

7. Wilbur Lang Schramm, "The Cost of Books in Chaucer's Time," *Modern Language Notes* 48, no. 3 (March 1933): 139–145, www.jstor.org/stable/2912154 (accessed 28 August 2009).

8. Jan Luiten van Zanden, "Common Workmen, Philosophers and the Birth of the European Knowledge Economy: About the Price and the Production of Useful Knowledge in Europe 1350–1800," *Global History Online* (Kyoto, Japan: Kyoto Sangyo University, 22 April 2006) (accessed 28 August 2009).

9. www.mprove.de/diplom/gui/kay72.html

10. Amazon, "Kindle: Amazon's 6" Wireless Reading Device (Latest Generation)," Amazon, www.amazon.com/Kindle-Amazons-Wireless-Reading-Generation/dp/B00154JDAI/ref=dp_ob_title_def/180-0805607-2865127 (accessed 28 August 2009).

11. Gadget Queen, "BEWARE of the SIGNIFICANT DIFFERENCES between Kindle 1 and Kindle 2!" Amazon, www.amazon.com/gp/pdp/profile/A3MDRBWMQBI2PS/ref=cm_aya_bb_pdp (accessed 28 August 2009).

12. Queen, "BEWARE of the SIGNIFICANT DIFFERENCES between Kindle 1 and Kindle 2!"

13. Hawkins, "Books: A Major Publishing Revolution," 15–28.

14. Authur Grebb, "The Showdown: Blu-Ray Versus HD-DVD," ecoustics.com, forum.ecoustics.com/bbs/messages/34579/129058.html (27 March, 4 September 2010).

15. Johnthan Dube, "Online Storytelling Forms," Committee of Concerned Journalists, www.concernedjournalists.org/online-storytelling-forms (31 August 2009).

16. Matthew Beacom and Youn Noh, "Cataloging Online Books: Born-Digital," Yale University Libraries, www.library.yale.edu/cataloging/Orbis2Manual/onlinebksnew.htm (2006) (15 August 2010).

17. William S. Baring-Gould, *The Annotated Sherlock Holmes: The Four Novels and the Fifty-Six Short Stories Complete* (New York: Clark N. Potter, 1967).

18. Hawkins, "Books: A Major Publishing Revolution," 15–28.

19. "Podcasting" University of Minnesota, dmc.umn.edu/technologies/podcasting.shtml (29 September 2010).

20. Jennie Johnson, interview with author, discussing Google Books (5 August 2009).

21. American Library Association, *Comments of the American Library Association on the Report of the Register of Copyrights to Congress—Library Reproduction of Copyrighted Works (17 U.S.C. 108)* (Washington, D.C.: ALA, 1983).

22. Michael Hart, "Gutenberg: The History and Philosophy of Project Gutenberg," Project Gutenberg, www.gutenberg.org/wiki/Gutenberg:The_History_and_Philosophy_of_Project_Gutenberg_by_Michael_Hart (28 August 2010).

23. Oxford-Google, "Oxford-Google Digitization Project Reaches a Milestone," Oxford University, www.ouls.ox.ac.uk/news/2009_mar_26 (28 August 2010).

24. Oxford-Google, "Oxford-Google Digitization."

25. Johnson, interview with author (5 August 2009).

26. *U.S. Copyright Act,* Public Law Title 17 (1976): 101.

27. John Lucas, "University of Wisconsin-Madison Expands Agreement with Google," University of Wisconsin-Madison, www.news.wisc.edu/16886 (9 July 2009).

28. Johnson, interview with author (5 August 2009).

29. Johnson, interview with author (5 August 2009).

Chapter Six

Libraries as Publishing Houses and the Long Tail Theory

In 2002, the Modern Languages Association's Ad Hoc Committee on the Future of Scholarly Publishing made several recommendations to university departments, administrators, and libraries, and publishers. Most of the ideas presented focused on a perceived crisis in scholarly publishing, as the committee's name would suggest. But the committee also noted the dilemma facing university faculty, especially since among their numerous roles and expectations was to publish. As faculty members are increasingly expected to publish more and more research papers, the avenues of publication have diminished. This holds true for both journals and monographs. Add to this an increased emphasis on publishing scholarly books by tenure committees, and academics seeking promotion are caught in a bind.

As of the summer of 2010, the Directory of Open Access Journals accounted for more than five thousand journals, with full access at the article level in roughly half of these.[1] This is small—in fact, very small—in comparison to the total number of academic journals, estimated at more than seventy thousand. So, while it is safe to say we are in the midst of a massive and rapid paradigm shift away from print to digital in all phases of academic research, from collection of data and its analysis and sharing, to the final published product, it is not occurring quite as quickly as might have been predicted in the late 1990s.

And yet, the shift seems irresistible, and with it an entirely new field of academic journal professionals may be necessary. New will be freelance editors and proofreaders. New will be rapid processing and rapid publishing. And some millennial libraries will be at the center of these changes. I suggest only some, because in the near term, issues of sustainability should inform some universities and their libraries that they are not suited to create and support new online journals over the long term. At the core of this new movement to create online journals should be a sense of responsibility to either commit to the long-term sustainability of the new journal, or to delay the idea until sufficient funding can be secured. This is not the time for academics, librarians, or their universities to run willy-nilly into the publishing business without a clear idea of what is at stake. Irresponsible efforts to create online journals will lead to scholarly disaster, not just for the journal, but also for the research entrusted to this new publishing format. We will discuss later in this chapter some of the commitments that a university, its schools and departments, and faculty must make to ensure the long-term sustainability of a new online journal. Suffice to suggest that this is not a simple task, though the existence of open source software may make it seem so.

Whatever the direction of this shift, from print to online, the academic publishing landscape will never be as it was. Research—while still under the auspices of major academic publishing houses as far as the eye can see—at a point in the not too distant future will no longer be presented on a printed page or a bound volume. Some of the practices in publishing decision making, especially within peer review, will cease to reside in a shadowy world of elites. Access to more and more research will be online, free, and readily available. Current print journals will be re-created online, and for the near term, offered both online and through the mail. Also in the near term, new online journals will continue to be created, whether their long-term sustainability has been carefully considered or not. And very many of these will be published within a structure established and maintained by university libraries, whether or not it is a wise decision to do so.

The longer-term issues at the center of this shift in academic publishing—probably the most significant change libraries and the academy have ever faced—are enormous. Decisions lay ahead, such as the form and nature of peer review, the role of journal editorial boards, and the value and commitment universities will place on these journals and their staffs. Libraries must address these issues, given that libraries are increasingly seen as a possible long-term player in academic publishing. As detailed earlier, millennial librarians are not just the future managers of information and data; they are the future managers of academic publishing itself, coequal to those publishing houses who have managed publishing for decades. As academic research moves to online outlets, some of these publication vehicles—especially university presses—will be taken up (or thrust upon) university librarians.

One way of deciphering the change that is upon us—a heuristic that we might employ to visualize the nature of future academic publishing—is Anderson's Long Tail Theory.[2] See Figure 6.1 for an example of the "Long Tail."

Applied to academic publishing, this economic model may help predict the changes in approach and thinking that will be necessary in a purely e-journal

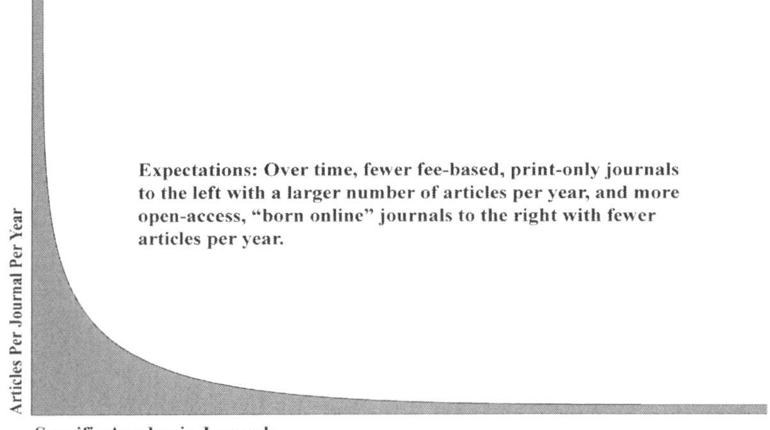

Figure 6.1. Long Tail Theory Applied to Print vs. Online Journals

world: the relevance of academic journals in an online archive environment; the economics and sustainability of online journals; the future of peer review; the ranking of online journals; and the role of libraries and authors as publishers. What can major journals do to reposition themselves to remain relevant to a new, demanding group of researchers who expect their sources of information to be free, open, and quickly accessible? How can new online journals overcome the low, but still significant, economic and university social barriers to publishing? What role will the millennial library have in helping academic departments evaluate the value of faculty publishing in an online world? What might happen to the culture of publishing, the role of peer review, as well as the previous assurances that only the "right" research is made public? And, what role does a university have in fostering the creation of online journals that are related to institutional missions, in rewarding faculty who spend time managing these new publications, and in assuring the long-term viability of the journals? Each of these questions is worthy of careful consideration.

The first domino has already fallen, though: print academic journals are moving online and new academic journals are being born online.

THE CURRENT SITUATION

The migration of print journals online is already taking place. The ARL has tracked the presence of online publications, including the method of delivery (print or online), since 1991. That first report counted 110 journals online.

By 1998, that number had jumped to more than 6,000.[3] By 2007, the ARL reported that 60 percent of the 20,000 peer-review journals were available in some form online.[4]

Some of the issues outlined at a Stanford University Libraries colloquium in 2006 addressing the online journal movement included:

- The 215 percent rise in cost of academic journals between 1986 and 2003
- Seventy-three percent of all articles in economic journals and 100 percent of the articles in the top four economic journals could be found free online[5]

Varian cited the costs of a quarterly, special-purpose, nontechnical academic journal publication as estimated by some researchers at $120,000 per issue, with an estimated per subscriber nonprofit fee of $200 and for-profit $600.[6] Varian went on to propose that the estimated annual increase in cost for this journal would be between 48 percent and 93 percent projected over a 10-year period. All of this, combined with an estimated per reader cost of $200 for some journal articles, produces an unsustainable economic model.

So, as noted earlier, existing print journals have moved online or are in the process of doing so. Some journals are offering open access abstracts, but requiring subscriptions or one-time fees to access the body of the article. Some are requiring some form of free registration to access articles. And some, similar to the practices of Google Books, are offering selected pages of works and a fee to access the remainder. But more important than that, new journals have been generated as solely online journals by off-campus nongovernmental organizations (NGO), on-campus interest groups, university committees, academic departments, and individual researchers. This shift defines more than just a change in journal ownership, but a significant redefinition in the culture of publishing. Given the new economics of online publishing, new journals will not need to appeal to a broad base of academia to generate a sufficient number of "readers" or to require subscriptions. Taken as a pattern of publishing, these new journals might fall more to the right side of Anderson's Long Tail—small readership, low cost, and self-defined. This trend is driven, at least in part, by the increasing number of articles generated by an increasing number of researchers worldwide. Some of these small journals are a "work around" for research that would otherwise never be available. Some are a shift from the print economic model to online. The latter of these, however, are still published much as their predecessors were: volume and issues of "bundled" articles that often have little or nothing to do with each other. It is a curious artifact of an economic necessity requiring publishers to maximize the efficiencies of bound journal printing. It has been rendered irrelevant by online search practices that only look for the cited article, ignoring whatever other journal articles it may have appeared beside in the bound version. Many former print journals are now online still reflecting this antecedent in organization. This shift away from the shape and protocols of print journals is not a proposed idea that will happen some vague and distant time in the future. This is—however slowly—happening now. And, as the creation of small journals continues, the tail to the right grows longer. What is remaining on the left of the chart by the ebbing tide will be an ever-decreasing number of "mass" journals covering many different areas of a broader research area, still in the volume-issue format.

Moreover, if we think of the Long Tail as extending to infinity, the furthest reach of the tail might include the appearance of lone research articles. Individual articles housed within a library's digital archives might be just as accessible to researchers as those within online journals. On the other hand, these "lone wolves" might be just as easily lost, either by poor application of keywords, or by more cataclysmic events, such as the corruption of a database.

This accessibility to individual research articles represents the threat to the new online journals mentioned at the beginning of this chapter. But it also provides potential opportunity for editors and reviewers that now form the backbones of these online publications to reformulate themselves within different roles and with new responsibilities. The information and formatting of the materials would still be necessary, as would the need to provide some form of review, peer or otherwise, that ranks the value of the published research. This review activity is not just a form of academic evaluation, but a certainty that vast numbers of research articles will not be effectively "lost" in the thin part of the tail, lost because no one knows about them, and no one can find them. For now, we know one thing is certain: in the not too distant future, research will be available online and (almost) free, with (minimal) barriers.

The Preference of Online Research

While concerns may exist as to the viability and sustainability of online journals, researchers, especially younger researchers as mentioned earlier, seem to prefer the ease of accessing online materials. And, despite the effort by some print-only journals to make their holdings accessible via subscription or "free registration" models, newer open and direct access journals are proving to be the preference of the next generation of academicians.[7] As noted by Timmer in 2009:

> Last week, the head of the U.S. branch of Oxford University Press noted an event that was striking, if unsurprising. When grading an assigned paper, a Columbia University professor found that the majority of his students had cited an

> obscure work of literary criticism that was roughly a century old. The reason? Because the work was in Google Book Search, while much other (more recent) work was not. The relative invisibility of offline information has an impact on almost all areas of life, but it's felt especially acutely in the academic world, where work builds on the existing body of knowledge.[8]

With off-campus logins to university libraries available to researchers working from a distance, along with such online (and free) research support tools as Google Scholar and RefWorks, the need for the individual researchers to subscribe to print journals clearly is minimized. In the case of this author, eliminating old, dusty print copies of mass communication journals now available online immediately called into question the need to subscribe to these publications in the first place. It is not a long reach to consider that the ease of access to online research will lead inexorably to the ability of many in academia to drop print journal subscriptions altogether. And, given the continued inflation of circulation numbers by journals that continue to mail print volumes to researchers who do not even take them out of their plastic wrapping, one would think the efficiencies of going online would become more persuasive.

As Johnson and Luther point out, the trend since the 1990s also has included a shift by publishers away from offering both print and online access, to a strictly Web-based publishing system. Consider the American Chemical Society's recent decision to suspend print and publish only online. Johnson and Luther go on to cite data that reinforces the notion that not only are the economics in favor of online publishing, but that users prefer electronic to print. Scholarship, particularly in science, is becoming increasingly born-digital and networked digitally and younger users of library and other research sources overwhelmingly prefer electronic access to journal research compared to print.[9] Ware quotes a conversation with a librarian at a large research institution: "The librarian concluded [from a study he had conducted] that on present trends, there would be little demand for print journals within five years."[10] Notably, those five years have passed and print species of academic journal remain in place in university libraries globally. But the shift—however slow—away from print cannot be denied, at least within some disciplines such as the hard sciences and some areas of the social sciences. (For examples, refer to Public Library of Science [PLoS] for journal access and Ensembl.org for database access.)

A study by researchers in 2002 at Drexel University shows a significant preference among graduate students, but less adoption among faculty, for electronic materials over print journals.[11] Two other researchers, tracking acceptance among faculty, found a much higher rate, due in large part because of the 24/7 availability of research materials.

> Our in-depth interviews with faculty indicate a high degree of comfort with electronic access to journal literature. The scholars we spoke with clearly recognized the convenience of 24/7 access from home or office. Like many librarians, most faculty would prefer to retain print just in case, but when confronted with forced choices, the overwhelming majority either supported more electronic access at the cost of print retention or felt unequipped to make this choice.[12]

And, in the midst of this movement to online research sources, in 2008 the NIH instituted a policy requiring all research using its funds to provide access to the resulting published materials (and the data related to these materials) in an open access format within one-year of publication in a private journal.[13] The effect of this rule cannot be overstated. Over time, publicly funded organizations and many private, nonprofit groups very likely will adopt this standard. The standard could be extended to include all past research created using public funds. And, while not a part of this discussion, changes in access to published materials spanning the past twenty to thirty years—that is, the research in massive databases owned by large private publishing houses—is a source of great concern to all. A great deal of it may migrate to e-reserves under the same auspices established by NIH. However, some research not funded by public resources—especially the situation with many projects in the social sciences and humanities—may not. The solution to this may lie in copyright agreements. If an author has not specifically and in writing signed away all copyright ownership to a journal interested in publishing the work, the rights return to the author after publication. This may allow past authors in the social sciences and humanities to republish their works within a library's e-reserves. Lacking this work around, some sort of buyout would be likely transferring past academic research from private publishing houses to universities.

Thus, while new publications may resolve access and budgets going forward, these new innovations do nothing to address establishing open access to existing databases and archives stretching back decades, to information that remains proprietary.

Yet, the signs could not be clearer: going forward, academic research will be sought online, created online, and migrated to online repositories and archives. The Long Tail model presents a pattern of this activity, predicting that more and more research will be generated in the right region than in the left. What remains to be determined are how university committees will value online research journals, the economics to support online-only open access journals, and the role of the university library in sustaining journals that they may eventually host de facto in their electronic reserves.

RANKING (AND VALUING) ONLINE JOURNALS

As millennial libraries consider their role in hosting online journals, one of the first challenges they will face is the value of the journal itself to the academic community. Significant push-back exists within some areas of the university, especially for born-online journals. A recent polling of 2,500 journalism and mass communication professors in the United States found that only 16 percent of the respondents believe their department tenure committees would accept a research paper published in a new, online-only journal as counting toward a candidate's progress.[14]

The challenge, it appears, is that established university faculty members have for years ranked a journal's value based on its reputation for rejecting papers. The logic seems to be that the more submissions rejected, the more robust the peer review, the better the editorial board and, thus, the better the journal. These new online journals are at the least a mystery and certainly suspect to these tenure committees. Several times in the last few years, I have been contacted by academic committees dealing with faculty tenure, rank, and promotion at other schools seeking guidance on how to evaluate online journals and the work that their faculty members have published. The "established" method of evaluating research publishing—a journal's rejection rate and reputation—seems out of step when considering online publishing. Revisiting Anderson's Long Tail Theory, it is reasonable to imagine that small, topic-specific journals would have lower rejection rates. That is, given that a substantial number of rejections are based on whether an article is appropriate for a potential journal, the numbers of such "bad fits" would be lower for topic-specific journals. Indeed, many traditional journals have such vague, almost indecipherable "rules" of what is considered appropriate, that authors almost always start with a query on whether their work is a good fit. The smaller, topic-specific online journal should be more transparent as to their purpose and what would constitute appropriate topics for submissions. Therefore, would the generation of higher incidences of "good fits" then lead to lower rejection rates? And, if so, would such a journal be penalized for exhibiting a low rejection rate or rewarded for reflecting a preferred match for a small group of researchers? Additionally, using rejection rates for an online journal, which has the option of virtually unlimited space, seems technologically antiquated.

As for "reputation," as we see thousands of more narrowly defined journals appear, how likely are any to reach a level of high esteem (or even awareness) in a general area of research such as mass communications if they are judged by their journal and not their own worth? What stands as the important element here, the journal that the work is published in, or the intrinsic value of the research itself? Attaching value to an article because of the reputation of the journal within which it is published has all the qualities of elitism.

One alternative proposed would be the citation rate of the articles published in a particular journal by other researchers, such as that provided by Thomson Reuters's Institute for Scientific Information (ISI). ISI provides an annual summary, called the "impact factor," of various scientific journals, generally within a specific field. Created in 1960 by Eugene Garfield, the ISI and its impact factor, calculates the value of a journal based on the number of times an article within it is cited by an indexed journal over a period of time, divided by the total number of journal articles, reviews, proceedings, and notes published by the publication in that same period. It generally does not include editorials or letters to the editor, though, if such writings included citations, it might. Criticism of the impact factor includes its lack of sensitivity to citation style differences between fields of research. In addition, the charges of manipulation and abuse of the impact factor of a particular journal and, in cases even a specific journal article, has led some associations and researchers to understandably suggest:

> The impact factor, however, is not always a reliable instrument for measuring the quality of journals. Its use for purposes for which it was not intended, causes even greater unfairness. Therefore the European Association of Science Editors recommends that journal impact factors are used only—and cautiously—for measuring and comparing the influence of entire journals, but not for the assessment of single papers, and certainly not for the assessment of researchers or research programmes either directly or as a surrogate.[15]

Indeed, even the factor's creator, Garfield, suggested in 2006, that "All citation studies should be adjusted to account for variables such as specialty, citation density, and half-life."[16]

This "impact factor" citation rating method comes with its own set of problems not mentioned in previous research. Given the likelihood that researchers will gravitate more and more toward open access publications to find research information, citation rates of articles published within anything other than fully open access journals are likely to fall, not because these journals are of a lesser quality, but instead simply based on ease of access.[17] Thus, citation of a journal would not reflect on the value of the journal itself, but whether it is an open access or even slightly closed publication. Add to this that the vast amount of research is unavailable online, specifically works published prior to 1980.

Finally, some journal articles are cited for their flaws, not their strengths in research. Using the citation method to rank journals and articles would mistakenly value these works as valuable additions to a body of research.

Varian suggested in 1998 a publication system for online journal articles that might be applied to the journals themselves. A board of scholars would rank a journal's articles on a scale from 1 (low) to 5 (high). All submitted articles, in this system, are published (with the author's permission) with an attached average ranking. This, according to Varian is a "model . . . unlike the conventional publishing model, but [one that] addresses many of the same design considerations."[18] The rankings of journals could then be established by averaging the ranks of the articles it contains. Tenure committees and researchers would be able to track the value of a publication based on these article rankings. The entire model outlined by Varian is fluid, interactive, and eliminates the economic barriers and potential biases inherent in the far more expensive, far-slower-to-respond traditional print and many online journal models.[19]

The open and free exchange of ideas and opinions might avoid these sorts of biases; but even this system does not answer the question of anonymity among those providing online peer comments. Indeed, the issue of anonymous peer review is a significant hurdle that libraries will face, if not in the short term, certainly when the migration to e-reserves picks up speed. The solution may involve UGC, as well as the author's ability to respond to criticisms posted online. The ensuing discussion (with moderation) would result in a rich, valuable exchange of ideas, the sort only imagined by Justice Oliver Wendell Holmes's "marketplace of ideas."[20]

The Future of Peer Review

> The Web journals are threatening to turn on its head the traditional peer-review system that for decades has been the established way to pick apart research before it's made public.[21]

No other tradition within academics is so revered and scorned as peer review. To some academics, no less than the future of civilization has rested on its shoulders. To others, the spirit of elitism, bias, and racism permeate its structure. Roughly a quarter of a century ago, two professors tested the peer-review process in place at a dozen highly regarded academic journals in psychology. Twelve articles in each of these journals that had been published earlier (between eighteen months and two years) were resubmitted under fictitious names and institutions. The researchers reported that three had been caught as resubmissions, one was accepted, and eight were rejected. The rationale for the rejections was, in many cases, that the articles contained "serious methodological flaws." As the researchers noted at the time, "a major portion of the criticism of the journal review system has concerned the reliability of peer review." The research suggests the high rejection rates of the previously published articles might be related to author standing, institutional standing, peer bias, or poor reviewer performance.[22]

Research published in 2001 suggests that women face a much harder time getting their articles published because of gender bias and nepotism on the part of reviewers and editors. These researchers suggested that to avoid the loss of a "large pool of promising talent," the peer-review process should be retooled to create "built in resistances to the weaknesses of human nature."[23] Other researchers have found similar weaknesses within the peer system, a system that is intended to ensure that only the best research is published.[24]

In 2000 Rothwell and Martyn noted in evaluating the peer review of papers submitted to two neuroscience journals that the relationship among the opinions of reviewers was little better than what could result from chance. In fact, their analysis suggested that the contents of the abstracts submitted for review accounted for only 10 percent to 20 percent of the variance in the opinions of the reviewers.[25] In citing this research, Horrobin concluded that the peer-review system itself was "rotten."

> These appalling figures will not be surprising to critics of peer review, but they give solid substance to what these critics have been saying. The core system by which the scientific community allots prestige (in terms of oral presentations at major meetings and publication in major journals) and funding is a non-validated charade whose processes generate results little better than does chance. Given the fact that most reviewers are likely to be mainstream and broadly supportive of the existing organization of the scientific enterprise, it would not be surprising if the likelihood of support for truly innovative research was considerably less than that provided by chance.[26]

However, despite its frailties, peer review is still valued as a method used to sift out research appropriate for publication and block what might be inappropriate or not rigorous. This is the model that academia has relied upon in one form or another for at least four hundred years.[27] As noted by Goodstein, peer review works "superbly" in identifying science from nonsense. It works less well in "choosing between competing valid ideas."[28] He goes on to note that peer review also fails to detect or account for "cheating or fraud, because all scientists are socialized to believe that even their bitterest competitor is rigorously honest about the reporting of scientific results, making it easy to fool a referee with purposeful dishonesty if one wants to."[29]

Although discussing issues of Internet commerce in the 1990s, O'Reilly may have put it best:

> Information has a funny characteristic. Up to a certain point, more choice is better. Then the situation flips. The user gets overwhelmed, and less is more. Publishing shows us the role not of the gatekeeper (who allows only certain

> content to be published), but of the adviser, whether that adviser is a trusted columnist or reviewer in a newspaper, or trusted clerk at the local bookstore.[30]

The question is not whether to eliminate peer review altogether, but whether the new forms of online publishing provide an opportunity to make peer review more robust, reliable, and useful. If the core value of peer review is its ability to identify weaknesses in research, then it would seem, logically, that more peer review would lead to better published research. This falls close to another of Justice Holmes's arguments that bad speech is cured by more speech, not less. That is, rather than restricting the "speech" of researchers, the "cure" for any errors in their publication would be a multitude of comments and suggestions for improvements.[31] In fact, along with the article cited earlier that dealt with the rejection of previously published research by psychology journals, four dozen responses from other researchers were included by the journal.[32] Given the year, which was 1982, this might be one of the very early examples of a blog, with all manner of positive and negative reactions presented in what amounted to equal time.

Online journals are uniquely positioned to offer much the same sort of enriched conversation among researchers. A research paper might be placed online and other researchers invited to comment on the strength of the data, the clarity of the writing, the reliability and validity of the analysis, or any other element of the work. These comments provided freely by other researchers could be weighted by editors, readers, and the author for their value and then used to improve the work in question. The net result would be stronger research, clearer writing, and presumably progress in the field of study. Such a structure would avoid the miscarriages of nonpublication or severely delayed publication as was the case with Einstein's works in physics, as well as other cases frequently alluded to in discussions of peer review. By its very structure, the peer-review process assumes that the scholar who is relied upon to review a work and provide advice as to whether to publish it is familiar with the field and capable of rendering an educated and measured opinion.

> Today, Einstein's papers would be sent to some total nonentity at Podunk U, who, being completely incapable of understanding important new ideas, would reject the papers for publication. "Peer" review is *very* unlikely to be peer review for the Einsteins of the world. We have a scientific social system in which intellectual pygmies are standing in judgment of giants.[33]

Another question regarding peer review remains largely sacrosanct and untouchable: the anonymity of the reviewers. The use of anonymity in peer review dates back to the mid-twentieth century.[34] The presumed value is that reviewers feel more comfortable with being direct and to the point in their opinions of a work. The obvious downside goes back to all the faults mentioned earlier: bias, competition, and jealousy. Without identification, reviewers with a personal agenda could suppress, or at least stall, the publication of works they either do not understand or do not like for a multitude of nonscientific reasons.

It could be argued that with an open review system as outlined previously, the cream of the crop could still be identified and, moreover, improved upon. Such rigorous debate over research in a transparent environment might be far healthier than the secretive machinations of a small group of reviewers. And given the presumed increase in comments and grading by peer researchers, the final product might be more improved in an open, identified system than a closed, anonymous one.

However, such an open peer-review system may cause trouble in an entirely separate area of academia. The presumed value of a journal is in the tendency of its editorial board to reject all but the best research submitted for review. Without that board, how can tenure and promotion committees evaluate a candidate's work? Providing the certainty of a strong peer review process—as reflected in a journal's rejection rates—offers a tenure committee an easy rubric. It moves the task of evaluation from the possible political environment of a faculty meeting to an outside board of experts.

Yet, an alternate method, and one that is close to the outside approach just mentioned would rest the value of an online journal on its board. A board consisting of the leaders in their academic or private fields would reflect the professionalism sought by tenure committees. These individuals may come from the core group that started the journal or may be recommended by that same group. This is a very important step. A new journal needs a strong board to support its credibility as a publication of worth to attract submissions, as well as potential funding. Tenure committees might also look to other factors to evaluate a publication's worth, such as citation rates of its published articles in other journals. However, such citation rates can only occur, of course, after the publication is underway. A strong, nationally recognized editorial board would attract submissions and aid in the recruitment of reviewers.

Having posed this possible method of evaluating an online journal, the door is open to ask why—in a strictly online world—the role of the editorial board could not be more of a rating of research, rather than a publisher of the actual research. That is, rather than strictly following the publishing patterns of today, including those within online journals, a board could offer its opinion on each article, perhaps even rate the article via some agreed-upon scheme. If this sounds more like commercial reviews of a book (or even a movie, for that matter), so be it. The space restrictions of print were not conducive to highly visible, if still anonymous, participation by editorial boards. The use of blogs by the editorial board to support online discussions of each published journal article in an almost side-by-side environment would provide immediate and lively feedback to the authors and researchers. And, if the actual goal of research is to assure progress by implementing the most critical evaluations of work, then the one hundred voices might be considered far more robust than that of three. Such critiques by the corpus of an academic field of study could result in not just a one-way flow of feedback to the author, but a second flow back to those posting their opinions, informing and educating even those who stand in judgment. The ensuing robust discussion, with careful, but not overly restrictive moderation, would educate all, and quite possibly result in better research, as well as better researchers.

Pulling together an editorial board might start with a small group of interested researchers within the field or within a university. Using a snowball method, each member of the small group could recommend other potential editorial board members. And these new board members could recommend others, and so on.

The role of the board would be largely to provide reviews of papers submitted. But such a board might also be called on for advice on special issues, staff changes/new hires, and other management issues. A new journal would be wise to create as large a board as possible to ensure a low annual review rate for each member (given that funding for such journals is likely to be very minimal). Large boards also push back any belief that the journal is exclusively for the benefit of only a few researchers. This is not to suggest that very narrowly defined subject areas might result in very narrowly defined editorial boards, of perhaps as few as five members. However, such a narrowly defined journal would approach the nature of a small academic commons, rather than an online journal. These boards would serve pro bono, especially important to these new journals whose funding would likely be scarce and their needs high. Such an arrangement feels like it would not appear for years, perhaps decades. Yet, if an association, such as the American Medical Association (AMA), were to see its role to evaluate all medical research, no matter where or by whom it is published, what other group could carry more weight? And, how could such an activity, if extended to all AMA members, not raise the standing of the association itself?

As the economics drive the creation of more and more new journals, and the likelihood of more and more individual publishing, the unique economic demands associated with these forms and forums of publishing will fall on the university and, ultimately, its library.

The Economics of Online Publishing

In "The Future of Electronic Journals," Varian proposes a supply and demand model for publishing scholarly work, concluding that, for most universities, "The ability . . . to attract top-flight researchers depends on the size of the collection of the library. Threats to cancel journal subscriptions are met with cries of outrage by faculty."[35] However, over the past few years, the merging of major publishing houses has resulted in extreme increases in the cost of subscriptions. For example, after Elsevier, a major publisher of academic research, acquired several smaller publishers, the fees for subscriptions for both their journals and those acquired in the deal shot up.

> According to these empirical estimates, each of these mergers was associated with substantial price increases; in the case of the Elsevier deal the price increase appears to be due to increased market power. For example, compared to premerger prices, the Elsevier deal resulted in an average price increase of 22% for former Pergamon titles, and an 8% increase for Elsevier deal titles.[36]

Varian concludes that to reduce the cost of academic communication, the manuscript-handling process would require reengineering. Using electronic distribution could cut costs within the editorial system by 50 percent. Add to this the reduction of shelf space in libraries, the costs to monitor holdings, the ease of online searches, and the ability to store accompanying support documents, such as images, datasets, and, though not mentioned by Varian, audiovisual files, and cost-savings could be significant. "When everything is electronic," Varian notes, "publications will have much more general forms, new filtering and refereeing mechanisms will be used, [but] archiving and standardization will remain a problem."[37]

Had the Long Tail model been available to Varian when he published his research in the 1990s, he might have used it to explain how hard costs (capital outlay) would drop to near zero on the right side of the curve. The Long Tail predicts the smaller the journal in the number of articles published annually, the lower the cash outlays required to establish and operate. Notably, recent thoughts from Anderson suggests that the Long Tail Theory might need some modification to include the possibility that a few already well-established journals online will become very, very large, literally sucking up all the available research that might be appropriate for publication.[38]

New software created in recent years to assist online journal editors has reduced the time necessary to manage a journal. This software allows editors to establish reviewers, provides for easy article uploads from authors, and manages the interaction of editors with the entire editorial team, all in online formats. A cursory search for such software packages found more than a dozen free and open source options:

ARNO: Academic Research in the Netherlands Online, www.uba.uva.nl/arno

CDSware: The CERN Document Server Software (CDSware) was developed to support the CERN Document Server, cdsware.cern.ch

CLEO: The University of Provence and the University of Avignon, cleo .cnrs.fr/
DSpace: MIT's DSpace was expressly created as a digital repository to capture the intellectual output of multidisciplinary research organizations, www.dspace.org
DiVA: Electronic Publishing Centre at Uppsala University Library, www .diva-portal.org/about.xsql
DpubS: Cornell University Library and Pennsylvania State University Libraries and Press, dpubs.org
E-Journal: From Digital Publishing Systems, drupal.org/project/ejournal
Eprints: Developed at the University of Southampton, the first version of the system was publicly released in late 2000; the project was originally sponsored by CogPrints, but is now supported by JISC, as part of the Open Citation Project, and by NSF, software.eprints.org
ePublishing Toolkit: The Max Planck Gesellschaft, www.mpg.de
Fedora: The Fedora digital object repository management system is based on the Flexible Extensible Digital Object and Repository Architecture (Fedora), www.fedora.info
GAPworks: German Academic Publishers (GAP), developer.berlios.de/ projects/gapworks/
HyperJournal: The University of Pisa, www.hjournal.org/download
Lodel: Publishing software behind Revues.org, www.lodel.org
MyCoRe: MyCoRe grew out of the MILESS Project of the University of Essen and is now being developed by a consortium of universities to provide a core bundle of software tools to support digital libraries and archiving solutions, www.mycore.de
OpenACS: Toolkit for online communities, openacs.org/
Open Journal Systems: The Public Knowledge Project, pkp.sfu.ca/?q=ojs
Online Publications of the University of Stuttgart (OPUS): elib.uni -stuggart.de/opus/
SOPS: SciX, a European Union funded research project, www.scix.net/sops .htm
Topaz: Public Library of Science, www.topazproject.org/trac/wiki

For example, OJS is a journal management and publishing system developed by the Public Knowledge Project, a federally funded organization intent on expanding access to information. Its features include,

- Local control by library staff
- Ability of editors to configure the required sections and review process
- Management of submission and review online

- A built-in subscription module
- Indexing
- Reading tools
- E-mail correspondence with authors and reviewers
- Help support
- Functionality on any standard server

What is does not allow (at least in a format that readers might recognize) is a UGC area. This is unfortunate. The Open Society Institute's *Guide to Institutional Repository Software* has identified several software platforms suitable to manage online journals, at least as of 2004.[39]

Depending on the size of its budget and the intended scope, amount, and depth of its publishing, the journal may require more than one editor, plus additional support staff, such as copywriters, Web managers, and staff to handle reviewer relations. However, it is just as likely that in its first year, only an editor and a graduate student will be required. The editor and student will be expected to have some Web skills, since almost all of the activity of the journal's maintenance will be online. In addition, at least some familiarity with the subject of the journal would be expected of the editor. And it will be up to the editor and the founding members—if present—to recruit the editorial board.

The journal would require technical support from the library, generally represented by a staff person or persons familiar with one or more of the many types of open access software platforms mentioned previously.

Another major technical challenge at the university level is the amount of space available for archiving. Given the significant drop in memory costs, a server for a small journal with 4 TBs of storage might cost as little as $1,500. The average twenty-page research paper with no charts might require 200 KBs of space as a PDF/A. Add in four or five color charts and the result might be as large as 2 MB. Assuming fifty articles a year, which is high for even a journal such as *Journalism and Mass Communication Quarterly (JMCQ)*, and you have hardware capacity of four years, or roughly $400 a year. Clearly, the barrier is not the software (no cost) or the hardware (minimal costs). The barriers are strictly a matter of desire on the part of faculty and the university, and the willingness of both to follow the open access, free model of publishing.

In addition, the traditional journal budget obviously would include the publication of printing, mailing, scanning, and all the other functions required to take a research paper to press. By ensuring that manuscripts are submitted electronically, reviewed electronically, and published electronically, these costs can be avoided.

However, while the low costs of online journals may be driving the engine of new journal creation, other significant issues have yet to be resolved. Issues of sustainability and the very ephemeral nature of HTML itself (as mentioned in chapter 2) have worried some researchers going back to the mid-1990s. As noted by Hitchcock, Carr, and Hall in 1997, the "bare facts of this change [are] a simple record of a short period which may or may not, with greater analysis and hindsight, prove to be an important pivotal moment."[40] Among the issues raised by Hitchcock's team were the questionable stability of online journals and, perhaps more importantly, the ability of online journals to carry more than merely one-dimensional, written content.

> In these projects lie the clues—information filtering, agents, links, multimedia—not just to the next generation of the digital journals but to the emerging shape of the digital library. Clearly these projects will not provide all the answers or the tools, but they are good starting points from which to understand how, also why, e-journals will change.[41]

JOURNAL SUSTAINABILITY: IS THE MILLENNIAL LIBRARY IN IT FOR THE LONG HAUL?

Oddly, the issue of journal sustainability is rarely cast in terms of a print journal's viability, but is always raised as a factor in discussing the value of an online journal. The fear is that the online journal, a mere collection of bits and bytes, could disappear should its sponsor drop its support. The print journal has its subscription base and the ability of large publishers to "bundle" less-favored publications with high-demand ones. The lone wolf online journal (or researcher) has neither of these. Its information, that is, its research articles, are available at no charge, in keeping with the free nature of the Internet itself. The free, online journal will always require sponsorship of some sort. And, while some author-fee structures have been proposed,[42] the reliance of new online journals on their hosting universities (specifically libraries) is a given.[43] The extent of this support can be focused on three essential items: a faculty member or members, some sort of academic support (most likely in the form of a graduate student or students), and archive server space and technical support. Lacking a strong commitment from universities, these small journals are likely to fail for a number of reasons.

It would be good to note that simply because one can do a thing (and quite easily at that), it does not follow that one should do that thing. Any faculty member, group, or committee considering establishing an academic journal online must first consider the long-term implications. Does the group have long-term funding established? Or is this the vision of a few or perhaps even the passion of one?

As mentioned earlier in this book, the ease with which an online journal can be launched belies the need to ensure that it will continue. A rash rush into launching a journal is not only irresponsible; it may present a real threat to the research it publishes. For, once an article is published, a certain trust exchanges hands between the researcher and the publication's administration. The former assures the publisher that the work is accurate and original. The latter assures the researcher that the work will remain available for decades to come. If this promise of sustainability can be established, and only when it can, then a new journal should not only be launched, it should be celebrated by the hosting library and its university.

For the faculty engaged in editing a new online journal, the reward for the hours or work in recruiting submissions, editing works, cajoling reviewers, and pushing the works through to the site must be more than a mark of service. The value a university gives to works published within its new journal must be equally extended to faculty willing to manage and edit such journals. Given the modicum of university financial support likely available to faculty wishing to act in online journal roles, the scholarly credit must be high for faculty willing to act as editors. If a department chair or college dean sees no or little scholarly value in the work by a faculty member as an editor, it is unlikely that the journal will find an editor willing to do the work without compensation. Yet, attaching performance rewards and rankings to journal editing is precisely what must happen if these new journals are to succeed.

Universities must highly value the editorial leadership positions of these new journals so as to ensure that succession from one editor to another is never in question. As vacancies occur, faculty members must be encouraged to compete for these posts. Universities cannot rest upon the zeal of the early builders of these journals for their long-term success. These leaders will retire or move elsewhere. Without a built-in aura of regard for online journal editors, the prospects for the publications' long-term viability will be short, shorter than necessary. Universities need not expend funds to reward editors beyond a small honorarium. It is the position itself that must be considered the reward.

In addition, universities must be full-throated supporters of the new models of rigorous online commentary on research beyond traditional peer review. Online blogs are a very new, very unconventional model for peer review of academic research. Yet, it holds great promise as a far more powerful factor in its immediate impact on the quality of research itself. Indeed, this new model of academic publishing relies upon the participation of faculty in the online comment blogs. A free exchange of ideas, if it is to be of any scholarly value, must accrue value to the participants in that exchange.

Such full-throated participation will accrue benefits to the university, the library as publisher, the research, and the researcher. By considering what has occurred in the past, we can see the value of a fully open, fully collegial exchange of thoughts on newly published research. Consider a journal article published in a standard print journal twenty years ago, complete with errors in statistics and citations undetected by the publication's editors and reviewers. No doubt the author would have the chance to improve upon these erroneous findings in later works. Yet, the original work would remain uncommented upon, standing alone in its place within a print journal bound within a volume in a library. It could be cited thousands of times by researchers unaware of the errors or of other works citing these flaws.

Now imagine such an article published within an online journal. The errors could not only be pointed out by other researchers, but could be presented in the same physical area where the article resides or linked to the published work. Further, the author of this flawed work could have the opportunity to not only offer comment to rebut criticism, but could correct flaws as they are verified. The result is better research, a better publication, and possibly a better researcher. And shouldn't that be a goal for any university?

UNIVERSITY LIBRARY AS PUBLISHER: TOP MILESTONES

1. The growth of online-only research journals is steady, but hardly close to a majority of all academic publications.
2. New online-only journals do not address the research published prior to the 1980s, which is largely still not digital, and may remain so for some time to come. Predictions of the passing of all academic journals from print to digital have been grossly overstated.
3. Future new journals, however, will most likely be born online only, with no paper artifact.
4. While it is true that researchers, especially younger ones and students, prefer to find their data online, it is also true that the vast majority use poor search skills.
5. The millennial library must be engaged in assisting university presses, many of whom may be moving under library administration, make the shift to online, including the digitization of past issues.
6. Acceptance of online journal publishing by tenure committees lags far behind the use of these journals by researchers. For its own online journal, the millennial library must ensure that the best editorial board is created, and that all editorial processes (proofing, fact checking, and peer review) are run accurately and ethically.
7. It is better to not start an online journal, than to start the journal and then let it drift for lack of funding or lack of academic support from the university.

8. Universities must be brought to understand that the editors who spend their time working on these journals, whether within the library publishing structure, or in various departments across campus, must be given credit for their efforts as scholarly research, not service.
9. The academic commons can provide a lively, engaging discussion about scholarly works through the use of blogs and other tools within the millennial library.
10. UGC can enhance and strengthen any academic journal and any publication within it.

SUMMARY

As universities struggle with the new publication model for researchers, it is key for them to be proactive in addressing their new role as publishers. At the same time, these universities must carefully examine whether they are ready to stand behind and sustain their newly created publications for the long term. New software has made the maintenance of online journal affordable. The economics of online publishing is making the creation of journals with narrowly defined subjects possible. Investments in storage space for archival materials must be extended to include as-yet-not-published material, specifically, research. The barriers to publishing are now more a matter of philosophy, not economics, as shown by Anderson's Long Tail model.

And, given the shift of publishing away from traditional large publishers to smaller, narrowly defined journals, the methods used to determine what is valued research must change. As has been shown, the likelihood that all future research will be published online, whether reviewed or not for its value, demands that we take a hard look out our evaluation systems. It makes sense that if all academic research eventually is stored within a university library's archival e-space, the role of journals as filters to that research is moot. Rather than acting as barriers to access, the new online journal will be asked to evaluate the already published, already accessible research. Arguments backing up these evaluations should be encouraged. Comments from others in the field will be encouraged. And revision and reconsideration of research by authors will be enhanced and strengthened.

All of this is at the heart of online access to academic research. The nature of this access is varied: from complete to limited, from registered to subscription. All of these represent a shift of more than ownership, but a redefinition in the culture of publishing. As we move forward, two scenarios are likely to play out: more and more small, narrowly defined journals will appear, and larger and larger massing of research will occur in fewer and fewer journals.

That is, having a journal dedicated to research involving the Great Plains of North America not only is possible, it has already happened. At the same time, when journals, such as *Journalism and Mass Communication Quarterly*, finally realize they need not be bound by the size of their presses, they will also realize they can attract and publish far more research.

Two forces drive this shift to online publishing. First, the economics of posting versus printing are clear and persuasive to any agency or group funding a journal. But, second and equally persuasive, is the preference that academics—especially younger academics—have shown for online accessible research. In fact, it is this younger researcher who is making it clear that all research must be accessible without even the hint of requiring a modest registration or logon.

Tenure committees are struggling to establish new standards, as well as evaluate new born-online journals. By and large—at least within mass communication faculty—less than one in six professors believes his school tenure committee places any value on publishing that appears in an online-only journal. As the rules shift in both journal evaluation and status, and in the peer-review process itself, research appearing online (and only online) will become more acceptable. One possible method of evaluating these new online journals might be Garfield's "impact factor." Another might be a simpler evaluation of the journal's editorial board.

Other changes in the way in which research is evaluated for publication might include more input from other academics. Expanding past the usual three anonymous peer reviewers to a system that encourages outside involvement might, logically, lead to better research and better researchers. In the opinion of some, any change to what they see as a biased, inept peer review "club" would be a welcome improvement. Errors in peer judgment, whether based on personal animosity or a simple lack of ability, stifle growth and progress and, in some situations, may prevent brilliant researchers from attaining a much deserved tenure status.

These new online journals—as well as traditional print publications who choose to move online—will find a host of online software options to support their staff activities. It is likely that even more than the almost two dozen that are mentioned in this chapter will come on the scene in the next few years. Whatever the package the new journal's staff choose, it is vital that some basic standards be held to, starting with the use of PDF/A for article preservation.

Universities must value online publication and publishers—not only the original work, but also the efforts of editors in publishing that work, as well as reviewers commenting with the intent to improve that work. Journal editors working for little or no pay are assets to any university. Failure to see their work as scholarly research is not only short-sighted, it is also counterproductive. Most of all, the university and its millennial library must be certain they are behind a new journal for the long haul. Abandoning a new journal financially, or failing to value the work of its editorial staff would not just be unfortunate, it would be a tragedy.

NOTES

1. Directory of Open Access Journals, www.doaj.org.
2. Chris Anderson, "The Long Tail: Forget Squeezing Millions from a Few Megahits at the Top of the Charts. The Future of Entertainment Is in the Millions of Niche Markets at the Shallow End of the Bitstream," *Wired* 12, no. 10 (October 2004).
3. Dru Mogge, "Seven Years of Tracking Electronic Publishing: The ARL 'Directory of Electronic Journals, Newsletters and Academic Discussion Lists.'" *Library Hi Tech* 17, no. 1 (1999).
4. Richard K. Johnson and Judy Luther, *The E-Only Tipping Point for Journals: What's Ahead in the Print-to-Electronic Transition Zone* (Washington, D.C.: Association of Research Libraries, 2007).
5. Barbara Palmer, *Ongoing Crisis in Academic-Journal Pricing Is the Focus of Recent Colloquium: Attendees Agree High Costs of Subscriptions Are Unsustainable and Electronic Distribution Has Radically Changed Publishing* (San Francisco: Stanford News Service, 2006).
6. Hal R. Varian, "The Future of Electronic Journals," *The Journal of Electronic Publishing* 4, no. 1 (1998) as cited by Carol Tenopir and Donald W. King, "Trends in Scientific Scholarly Journal Publishing," *Journal of Scholarly Publishing* 28, no. 3 (April 1997): 135–170. Note that the Varian article was presented at a conference the year before that Tenopir attended. Varian's article can be accessed at http://quod.lib.umich.edu/cgi/t/text/text-idx?c=jep;view=text;rgn=main;idno=3336451.0004.105.
7. Irma F. Dillon and Karla Hahn, "Are Researchers Ready for the Electronic-Only Journal Collection? Results of a Survey at the University of Maryland," *Libraries and the Academy* 2, no. 3 (2002): 375–390.
8. John Timmer, "Science Moves from the Stacks to the Web; Print Too Pricey," *Ars Technica,* 6 July 2009 (accessed 7 July 2010).
9. Mike Ware, "E-Only Journals: Is It Time to Drop Print?" *Learned Publishing* 18, no. 3 (2005): 193–199.
10. Ware, "E-Only Journals," 193–199.
11. Dillon and Hahn, "Are Researchers Ready," 375–390.
12. Janet P. Palmer and Mark Sandler, "What Do Faculty Want?" *Library Journal* 128, no. 1 (2003): s26–s29.
13. *The National Institutes of Health Public Access Policy,* Public Law 2008 (8 June 2008).
14. Thomas Gould, unpublished data based on an online survey of 2,500 mass communication professors, 2009. Currently under review.

15. "Statement on Impact Factors," European Association of Science Editors (European Association of Science Editors, 2008), www.ease.org.uk/statements/EASE_statement_on_impact_factors.shtml (15 August 2010).

16. Eugene Garfield, "The History and Meaning of the Journal Impact Factor," *Journal of American Medical Association* 295, no. 1 (4 January 2006): 90–93.

17. J. Peters, "The Hundred Years War Started Today: An Exploration of Electronic Peer Review," *Internet Research: Electronic Networking Applications and Policy* 5, no. 1 (1995): 3–10.

18. Varian, "The Future of Electronic Journals."

19. Varian, "The Future of Electronic Journals."

20. *Abrams v. United States,* 250 U.S. 616 (1919).

21. Alicia Chang, "Web Threatens Peer Review System," *USA Today,* 2 October 2006 (accessed 7 July 2010).

22. Douglas P. Peters and Stephen J. Ceci, "Peer-Review Practices of Psychological Journals: The Fate of Publishing Articles, Submitted Again," *The Behavioral and Brain Sciences* 5 (1982): 187–255.

23. Christine Wennerås and Agnes Wold, "Nepotism and Sexism in Peer Review," in *Women, Science, and Technology*, eds. Mary Wyer, Donna Giesman, Mary Barbercheck, Hatice Ozturk, Marta Wayne (New York: Routledge, 2001), 46–52.

24. Rex Dalton, "Peers Under Pressure," Abstract. *Nature* 413, no. 6852 (13 September 2001): 103; Tom Jefferson, "Peer Review and Publishing: It's Time to Move the Agenda On," *Lancet* 366, no. 9482 (2005), 283–284; Michael J. Mahone, "Publication Prejudices: An Experimental Study of Confirmatory Bias in the Peer Review System," *Cognitive Therapy and Research* 1, no. 1 (June 1977): 161–175; Bryan D. Neff and Julian D. Olden, "Is Peer Review a Game of Chance?" *Bioscience* 56, no. 4 (April 2006): 333–342; Peters, "The Hundred Years War Started Today: An Exploration of Electronic Peer Review," 3–10; David Shulenburger, "On Scholarly Evaluation and Scholarly Communication," *College Research Libraries News* 62, no. 8 (2001).

25. Peter M. Rothwell and Christopher N. Martyn, "Reproducibility of Peer Review in Clinical Neuroscience: Is Agreement between Reviewers Any Greater Than Would Be Expected by Chance Alone?" *Brain* 123, no. 9 (September 2000): 1964–1969.

26. David Horrobin, "Opinion: Something Rotten at the Core of Science?" *Trends in Pharmacological Sciences* 22, no. 2 (February 2001).

27. "The Origin of the Scientific Journal and the Process of Peer Review," Select Committee on Science and Technology of The United Kingdom Parliament, eprints.ecs.soton.ac.uk.er.lib.ksu.edu/13105/1/399we23.htm (25 October 2008).

28. David Goodstein, "How Science Works," *U.S. Federal Judiciary Reference Manual on Evidence* (2000): 66–72.

29. Goodstein, "How Science Works," 66–72.

30. Tim O'Reilly, "Publishing Models for Internet Commerce," O'Reilly Network, www.oreillynet.com/pub/a/oreilly/tim/articles/pubmod.html (11 August 2009).

31. *Abrams v. United States*, 616–630.

32. Peters and Ceci, "Peer-Review Practices of Psychological," 187–255.

33. Frank J. Tipler, "Refereed Journals: Do They Insure Quality or Enforce Orthodoxy?" ISCIS Archive (30 June 2003), www.iscid.org/boards/ubb-get_topic-f-10-t-000059.html (accessed 15 August 2010).

34. Alexander Berezin, Richard Gordon, and Geoffrey Hunter, "Lifting the Pernicious Veil of Secrecy," *New Scientist* 1964 (11 February 1995): 46; Harry Morrow Brown, "Peer Review Should Not Be Anonymous (Letters)," *British Medical Journal* 326, no. 7393 (12 April 2003): 824, find.galegroup.com.er.lib.ksu.edu.er.lib.k-state.edu/itx/infomark.do?&contentSet=IAC-Documents&type=retrieve&tabID=T002&prodId=EAIM&docId=A100960008&source=gale&srcprod=EAIM&userGroupName=ksu&version=1.0 (15 August 2010); "Bad Peer Reviewers," *Nature* 413, no. 6852 (13 September 2001): 93.

35. Varian, "The Future of Electronic Journals."

36. M. J. McCabe, "Journal Pricing and Mergers: A Portfolio Approach," *American Economic Review* 92 (2002): 259–268.

37. Varian, "The Future of Electronic Journals."

38. Chris Anderson, "The Web Is Dead, Long Live the Internet: Who's to Blame?" *Wired* 18, no. 9 (September 2010): 118–127, 164–166.

39. Raym Crow, *A Guide to Institutional Repository Software* (New York: Open Society Institute, 2004), 28.

40. Steve Hitchcock, Leslie Carr, and Wendy Hall, "Web Journals Publishing: A UK Perspective," *Serials* 10, no. 3 (1997): 285–298.

41. Hitchcock, Carr, and Hall, "Web Journals Publishing," 285–298.

42. John Willinsky, "The Nine Flavours of Open Access Scholarly Publishing," *Journal of Postgraduate Medicine* 49, no. 3 (2003), www.jpgmonline.com/text.asp?2003/49/3/263/1146 (accessed 15 August 2010).

43. Leslie Chan, "Nurturing Online Journal Publishing," *Canadian Journal of Communication* 29, no. 3 (July 2004): 250–252, search.ebscohost.com.er.lib.k-state.edu/login.aspx?direct=true&db=ufh&AN=14800387&site=ehost-live (accessed 15 August 2010).

Chapter Seven

Access, Security, and Funding Options

CHALLENGES TO E-RESERVES AND THE ACADEMIC COMMONS

Balancing the need for access with the need to protect the information, while also assuring the long-term financial viability of e-reserves challenges every library's technical and administrative staff as it seeks to establish and maintain a free-flowing academic commons. All three of these issues—access, security, and funding—directly affect an e-reserve's value to the user, its reliability, and its sustainability as a resource for research.

And all three can be threatened by campus-wide turf battles, as well as the general inability of many universities to follow through on the adoption of new ideas and, at times, the irresistible desire to chase after the creation of perfect plans at the cost of more immediate action. I cannot provide advice on how to overcome any of these all-too-common issues. One suggestion would be to have the university library's academic commons development team recognize where the issues lie and attempt to either neutralize them or avoid them altogether. In some situations, victory can be attained within the simple issue of nomenclature. For example, a Midwest university library recently reconfigured its administrative structure in such a way as to deliver the services and support of an academic commons. It did not, however, call the new administrative structure an academic commons, thus avoiding the political issues that might have arisen. If your team feels that it may hit barriers because of what it is attempting to create, at least one answer might be to avoid calling the new creation an academic commons. As posited by David Bollier soon after he started teaching:

> As a newcomer to Amherst College (at least as a faculty member), I won't pretend to know the institutional history and habits, faculty and library politics, technological capacities, and—let's be frank—the sheer inertia—that may complicate any attempts to move forward into the digital frontier. But I do know enough about the larger trends in "open education" (as it's often called) to suggest that they will transform higher education. They already are. Our stance shouldn't be one of reluctant accommodation to the new realities, but rather spirited leadership in making the most of them.[1]

The inertia can be discouraging at times. It may be that all a university library need do is cajole and encourage faculty and students by showing them the advantages of an academic commons. On the other hand, these old, rooted prejudices against online scholarship are not the sort of barriers that can be overcome with ice cream socials or warm and fuzzy PowerPoint encounter sessions. It is likely to be a real struggle against immovable resistance, and deciding who has the best plan to overcome these barriers is likely to be the first barrier to encounter.

Each of these three areas—access, security, and sustainability—come with their own set of issues. Access not only involves the nature of the information itself, such as the formatting of data, but also is affected by requiring user registration or subscription. Security results directly in the long-term trust a researcher develops that data is stored accurately, is available easily, and is preserved from tampering, such as malicious "graffiti" or the intended desire of a competing third party to modify research results. And, finally, financial support for any project—new or otherwise—is an issue for all institutions. It is almost a given that the library's proposal for an academic commons—a vague term often misunderstood by the university's central administration and potential donor—will face significant fiscal challenges. This is despite the relatively low costs associated with construction and maintenance.

These three factors are intertwined, each representing issues that impinge on the other two. At the cost of easy access, security might be increased, but the effect on use could result in a drop in use and with that a drop in funding. And any damage to the database records themselves would result in a desire to increase security barriers to access and, again, potentially decrease usage, which would, again, lead to reduction in funding. A loss of funding on its own would likely degrade security and the value and confidence in the academic commons and its e-reserves. But a shift in the funding source, such as to a private corporation, could have just as much damage than any loss of data. A perceived lack of independence could lower trust and use. At the core of expectations of an academic commons within any university library is the free flow of ideas, comments, and suggestions. Locking down on this exchange may be preferable from a security standpoint, but would result in a dampening of discourse and a resulting chilling effect on research, both key to the very life of the academic commons itself.

Balancing these three issues—access, security, and sustainability—within the overarching mission of the academic commons falls within the purview and responsibility of the millennial library. Access is a factor within the scope of security, which in turn can be a factor in funding. Early decisions in all of these areas can have long-term effects on the success and viability of a library's e-reserves, which can result in dire consequences for a library's academic commons.

Other issues can affect the scale of access, such as language, file formats, reader devices, and network capacity. For example, in academic research, the use of English tends to be a one-way street. Non-native English researchers are expected to publish in English, while the opposite is not generally the case.[2] Considering that the most popular language on the planet is Mandarin Chinese, the bias in favor of English (almost presumptively) presents interesting challenges for any e-reserve librarian. Should the research be published in only English or translated into other languages? And, if translated, who would be responsible for such translations and the verification of the translations, and at what costs? On the other hand, all indications are that English is becoming the dominant language of academic research.[3] Even given this, however, it may at least deserve more than just a passing thought as a library establishes an academic commons.

But first, let us consider these three areas: access, security, and sustainability.

Access

While issues of security establish who can use the e-reserves and the university academic commons, other challenges revolving around access have more to do with the nature of the access itself. As mentioned earlier, direct and simple access to research data is the preferred model among academics, especially younger faculty and students. Any barrier, even as benign as a simple and free registration form, can drive many younger researchers and virtually all students away. This issue of registration is more complex than just a matter of inconvenience. It is a given that the very nature of an academic commons suggests that it should have the capacity to allow researchers to invite collaborators from other institutions outside the university network into online meetings and discussions.

Consider the nature of one component of an e-reserve—online academic publications—and how researchers might access them. To date, publishers have provided online access to research articles in more or less three formats: full, partial, and subscription. Full access requires no registration and no user identification. The advantage here is obvious to the researcher: quick, unfettered access. The disadvantage to the publisher is equally as obvious: no real idea who is accessing the research and no idea of the user's affiliation. For publications relying upon outside funding sources, this can be a very real challenge. Grantors have a stake in knowing who is using the information that their funds help publish. Lack of this data can lead to funding cuts.

Partial access certainly may help resolve a grantor's concern: researchers must log in to access the publication's data. This provides the grantor a sense of who is using the information, how often they are using it, and where the inquiries have originated. However such registration slows the researcher's access, a delay that some academics reject unless the information sought cannot be found at any other, more open location. That is, the researcher foiled (or perhaps just inconvenienced) by a registration requirement may simply "bail" to a known open access pathway, such as Google Scholar, or use a library's subscription to a research aggregator of several journals, such as ProCite. The arrangement on subscriptions most often has to do with timely usage, as well as an understanding that users must be authenticated as members of the subscribing university or provided temporary e-passes.

Subscription-based access also is provided in three formats: bundled subscriptions, individual subscription, and individual article. The bundled database is typical of a university library, which bears the cost of the subscription and then offers direct access for researchers on campus. Those university researchers working at a remote site, such as at home, can access their university's databases through a single logon using the institution's authentication system.

Individual researchers can also access data directly with individual subscriptions, specifically necessary for nonbundled material available only within specialized data collection sites. Such arrangements are driven not by easy and direct access, but by the value of the data sought. And this data may be in the form of an archive of rare documents or a private company's research database. The need for the data renders moot the issues a researcher may have with delivery delays in such cases. The researcher most often is willing to wait. A variation of this might be the single article purchase system, where individual articles are offered by a collecting service.

This scheme of payment for levels of involvement may be applied to a library's academic commons. Some users may have full access at one level, must register at another, presumably deeper level, and finally may have to show proof of having paid a subscription fee to access a very deep level. Such a scheme would ensure that the causal user pays little if anything and not be delayed in accessing the data by a registration form. It also assures that the most-specialized data would be available to partially fund the cost of the overall academic commons. Of course, it might also result in researchers using only the upper, surface layer of data, thus resulting in weaker, less profound ideas and conclusions.

Fee-for-data is not an activity with which most librarians are familiar or, frankly, likely to embrace. Charging users for access to all information is an anathema to many librarians, who see their roles as facilitating access to data, not creating funding schemes. Yet, predictable and stable funding sources must be established and those wishing to access the rarest of information—as defined by its use—logically should pay more than first-level researchers accessing heavily used databases. This is a "cost-per-reader" model already in place at some institutions and used to eliminate journals that are rarely accessed.

This same pay-as-you-dig method for funding a university's academic commons could be applied to other areas that will be discussed later, including chat rooms, whiteboards, and other collaborator areas. Fees could be assessed based on the nature of the user—whether a member of the faculty or a cohort at another institution. Elaborate agreements for specific areas of research of interest to two or more institutions might be established to eliminate or lower these fees. Given the current environment of ever-decreasing government funding for higher education, such fee arrangements for the information that is in the highest demand may be the only way some universities can fund and sustain an academic commons. Of course, "information is free" has been the motto of the Internet since its inception. Adding this layer of entrepreneurialism to what has been an open door will be difficult for many to accept. Establishing a funding source that will provide the necessary support to maintain a millennial library may be harder in these distressed economic times. Any millennial library considering a fee-for-use model should be prepared to make a clear, convincing argument to their university faculty members and students.

Security

The illegal invasion of computer servers by hackers is a constant threat and is especially worrisome for those responsible for maintaining the integrity of databases containing original research. And, while an attack on a company website like Cisco's, might cost that company millions of dollars in lost revenue, the long-term damage to a library's e-reserves can be far more horrific. Indeed, this may be the main concern raised by those who do not trust electronic storage of research data. After all, it is not the obvious attacks that hackers might wage against a private company's reserves that academia fears. It is the undetected attacks that result in the manipulation of data and results that present the biggest challenge to e-reserves and to scholarship, in general. A hacker can enter a database site, make minor but crucial changes to formulae, and leave undetected. And, while it is true that all such databases would be backed up elsewhere, a sophisticated attack would leave server administrators wondering which is the correct, untampered file.

In addition, funded research conducted by university researchers for outside patrons must be protected as the intellectual property may be owned, at least in part or in all, by the funding group. Losing data funded by a patron corporation to the tune of millions of dollars is not only a severe blow to the funding group, but it also dampens the enthusiasm of such economic activity going forward. In addition, the researchers themselves would suffer a crushing blow were their research effectively stolen from them. Any academic commons that cannot provide an effective level of security for sensitive datasets in a group activity area, for example, would likely not be used except for the most mundane of activities. Again, this is an issue of trust that relates to the brand created by the users of the academic commons.

To thwart such attacks, data must not only be protected with the use of firewalls and other standard security measures, but also must be stored on offline, locked-down hard drives. The issue here is not a matter of cost, but protocol. All data, no matter its nature, must be secure not only for the present, but also the future. And, all assurances must be made that the data available to researchers is precisely what was first loaded to the site. This is one of the core values of a university academic commons: Confidence that engenders data sharing must flow from data protection, and data protection must engender data sharing. If researchers have even an inkling that their raw materials might be corrupted or stolen, the resulting suspicions will kill the trust required to fuel healthy exchanges with an academic commons.

Yet, in some cases it is how universities have added new servers to their networks that has created the greatest threats. As university systems expand, the proliferation of new servers—usually created to serve specific needs, such as a department's intercommunication—can create havoc within the technical maintenance staff. As noted by Huwe in 2003, the management of this growth of subnetworks is often decentralized and not well coordinated or planned. Each department goes about setting their servers with their own protocols, including how some users are allowed access. This protocol may work fine for years, only to be found deficient after a hacker's attack, or until some new, university-wide software is installed. The former situation results in ever-increasing staff time dealing with these ever-increasing system attacks. The University of California–Berkeley, for example, experienced roughly three thousand virus attacks a day to its multitude of servers in 2002, each requiring substantial time and effort by staff members to ward off.[4] Add to this the thousands of spam messages that pummel systems on a daily basis, and you have not only a very real challenge for system administrators, but also a real resistance to new system adoption or manipulation. For any library looking at starting an academic commons, with its requisite e-reserves, the planning to deal with system authentication alone can take months, if not years.

This authentication ensures that only authorized individuals with approved identification and passwords can access the network. Thus, the very idea of installing an academic commons—with varying access points, both on and off campus, plus the need for outside, nonuniversity collaborators to access parts of the shared space—can generate significant resistance, both among the system administration and university budget planners. As Huwe notes, attempting to stay ahead of the curve in a dispersed computing environment, such as that typically found within a university, can be a lot like herding cats.[5] Yet, the strength of the system's authentication system and the planning that creates that system are the keys to how fast a university can adopt a new network feature, such as the academic commons.

A possible solution to this multiple point and multiple permissions need for a shared worksite online may be similar to the access structure suggested previously. For example, the required security might be maintained, while promoting the requisite file sharing, by relying on the secured users to provide nonsecure collaborators—such as those off campus—access to duplicated datasets. That is, the secure user literally "places" a copy of a secure file in a nonuniversity secure area, thus eliminating the need for authentication of the off-campus user by the university. The file can be manipulated, edited, and then stored as an iteration of the original. Date-based nomenclature might be used so that other users touching a file being manipulated are accessing the original. Or a check-in, check-out system might be used similar to that used by website management software, such as Dreamweaver. In this case, the file that is checked out is not available to another until the user checks the file back into the site. A system like these—date defined or check-out formatted—assures that the primary researcher or primary investigator (PI) would reserve the authority to make any updates to an original file, and then post that file to an area within the most secure area of the commons. This protocol, obviously, is more cumbersome than the previous one of on-campus authentication and access. However, a system that relies on off-campus secure sites could be implemented far faster and with fewer concerns than meddling with a university's authentication protocols.

The challenges surrounding file sharing within an academic commons, for some universities, may delay or outright kill the implementation of such a project. Allowing nonauthenticated users within any layer of a university's server network is more than just problematic, it is a source of great concern. The millennial librarian must understand that administrations—both within and outside universities—when faced with a potential security risk, almost always opt to the prudent path: allow no access at all. It is much like the risk-averse nature of some corporate lawyers who advise no involvement in any situation that might involve court action, no matter how worthy the proposed action might appear. No action results in no financial loss. No access would also result in no financial loss. Those seeking to establish a university academic commons must be prepared to make a strong argument for access and present the potential results that can overwhelm the issues of security. And, given that in most universities, personnel resources are stretched thin already, adding a project of this magnitude would also require a very strong argument for new funds or redirected funds to provide for construction and maintenance.

As noted earlier, the steadily declining financial support provided by state legislatures to their state universities since the 1980s has put many universities in a funding bind. Many have eliminated or severely reduced new hires. Some have delayed the replacement of retired or transferring faculty. Some have even resorted to faculty and staff furloughs. The support by legislatures of universities within their states has fallen even further and faster since the 2008 recession. As noted by the president of a Midwest state university at his inaugural in 2009, the steady decline nationally of state support for higher education is likely to create in the near future universities run by state legislatures, but not funded by state legislatures.

In such an environment, any new endeavors on the part of the university will be in competition with other much-wanted proposals within the institution. This highly competitive environment will require each proposal be carefully outlined and supported with detailed and powerful research. The millennial library must put its best foot forward, armed with the strongest argument it can craft if it seeks university support. Logic alone will not carry the day. Cost-savings in faculty travel, mailing fees, and increased grant funding must be clearly argued as a rationale for the commons.

Sustainability

The university library's first decision should be to determine if an academic commons is a feature its faculty and students would find useful. Without a clear understanding of the role of such a resource, it is unlikely such support will be forthcoming. And, without a clear mission for a university library's technical staff, communicating the advantages—concrete and concisely stated in nontechnical terms—will be lost in a forest of tech talk. This clarity of purpose is an especially challenging goal for some university technical teams because they have rarely been required to gauge support for their work. Unlike university librarians who are constantly tracking usage of resources, university technology groups are sometimes guilty of pushing a new service out to students, faculty, and staff with little or no idea of whether the new software is needed by the potential users. A university library's computer and online communications team often has some experience actually talking to faculty and students. The feedback this library team can gather from the potential patrons can be more far more useful in the long term than the "create it and they will use it" approach often employed by campus technology groups.

Perhaps this would be a good place to raise an issue that has plagued many a library for years: unfunded mandates. When a research project is developed, budgeting for all manner of costs is included. But rarely are the costs provided to the library for the required new materials and databases, or the storage and transfer of these materials via a system such as an academic commons. In addition, these research projects may be budgeted for unnecessary services, such as mailing materials and data between cohorts. If these funds were pooled to support an academic commons, the outcome would not only be improved by the ease and speed of data sharing online, but the funds would provide far more collaborative support. That is, two hundred projects budgeting $10,000 each to send and receive materials via postal mail could divert these funds to an academic commons. This funding would not only provide for the online transfers for these projects, but would open up the service to many others. Including the library in all grant applications would not be politically popular, but it would be fair and long overdue.

Avenues of possible funding, including the use of grant funding, should be tested through some type of dialogue with faculty and administrators. Ask any researcher in the hard sciences and social sciences about collecting data and she will start by suggesting a survey. Surveys are a popular and effective method of determining need. However, an assessment of needs can be simplified if the goals of the academic commons are communicated in direct terms, usually through one-on-one discussions with faculty and student groups. These meetings can be especially useful if the research team uses the opportunity to poll potential users regarding the problems they are routinely encountering. For example, when this author was putting together a proposal for an academic commons at his university, he interviewed dozens of faculty members in all but two academic colleges on campus. What was found was that faculty knew quite well the problems they were encountering, but had no idea how to solve these problems. They knew their need, but not its cure.

Thus, the library development team should not ask: "What do you need?" and expect the faculty to identify the kinds of tools actually needed. Questions might be better structured around what issues have come up in working with other researchers, for example. Students might be asked to identify a few problem courses they have had. In many ways, for both students and faculty, these focus group encounters may seem like gripe sessions: an opportunity to vent frustrations with teachers, students, and researchers, as well as class, projects, and grades. All manner of problems may and should arise. It is the problem that the academic commons seeks to resolve, not the undefined need for an academic commons just to have one.

Asking for input—in whatever form it may be posed—rather than announcing new services and software almost always leads to higher adoption rates, if only because the tools actually needed for learning and research are the tools provided. Making the case based on actual faculty and student demands (shaped, of course, as problems) will underscore the argument for an academic commons and, at the same time, provide a roadmap for what potential users will find most helpful.

The knee-jerk opt-in for massive surveys is largely unnecessary within a university environment that typically is smaller than that of a town. That is, surveying a community ranging between twenty thousand and fifty thousand fairly homogenous individuals amounts to a waste of dollars. The target consumer group—faculty and students—are so small in numbers and so similar in expectations and behavior that a full-fledged survey rarely will generate the kind of rich data that can be captured by focus groups. For example, it's a good chance that the student body of a university has more in common when it comes to behavior than the general population. They all need to read with comprehension, write with conciseness and clarity, and pass examinations. In focus groups, they may also talk about difficulties in group projects, fitting everything they have to accomplish into a schedule, or troubles with a particular teacher. They may even wander off into discussions about their personal life. Focus group leaders must help the students stay on topic, of course, but should be ready to allow some discourse that may not, at first, seem relevant. That personal life issue may be something that touches on other areas of the student's life at the university, and may be as simple as arranging a way the student can communicate with his parents using instant messaging.

Similar issues may arise with faculty: a seemingly personal problem that a researcher has with a cohort might have more to do with the way the editing of a grant proposal is handled. It is important that focus group leaders consider that every faculty person may know of a need they have, but every faculty person might also use a different nomenclature to describe that need.

Universities with much larger populations, such as those approaching or exceeding one hundred thousand users, are likely to have already established or are close to establishing an academic commons. If they have not—which, frankly, is hard to imagine—then a well-crafted survey using appropriate nontechnical terms could assist in the services and support identification-of-needs process. At the very least, any survey will generate numbers, and—without being too cynical—many university administrators love numbers. But surveys are poor at identifying a need when those surveyed cannot match their needs to a common set of terms. Even within large universities, a survey should be followed by focus groups to probe into the nature of the needs that faculty have in teaching and research.

A gauging of faculty and student needs or problems is a critical component of the marketing plan. Ideally, the development team would start with a small number of users, perhaps six to eight participants, in focus groups in various units in the university. The data gathered from these groups will prove invaluable to the creation of a concise list of initial needs. This stage of the research should be as transparent as possible, with calls for possible focus group participants made university-wide. It cannot be stated strongly enough that every effort should be made to allow the patrons to define their needs through this research. It is one thing to suggest that the development team has listened to the needs expressed by potential patrons. However, walking into a focus group with a set agenda intended to validate the need for a particular feature or service by falsely creating that demand renders the gathered data useless. The focus group members must be allowed to present needs without the research team leading or prodding them in any particular direction. This is especially important because the very nature of what an academic commons can accomplish may be unknown to the focus group members. Directing the focus group in one direction or another does not allow them to simply express their needs, which might seem like "wishful thinking" of what they would like to be able to accomplish, but can't. Focus group leaders should not expect to hear "I want the academic commons to include . . ." In most cases, these members have little or no idea of what might be accomplished in an academic commons, whether that is in the form of advances in software or hardware, or the opportunity to use massive file transfer stations. The focus group leaders should make it clear that almost anything is possible and that every situation that has resulted in less-the-optimal results should be discussed. One of the worse outcomes of a focus group is for members to self-censor their needs on the basis that those needs could never be satisfied. An open approach not only provides good ideas but also targets potentially new products and services the marketing team had not considered.

FUNDING OPTIONS: UNIVERSITY, AUTHORS, SPONSORS, ADVERTISERS

Having identified and, by way of that, established a concrete need for an academic commons through surveys or focus groups, the millennial library's academic commons development team might consider approaching for funding the unit most likely to reap the highest rewards from this project: its university. However, before any request is made, the library's team must create a solid argument in the form of a business plan that outlines not only costs, but also the intended future marketing plans to promote the advantages of the learning, research, and teaching commons. In a nutshell, the plan must make a sound argument for need, identify the targeted patrons, and provide a timeline for implementation. Collaborators must be identified and the plan should include examples of similar efforts at other universities. The case studies offered throughout this book represent a good start, but a library development team might wish to take a closer look at efforts made at cohort universities. Visits to other facilities are a good idea and, at the minimum, development team leaders should at least engage academic commons leaders at other institutions whether by telephone, e-mail, or Skype.

In addition to the surveys and focus groups discussed earlier, the library's academic commons development team should attempt to identify the leaders in the various target patron groups and seek out individual interviews. Such leaders should be developed as stakeholders in the project. These stakeholders will be invaluable ambassadors, ready to argue for the funding, and helpful as potential future trainers in the implementation phase of the academic commons.

The development team also should be prepared to present preliminary results at faculty, student, and administration meetings throughout the campus, ever mindful that new ideas may arise even in these discussions, as well as unexpected new objections raised. This is a very important part of the process of moving toward the ultimate success in the funding (and, frankly, in the long-term usage) of the academic commons. Providing buy-in by the key patron groups ensures long-term support and use, as well as communicates to the university administration that all groups have been included in planning the structure and nature of the academic commons.

The budget may include a number of income streams in addition to the outright direct funding from the university's administration. Among the most prevalent—outside of direct university support—are author publication fees, off-campus sponsors, and advertising schemes focused around the online traffic within the academic commons.

The ability of a university online publication to generate actual income through the use of author fees may not be the strongest reason to apply such a plan to an academic commons. Yet, as we have discussed, the university library as online-only publisher is just around the corner for most universities and already a reality at a few. Author fees for publishing have a long tradition in the print academic journals serving the hard sciences. This is not the case in the humanities and social sciences. Asking chemistry and biology researchers to pay a per-word fee is unlikely to raise a ripple. Doing so with a sociology or English researcher without some prior explanation would very likely set off a storm of protest. In addition, it is arguable that such fees would likely diminish participation of collaborating off-campus researchers, especially those from smaller schools. This may be a sufficiently strong objection, to give a university's academic commons development team cause for a second review of this revenue stream.

As an alternative, charging outside participants a fee to work within a collaboration project might be based on a financial scale tied to that visiting researcher's university student population, department size, or even library holdings. Such a scale would significantly lower the cost for collaborative researchers working at schools with student enrollments under five thousand, for example, while placing the highest fees on those working at schools with enrollment over forty thousand. Larger schools are possibly more capable of supporting their research authors with publishing grants. Of course, this does not account for small, private well-funded universities whose small student and faculty numbers and limited library holdings may place them in the same fee categories of small public colleges. In such circumstances, the fees for faculty publishing may require a case-by-case analysis. Similar scales could be developed to work with these that would take into account small departments within large universities, or vice versa. Such schemes might be developed across various peer institutions, with a goal of creating fairness and openness, and reducing hardship on those researchers at schools with limited financial support for research.

Perhaps more challenging for most institutions would be the ability to attract enough private or public sponsors of academic activities sufficient to generate the financial support necessary for a university's academic commons. This is a sensitive issue: the role of private industry in university research has been controversial at least as far back as the 1960s, when Mario Savio, the leader of the Berkeley Free Speech Movement, argued that his university was nothing more than "a factory that turns out a certain product needed by industry."[6] Left with little or no state funding, universities may be forced to look to the only two other options: higher tuition and private funding sources.

Naming various buildings and programs within a university is a long tradition. Earlier in the twentieth century, the naming generally followed the template of identifying a past university leader, such as its first president. In the past few decades, perhaps magnified by the rise in massive college sports budgets, the inclusion of potential private corporation naming schemes has generated millions in new revenue used to build stadiums, theaters, and other campus facilities. Involvement of private sponsors in supporting university research may generate significant concerns that the sponsor may be attempting to shape the research methods and results of projects of interest.

Yet, university colleges, schools, and departments have long practiced building and program naming available to powerful alums willing to provide much needed and ongoing financial support. This type of family giving undoubtedly presents significant challenges to any institution seeking to change its purpose or modify its goals. Finding alumni who are both understanding of a new media need and willing to provide significant funding to back an academic commons is not a simple task. This can be especially difficult for universities faced with a changing environment and role within a new media world, such as distance education. Modifying the curriculum and procedures of a college within a university to address new media pedagogy may present a serious fracture with the existing patrons of the school. This is, in some ways, equivalent to tearing down a building or changing the name of a program to accommodate a new approach. For example, the University of Colorado at Boulder recently announced it would be closing its School of Journalism and Mass Communications in order to create a new, repurposed program targeting the demands of new media.[7] The effect on students within an academic program that is shifting can be massive, both emotionally and academically. If the change in a library's direction or goals is presented as a positive reconfiguration, it may not generate as much angst among students or faculty. Yet, resources will very likely be reallocated, and some services and collections either digitized or eliminated.

Involving an outside private entity in this shift is almost certain to generate concern. The obvious possible conflict of interest of having an outsider at the heart of a university funding change within the library's structure and purpose is certainly magnified by the certain knowledge that the private donor's funds—should a philosophical breech occur in the future—will not be matched by state funding.

Such potential conflicts of interest are certainly at play in the dependence of any university's academic commons—and the online publications that may be part of this research commons—on private corporate support. Such a "naming" relationship may be the only option that the university has to create the much needed teaching and research commons. If a potential donor is unwilling to accept that the funding of an academic commons and its publications must be fully independent of even the perception of influence, the resulting agreement may be unworkable.

A third way also involves potential conflicts of interest: advertising on a university academic commons website. Google AdWords, an existing model of how to implement such a revenue stream, generates revenue based on the use of search terms within a database search. In the case of Google, each search costs the advertiser anywhere between a few cents and a few dollars per thousand pageviews. That is, each time Google is searched using a particular set of words, an advertiser is allowed, for a small fee, to present a link to its website on the right side of the search results page. The advertiser pays only when those particular search terms are used.

This can be a useful, if not high revenue, source of financial support for an academic commons. A student or faculty person using a search term such as "mass communication and women" and then clicking on the resulting "ad words" that might appear on the right side of the search screen might generate only a dime in advertising revenue to the library for each search. Yet, the potential numbers of searches might be in the tens of thousands. The resulting revenue could easily provide the necessary support of a university library's academic commons or bridge a funding gap. In addition, the nature of the user, such as faculty, administration, or student, could define the trigger for a set of ad words. Thus the resulting set of ad links would target a particular group, as well as a particular area of interest, and generate higher per search rates.

In addition, banner ads and other traditional online advertising platforms could be used by a library's website, such as that used by commercial search engines. After all, a library's database is nothing less than a specialized search engine. The idea of advertising on university websites may seem foreign to a university's teaching and research mission. Yet, few universities have not already completed agreements with soft drink bottlers for exclusive on-campus rights. Advertising is a part of many functions held on campus, whether university-sponsored or private. Consider the advertising placed at university football stadiums and other sports arenas. Given the demographics of campus populations, whether students or faculty, some advertisers would be very motivated to reach these much-sought-after targets.

The university library's administration could certainly establish rules regarding acceptable advertising messages and acceptable advertisers. The number of paid linking could be limited to three or four a page, as banner ads could be limited. Other standards could be adopted with an eye toward protecting users. Yet, to reject such an advertising scheme would be shortsighted, especially in an era of rising tuition costs and falling state revenue support.

SPECIAL SERVICES

A few more easily defined concerns also face a university academic commons development team: language, file formats, reader devices, and network capacity. The language of portions of the commons might be specifically and purposefully non-Anglo. For example, special collections of Hispanic literature or the Norse *Edda* may require the inclusion of translated sections of the academic commons. Also, faculty may request multilanguage collaborative areas for use by teams that include non-English readers. Modern language instructors may request special team areas with multilanguage software support. Decisions to include these areas would generally be in response to specific requests and can be accomplished with the assistance of the requesting faculty or administration.

The decision to provide the entire academic commons in a second language might be in response to a local linguistic need, such as a large Thai student population. This need could only be met through a dedicated translation staff, paid for by the academic commons budget. Given that English is not the most-used language worldwide, and given that all areas of the university academic commons would be globally accessible at varying levels of security, the failure to consider other languages on the site might be shortsighted and overly presumptive. Consider than Mandarin Chinese is used natively by more than a billion people. The number of native English speakers is far less. The millennial library must seriously consider at least offering links on its website in other languages than just English if it wishes to offer a truly global academic commons.

Users of the academic commons could define the necessary file types. Generally, a library staff can expect to deal with everything from image files such as jpeg, tiff, and gif. Two of these, jpeg and gif, tend to be manageable in size and available to a multitude of software readers. Tiffs are larger in size, but also universally compatible. Other more commonly used file formats, such as Adobe Illustrator (ai) or Photoshop (psd), are proprietary file types and can be much larger in size, especially Photoshop files. Guidelines on acceptable file types must be established and clearly stated for users. For example, a university library's commons administration may wish to forbid the posting of music files or certain video files, without advance permission. These files can generate not only space issues, but also potential copyright violations. The academic commons administration may also consider restricting the use of some software platforms to lower traffic times of day, such as in the case of streaming files.

Whether a university library's academic commons is available to handheld devices, such as iPods, should be established based on need. Establishing whether a significant percentage of users would access the resources via handhelds could be part of the initial needs-based surveys and focus groups discussed earlier. If the demand is perceived as high, such as 10–15 percent of the potential users, then formatting of the site should include an auto-detection code to route such users to pages with readable formats.

Network capacity issues are not as easily resolved. An academic commons area can expect to be asked to handle large file transfers, transfers that would demand a significant part of a standard Internet "pipe." Many universities already experience network slowing at peak use times, such as at 8:00–9:00 A.M. and 4:00–6:00 P.M., as users check their e-mails. The use of network-intensive files transfers, therefore, may require restrictions based on time. Attempting to limit the size of files would most certainly generate complaints, especially from areas such as the hard sciences, art, and architecture. The value of the academic commons is linked directly to its networking capacity. If certain file sizes, such as those over 1 GB, are not allowed, the collaborative works of many teams would be severely hampered, if not eliminated. And while the file size needs might be established in the needs research mention earlier, the resulting stated demand would likely only be a snapshot—a demand that is certain to grow in time as academic commons users discover what can be done in this new environment. One possible stopgap would be to route users to sites that specialize in storing and transferring large files, such as transferbigfiles.com, which can handle up to 2 GB files at no cost. Sites such as this generate revenue by charging for much larger file transfers.

Another solution may be to merely create a single, massive academic commons available to all universities, inside and outside North America. The idea of taking all university academic commons into their own network, a sort of Internet II arrangement, is very appealing. Discussions are already underway for a federally funded broadband expansion to the tune of $7 billion. Providing a dedicated network for the healthcare industry could run as high as $500 million over three years. The Internet II concept would place science research on its own, dedicated network, thus speeding up file transfers and allowing for more international collaboration.

How an individual university library's academic commons might plug into such networks is unclear, but not impossible. In its working form, the cloud feature we've already discussed could be rededicated to allow for only users with edu domains or university authenticated access. However, discussions of all of these proposals should include a teaching and faculty needs component as part of the federal government's support of higher education. And, the needs for other features, such as faculty teaching mentors, localized research areas, and student search training, to mention only a few, would still require each university to establish its own academic commons.

SUMMARY

Balancing the need for access with the need to protect the information while also assuring the long-term financial viability of e-reserves challenges every library's technical and administrative staff as it seeks to establish and maintain a free-flowing commons.

Library and university administration must be prepared to deal with issues of security: who can access the e-reserves and the commons, and in what form.

Access to holdings could be based on the nature of the material requested: the rarer the holding, the higher the access fee.

At the same time, direct, simple, and free access to research data is the preferred model of academics, especially younger ones. Any barrier, even as benign as a free registration form, can drive younger researchers away.

A commons' publication area could be accessible fully, partially, or through subscription. Full access would require no user identification. For publications relying on outside funding sources, this may not be preferable given that grantors have a stake in knowing who is using the information. Partial access certainly may help resolve a grantor's concern: researchers must log in to the publication. Subscription-based access may be bundled, by individual user, or by individual article. The bundled database is typical of a university library, which bears the cost of the subscription and then offers direct access for researchers on campus. Individual researchers can also access data directly with individual subscriptions, specifically necessary for nonbundled material available only on specialized data collection sites. This scheme of payment for levels of involvement may be applied to a library's commons. Some users may have full access at one level, must register at another, presumably deeper level, and finally may have to show proof of subscription at a very deep level. Such a scheme would ensure that the average user would pay little if anything, while the most-specialized data would be leveraged to pay for the cost of the overall commons. The idea that "information is free online" has been the motto of the Internet since its inception. Adding this layer of entrepreneurialism to what has been an open door will be difficult for many. Establishing a funding source that will provide the necessary support to maintain a millennial library may be harder in these distressed economic times.

To thwart security attacks, data must not only be protected with the use of firewalls and other standard security measures, but also must be stored on offline, locked-down hard drives. The issue here is not a matter of cost, but protocol. All data, no matter its nature, must be secure not only for the present, but also the future. And all assurances must be made that the data available to researchers is precisely what was first loaded to the site.

As university systems expand, the proliferation of new servers—usually created to serve specific needs, such as a department's intercommunication—can create havoc within the technical maintenance staff. For any library looking to start a commons, with its requisite e-reserves, the planning to deal with system authentication alone can take months, if not years. This authentication ensures that only authorized individuals with approved identification and passwords can access the network. Thus, the very idea of installing a commons—with varying access points, both on and off campus, plus the need for outside, nonuniversity collaborators to access parts of the shared space—can generate significant resistance, both among the system administration and university budget planners.

The challenges surrounding file sharing within a commons may, for some universities, delay or outright kill the implementation of such a project. The millennial librarian must understand that when faced with a potential security risk, the prudent (but ill-advised) path is to allow no access at all.

The university library's first decision should be to determine if a commons is a feature its faculty and students would find useful. Without a clear understanding of the role of such a resource, it is unlikely such support will be forthcoming. Surveys are a popular and effective method of determining need. However, an assessment of needs can be simplified if the goals of the commons are communicated in direct terms, usually through one-on-one discussions with faculty and student groups. Making the case for need will underscore the argument for a commons and, at the same time, provide a roadmap for what potential users will find most helpful.

Having established a concrete need, the millennial library's commons development team might consider approaching for funding the unit most likely to reap the highest rewards: its university. However, before any request is made, the library's commons development team must create a solid argument, a business plan that outlines not only costs, but also the planned marketing of the research and teaching tool. A survey of the faculty and students is a critical component of the marketing plan. Ideally, the development team would start with small six to eight participant focus groups in various units in the university.

The ability of a university online publication to generate actual income through the use of author fees may not be the strongest reason to create such a publication. Yet, as we have discussed, the university library as publisher is just around the corner for most universities and already a reality at a few. Financial scales could be developed that raised the costs based on university student population, department size, or even library holdings.

Perhaps more challenging for most institutions would be to attract private or public sponsors of academic publishing to generate the financial support necessary for a university commons. This is a sensitive issue: the role of private industry in university research. University colleges, schools, and departments have long practiced building and program naming for powerful alums willing to provide much needed and ongoing financial support. Potential conflicts of interest are certainly at play in the dependence of any university's commons—and the online publications that may be part of this commons—on private corporate support.

A third way also involves potential conflicts of interest: advertising on a university commons website. Google AdWords, an existing model of how to implement such a revenue stream, generates revenue based on the use of search terms within a database search.

A few more easily defined concerns also face a university commons development team: language, file formats, reader devices, and network capacity. The language of a site might include specifically and purposefully non-Anglo sections. The decision to provide the entire commons in a second language might be in response to a local linguistic need, such as a large Thai student population. This need could only be met through a dedicated translation staff, paid for out of the commons budget.

Users of the commons would define the necessary file types. Generally, a commons staff can expect to deal with everything from images files such as jpeg, tiff, and gif. Two of these, jpeg and gif, tend to be manageable in size and available to a multitude of software readers. Tiffs are larger in size, but also universally compatible. A university library's commons administration may wish to forbid the posting of music files or certain video files, without advance permission, due to inherent potential copyright violations. Or, it may wish to divert such traffic to outside service providers, such as transferbigfiles.com.

Whether a university library's commons is available to handheld devices, such as iPods, should be established based on need. Establishing whether a significant percentage of users would access the commons via handhelds could be part of the initial needs-based surveys discussed earlier.

A commons area can expect to handle large file transfers, transfers that would demand a significant part of a standard Internet bandwidth. Many universities already experience network slowing at peak use times, such as at 8:00 A.M. and 5:00 P.M., as users check their e-mails. The use of the commons, therefore, may require restrictions based on time. A dedicated Internet II arrangement is a very appealing solution to broadband availability.

ACCESS, SECURITY, AND FUNDING OPTIONS: TOP TEN STRATEGIES FOR SUCCESS

1. Sometimes the most successful path to a new academic commons is to avoid using the term, which has become a target of some faculty fears and concerns.

2. The balance struck by the millennial library must take into account:

   (a) access to the academic commons: will it be open to collaborators outside the university? (b) security of files and data: can researchers be assured that their work will be protected? (c) funding of the necessary tools and staff: can the university step up and support the academic commons or can the library configure a tiered subscription system that will provide long-term financial stability?

3. The university administration might consider putting flesh to bone over a long-standing issue of fiscal support for libraries: require that the cost to the library of research projects be included in grant funding applications.
4. Libraries seeking to find possible avenues of funding should consider talking with faculty and administrators in small focus group settings. These can provide a wealth of information that could be used in marketing the academic commons to patrons, as well as identifying possible funding options.
5. All e-reserves must be backed up on devices that are extremely secure and, most likely, offline. This can be done internally by the university technology team, or through an off-campus private company.
6. The university technology team must be under the administration of the library. The success and growth of the millennial library rests, in part, on its technology and the ability to shape it in the direction required to maximize the effectiveness of the academic commons. This is no time for university turf wars.
7. The academic commons team must listen rather than proscribe. Allow the potential patrons of the learning, teaching, and research commons to dictate what they feel they need, rather than telling students and faculty what is "good for them." Buy-in is enhanced by a sense that needs are being addressed.
8. All options for funding should be on the table:

   (a) direct state/board of regents/university support—university libraries are more and more the center of learning and the key to long-term success. (b) subscriptions based on use—a tiered system would put the heaviest load on those who use the academic commons the most. (c) private foundation grants—this is clearly a good idea, but does it ensure long-term sustainability? (d) alumni—perhaps it is time to consider funding learning over athletics.

9. The millennial library should consider how it can use advertising to support its academic commons. This is a tough pill to swallow for some

in academia, but it may be the only option for some universities. Much of this could be accomplished via AdWords and banner ads on library search sites.

10. The university library should offer its support to the creation of Internet II, a strictly academic pipe for research, teaching, and learning.

NOTES

1. On the commons, 26 April 2010, onthecommons.org/academia-commons (accessed 15 August 2010).

2. John Flowerdew, "Problems in Writing for Scholarly Publication in English: The Case of Hong Kong," *Journal of Second Language Writing* 8, no. 3 (1999): 243–264.

3. Jacques Mélitz, "English as the Global Language: Good for Business, Bad for Literature," Centre for Economic Policy Research, January 1999, www.cepr.org/press/DP2055PR.htm (accessed 28 August 2010).

4. Terence K. Huwe, "Managing a 'Forest' of Servers and Documents," *Computers in Libraries* 23, no. 5 (2003): 31.

5. Huwe, "Managing a 'Forest' of Servers and Documents," 31.

6. Eyal Press and Jennifer Washburn, "The Kept University," *The Atlantic Monthly,* March 2000.

7. Stefanie Chernow, "University of Colorado May Shut Down Journalism School to Create a More Tech-Oriented Degree Program," editorswebblog.org (August 2010), www.editorsweblog.org/newsrooms_and_journalism/2010/08/the_digital_trends_in_the.php (accessed 10 September 2010).

Part Three

EVOLVING ISSUES FACING THE ACADEMIC COMMONS MOVEMENT

We have considered the role the millennial library could play in improving how learners learn, teachers teach, and researchers research. We have examined the expanded role of the library as publisher, both in academic journals and monographs. And we have considered how the academic commons development team can best identify needs and communicate the solutions that will be available. Several additional challenges remain. While libraries have a long history with issues of copyright, rarely have they been asked to consider issues of intellectual property. Yet, if it is very likely that as completed research publications migrate to an e-reserve managed by the campus library, so it is also likely that the data that formed the basis of those articles will also be posted in open access. However, the issues surrounding ownership of research articles is relatively clear compared to that of research data. And, there are many interested parties—including the university, the researcher, and grant-funding organizations—which will want a seat at the table. And what of the author's privacy? Should the detailed notes and e-mails of a researcher be included in an open access platform?

This is a rapidly changing environment, perhaps best exemplified by the introduction of a bill—the Combating Online Infringements and Counterfeits Act[1]—in the fall of 2010 that would, according to some, "put America into a league with China and Saudi Arabia, among others, as a nation that makes sure most of its citizens won't find information that a tiny, elite group deems improper for their eyes."[2] Of course, others argue that the bill would better protect property rights that are now under pervasive attack from well-organized piracy groups.

> While many of these rogue sites strive to conceal their true nature and thus may appear legitimate to consumers, they are devoted almost exclusively to offering or

> enabling unauthorized downloads or streaming of copyrighted material —including the latest movies and music hits—or to trafficking in counterfeit products, from pharmaceuticals to luxury goods.[3]

The dialogue surrounding this one act reflects the demeanor of all discussions regarding copyright and intellectual property rights: a great deal of heat and very little light. Just consider that those lined up in support of the bill include the U.S. Chamber of Commerce, the Screen Actors Guild, Viacom, the Motion Picture Association of America, the International Alliance of Theatrical Stage and the Employees, Moving Picture Technicians, Artists and Allied Crafts of the United States. Those against it include the Electronic Frontier Foundation, the Distributed Computing Industry Association, and dozens, perhaps hundreds of blog sites.

This is a very complex issue with competing interests and no simple answers.

NOTES

1. 111th Congress (2009–2010) S.3804.
2. Dan Gillmore, "Hollywood Wants to Censor the Internet, and Congress Is on Board," Salon (24 September 2010), www.salon.com/technology/dan_gillmor/2010/09/28/worldwide_authority_for_american_copyright_cops (accessed 30 September 2010).
3. "Letter Supporting S. 3804, the 'Combating Online Infringement and Counterfeits Act'," U.S. Chamber of Commerce (21 September 2010), www.uschamber.com/issues/letters/2010/letter-supporting-s-3804 (accessed 30 September 2010).

Chapter Eight

Copyright, Intellectual Property Rights, and Privacy

Shifts in the application of copyright law in this country and internationally, combined with the shifts in the method and styles of publishing and the misguided sense that anyone with a computer can violate intellectual property rights with impunity has created a challenge for universities, publishers, and librarians. The inclusion of libraries in this discussion may seem to some odd or even inappropriate. We suspect that those who see the issues surrounding copyright and intellectual property rights to be a nonstarter for libraries are the same who see libraries as mere catalogers of journals and monographs. This would have seemed agreeable twenty years ago. Today, however, libraries must be part of all discussions regarding research. This is especially true when we consider access to data developed as part of the research publishing function. We must embrace the millennial library as the center of every university and every university activity to a degree that would have seemed bizarre just two decades ago.

Thus, a challenge that librarians may have only been aware of peripherally in the past is now front and center on their agenda. How can librarians post faculty-developed information within a learning, teaching, or research commons and still assure the creators of this material that it will be protected from unauthorized use? How can librarians ensure that faculty members are not overly restrictive in their use of materials, especially in situations where the proposed use would be allowed via the fair use exception? The typical answers can be found in the application of copyright and intellectual property rights. These laws are old, both derived from common law, and both evolving from the general precepts of individual property rights.

The two methods by which invention and creativity typically have been protected—copyright and intellectual property rights—often are treated as if they are one in the same. They are not. For example, copyright provides a fair use exemption that allows the reuse of some portions of a work. Intellectual property rights provide no such safe harbor, except as part of a mutually agreed upon use, typically involving some sort of contract, or intervention by way of a fiat by grant funding institutions, such as the NIH. Additionally, the types of information covered by each of these laws differ significantly. One of the important areas of different research data is of particular interest to millennial libraries as they consider the storage of research materials and the standards of access applied to each work. In fact, in many ways the issue of copyright has been resolved—if not always protected. Intellectual property rights is an unsettled area in practice, most especially given the latest move to make research data available online via open access.

And this is the crux of the matter. For now, far more than in the past, a millennial library can store and deliver all manner of notes, voice recordings, even e-mails associated with a research paper, as well as its datasets, all in one place, all with varying levels of accessibility. This is a truly profound change. Yes, notes of scientists and writers have been available, but usually not with the published work. E-mails, or what would have been letters, are the stuff of special publishing volumes, often years later, after the death of the author. The ability to publish, literally, everything immediately opens up the possibility of looking into the very heart of a researcher via her personal notes and e-mails to other researchers. Will this be some sort of new requirement attached to all funding grants? Will it be required that all communication regarding a project will be the property of the grantor, and thus available for publishing?

COPYRIGHT

Copyright, found in Article 1, Section 8, Clause 8 of the U.S. Constitution, provides: "To promote the Progress of Science and useful Arts, by securing for limited Times to Authors and Inventors the exclusive Right to their respective Writings and Discoveries."[1] The provision was intended by the crafters of the Constitution to allow for the dissemination of information, as well as provide some incentive to the authors who created this information. The notion was that locking up the ideas that flow from information would stifle progress. At the same time, providing no protection to the authors who created the information would, logically, dampen creativity.

Internationally, copyright is covered country by country, with no broad agreement on the length of time a work is protected.[2] The length of time of copyright protection in this country has expanded from fourteen years to the span of the author's life plus seventy years. The latest significant expansion, the Sonny Bono Copyright Term Extension Act of 1998, is often referred to by some as the Mickey Mouse Protection Act, in reference to the cartoon it was ostensibly designed to protect. Whatever the intent, the extension locked up most of the works of the past century. However, the law is not very clear as to specific years of protection. For example, many works published prior to 1923 (the date Google Books is working with) are out of copyright, while others published before or after are not. The vagaries and suspected corporate tinkering with the law has created its own pushback from those who see the constant lengthening of the years of coverage as a violation of the spirit of the constitutional standard of "limited times." Taking the copyright and expanding it from fourteen years to what might be five to eight times that might seem to some as egregious and anything but "limited," especially given the sense that, when Mickey approaches copyright expiration, the law will be extended again. At some point, the idea of an actual expiration of an author's copyright may be moot.

Protecting music, movies, and print rights from unlawful use is the intended purpose of copyright laws, both in the United States and internationally. This is especially true in music and movies, where an entire cottage industry has sprung up creating unauthorized copies of works moments after they are released. In fact, in some cases, the copies of some movies have made it into the market prior to their release as DVDs. The loss to copyright holders is measured in the millions of dollars. And the Internet has provided the most efficient delivery system for the ill-gotten treasures. Countless lawsuits have been brought against these e-thieves, though few, if any are actually taken to trial.

A smaller, though perhaps no less pursued, violation of the amended 1976 Copyright Act revolves around the use of large sections of scholarly works, specifically research articles and books, by academics without proper permissions from or remuneration to the copyright holders. Much of the activity of academics in using copyrighted material without the owner's consent revolves around the much-misunderstood section of the law providing for fair use. The intent of this section of copyright law in this country is to protect, in practice, the educational use of copyrighted material intended for the classroom or other educational purposes. At its core, though, fair use assures the possibility of progress by allowing the sharing of ideas. Locking up an idea to assure that the maximum amount of profit can be gained from it is not only contrary to the spirit of the copyright provisions in the U.S. Constitution, it flies in the face of any model for progress. How can society expect its scholars to create new ideas (progress) without the grist necessary to do so? Perhaps the Copyright Act needs a special "mouse" provision that does not impede the sharing of academic ideas.

For the millennial library, the issue of academic sharing of information has reached a boiling point in teaching, as we discussed in the previous chapter, and in the area of published research. In pedagogy, academics are encouraged to allow access to their syllabi and teaching materials to other educators as part of a universal effort to improve student outcomes and progress. The educators who authored the works retain ownership of the materials, with the expectation that those teachers using the works would cite the creators and not attempt to present themselves as the authors of the work. This is an important issue. The evaluation of a faculty member's performance is annually based on research, teaching, and service. At schools that value teaching evaluation as more than just a function of student feedback, examining the syllabi and test materials is a critical part of an educator's performance. As more and more sharing of materials takes place and more and more value is placed in teaching outcomes, educators must, literally, "show their work." That is, what part of a syllabus is original and what portion is based on another's work. Thus, careful citing of all teaching materials is critical to an educator's job performance evaluations.

More traditionally, the same approach has been used in research. Authors are cited and a portion of their works used. The major difference is the amount shared: 100 percent of teaching syllabi, test platforms, and lecture guides are placed in the teaching commons expressly for use in total by all. Only a portion of a research article may be cited. Taking an entire research work and making copies for classroom use—a common practice in many universities—has generated a few legal actions, if only in some of the more publicized cases. Academics taking the research of others and passing it off as their own has justifiably generated far more heat and attention.

Copyright and intellectual rights laws in the United States have dealt not just with ownership and attribution issues, but also access. It is this area that may prove to be of greatest interest for millennial librarians. For example, with the academic commons movement, the effort to make research available in an open access format has generated interesting arrangements between authors and their publishers. Publishers such as Springer offer their authors the option of making newly published research open access for a fee. Otherwise the work will be accessible only through the more traditional subscription service, usually paid for by the university library. This shift to open access has also created a new relationship between libraries and university faculty, though one that is likely more profound on the library side than the faculty. As I found in an exchange with a cohort regarding the new roles of the library, there is a sense among some faculty that the only true role for librarians is to collect and catalog books and journals. Anything beyond that is a violation of the true nature of libraries and their staff, at least as that nonlibrary faculty person believes.

Setting aside the quaint longings among some faculty for a library (and a librarian) that very possibly never truly existed, we will examine three areas of the copyright law as they are applied in this country's universities and then consider the long-term tracks of each: the nature of work, specified levels of access to the work, and its authenticity. But first, we will briefly review the elements of copyright, with special attention to fair use. Of note, any library contemplating establishing an e-reserve should consult with its own university attorneys or other professionals in law regarding its liability in the area of copyright and fair use.

FAIR USE

In August 1998, I sent a graduate student to the campus copy center with instructions to photocopy three chapters of *The Mirror Makers*, make four copies of these chapters, and then put them on reserve for 190 students in his principles of advertising class. The graduate student shortly returned a bit shaken: the copy center staff (mostly comprised of undergraduates) had refused to copy the chapters or put the copies on reserve because, as the graduate reported, "They said it's a violation of the copyright law." Apparently, the student reported, the copy center staff had instructions to limit copying of any published work to 10 percent of the total number of its pages or 10 percent of the total number of chapters, whichever was smaller.

We were baffled. Somewhat familiar with the copyright law, we could not recall any provision specifying any such 10 percent limit. So we called the center, only to be told that it was the university administration's contention that the 10 percent rule was law, not policy. The staff was not forthcoming on citing any particular case or section of the law dealing with the limitation. They were also not bending on the rule. Spurred on by the encounter, we launched a research project that found that roughly one-quarter of the slightly more than one hundred academic research libraries in the United States reported they were using the 10 percent rule as "law," and, thus were misunderstanding and misapplying the 1976 Copyright Act.[3]

The Copyright Act of 1976, as amended, does not contain a single phrase that explicitly forbids copying in excess of 10 percent. In fact, it does not in precise terms define what is specifically allowed. The errors in how the law was applied as revealed in the survey were to be expected with a law that is seen by some as vague, abused, and constantly under review. As noted in a ruling regarding improper use of lyrics in a song, the judges on the 6th Circuit Court of Appeals noted: "Finally, and unfortunately, there is no Rosetta stone for the interpretation of the copyright statute."[4]

This issue of fair use is of particular interest to librarians, educators, and researchers. But the law itself provides little more than hints at what is allowed and what is not. As noted by the U.S. Copyright Office, Title 17:

> Section 107 contains a list of the various purposes for which the reproduction of a particular work may be considered fair, such as criticism, comment, news reporting, teaching, scholarship, and research. Section 107 also sets out four factors to be considered in determining whether or not a particular use is fair:
>
> 1. The purpose and character of the use, including whether such use is of commercial nature or is for nonprofit educational purposes
> 2. The nature of the copyrighted work
> 3. The amount and substantiality of the portion used in relation to the copyrighted work as a whole
> 4. The effect of the use upon the potential market for, or value of, the copyrighted work

Put simply and directly, no simple test to determine what is fair use has ever been devised or outlined by any higher court. As noted by the U.S. Copyright Office: "The distinction between fair use and infringement may be unclear and not easily defined. There is no specific number of words, lines, or notes that may safely be taken without permission."[5]

Given this vagary, it is not a surprise that copyright infringement and fair use in practice have crossed paths in court on multiple occasions. The case records are filled with instances of copyright holders bringing action against educators and those acting for educators. Perhaps one of the most well-known of these, involving coursepacks and Kinko's,[6] turned on the fees the printer charged students for materials required by a university professor. The court ruled that Kinko's violated the copyright holder's rights to the published material. However, it is interesting that the court also noted that "The search for a coherent, predictable interpretation applicable to all cases remains elusive."[7]

And, it may be the vagueness of the fair use provision that has led so many university libraries to set such a broadly (and erroneously) interpreted policy such as that outlined previously. The degree to which such a 10 percent maximum policy exists at major universities is unknown, but it certainly poses an interesting problem for academics seeking to use materials for "education purposes," a use specifically sanctioned in the Copyright Act. As a library seeks to accommodate the needs of faculty and also create packets of bundled resources for students, it is important that it understand the four defined areas set out in the act, even though few bright lines exist between what is and what isn't fair use. Again, this is just a brief summary of the four areas. University librarians seeking a more expansive reading of fair use will find no end of sources.[8]

The Purpose and Character of the Use

This first rule targets the for-profit reuse of a copyrighted work. In a nonprofit setting, such as a university classroom, the use of materials as part of an educational activity is generally allowed by fair use. This is especially the case when the use is spontaneous, suggesting that time restrictions prevented the educator from seeking formal permission from the copyright holder. Use of the material in a coursepack or as a requirement for the course might violate fair use. If the library uses an external for-profit entity (a printing shop or office store) to manage the class archives of its teaching commons, that outside vendor would very likely run into difficulties if it attempted to charge any fee for access to materials for which it does not hold copyright.

Actual access and use of the materials within an e-reserve can be set at varying levels. A copyright holder might place no limitations on how much of a work is used, but would require that the source be identified in that use. This open use–clear attribution might occur most often with syllabi and other in-class materials. Here the copyright holder of the materials wants to assist other educators and looks only for recognition of authorship. The copyright holders of other types of works—such as research articles or diagrams—may require a more restrictive use in quoting passages of the work. Significantly, especially in this area of copyright holders, the library must be prepared to ascertain who holds the rights. Many faculty members sign contracts with publishers ceding all reproduction rights, sometimes unknowingly. Setting standards for use requires ascertaining who actually holds the rights to the work.

The Nature of the Copyrighted Work

To be considered copyrighted, a work must be original, and perhaps that part is the only element that can be protected from unlawful use by others. That is, simple statements, such as this one, would likely fail any copyright challenge given its mundane nature. The spirit of copyright protection is the protection of ideas, not the applications and inventions that are protected under other areas of law, such as trademark or patent. Nor is copyright intended to protect simple listing of commonly accessible information, such as that found in a telephone book or a listing of the types of trees in a particular town.

Virtually every form of publication has different standards for fair use. Use of material from a newspaper differs from that appearing in a movie or photographic essay. And the amount used from each, whether a poem or research article, would also vary. Libraries must be careful in making both the standards clear as to potential usage, whether open or restricted, in every document it stores within its e-reserves. However, the library can make it clear that it is the copyright holders whose works appear within the e-reserves who must take action to protect the copyright against abuse, such as plagiarism. Given the expense involved in such legal actions, a library may conclude it cannot act to protect its e-reserves content, but must depend on the copyright holders to do so. Many libraries already have accomplished this, to some extent, by notifying the users of copying equipment of the Copyright Act's standards—most often by posting a sign or inclusion of a statement on their ILL Web page. However, the efficacy of these notices has not been tested in court. Thus, while posting a Copyright Act warning on each page of the e-reserves may help librarians sleep better at night, it is not clear that this will suffice against potential legal actions.

The Amount and Substantiality of the Portion Used in Relation to the Copyrighted Work as a Whole

Many believe it is this third part of the act that has generated the most legal interest. The 10 percent rule that so many research libraries inappropriately were applying in the latter part of the 1990s is not part of the law. It derives from a letter sent by various publishing groups to the Congressional subcommittee revising the act. That letter clearly states that, as far as these publishing groups are concerned, copying a *minimum* of 10 percent of a work would be accepted as legal on its face. That is, the letter sought to establish a baseline, while at the same time noting that more than 10 percent might be acceptable in some situations. The letter, which was included in the legislative history of the subcommittee's actions, is not considered part of the final act itself, and only very rarely has been cited by a judge in any legal action.

What is required by this part of the law is an examination of the actual amount of the work used compared to the overall work and how that use compares to the work itself. That is, does the use include so much of a work that using the original work itself is no longer necessary. Or, does the use focus on the heart of the copyrighted work, a portion far less than the 10 percent baseline. For example, if one uses without permission the two lines of an epic poem that sum up the entirety of the work, would that constitute a violation? If one used the two pages of an Ernest Hemingway novel that typically represents the essence of the work overall, does that still automatically fall within fair use? Probably not.

Again, this may not be an area that a library wishes to expend its legal budget. But, the library must—at the least—notify the copyright holders and those using the e-reserves of the law and its guidelines.

The Effect of the Use upon the Potential Market for, or Value of, the Copyrighted Work

Copyright does not apply, generally, to works published prior to 1923. Should the library choose to place in its e-reserves a work published prior to 1923, that book—again, generally—would be considered out of copyright. The word "generally" being inserted here because copyright, as mentioned earlier, is not clear on many issues. For example, it might be reasonably assumed that copyrights on the works of Shakespeare would have expired many centuries ago. However, a book that not only presents the plays of Shakespeare, but also commentary about the plays, and is published after 1923, would fall under copyright protection for the commentary portions of the book.

Also, updated editions of works published prior to 1923 are also covered under the new edition, if the updating is significant (again, a vague word). Finally, logic would suggest that if a book published after 1923 is now out of print, the result of any copying of that book by others on the rights of the copyright holder would be minimal. After all, no copying would affect the potential profits of a book the copyright holder is not marketing at the time. However, there exists no carte blanche on the copying of a book out of print. The book may be produced one at a time through companies that specialize in single copy publishing. Such companies render the concept of "out of print" moot.

Fair use of a library's e-reserves is best handled, as some universities now are doing, case by case. Establishing a specific rule, other than the posting of copyright notices, on what constitutes fair use is likely to be in error. Note Duke University's advice to its faculty regarding copyright within its commons:

> For other uses of materials from this web site, i.e., commercial products, publication, broadcast, mirroring, and anything else that doesn't fall under either "fair use" or the terms of the Creative Commons license found on most pages, we require that you contact us in advance for permission to reproduce.[9]

This case-by-case approach seems to fit well within the strictures of the fair use component of the copyright law. Each "questionable" case is reviewed by a committee at the library to determine if it meets the fair use rules, as determined by the committee. No specific set of rules are offered. This has all the look and feel of other areas of the law—such as obscenity—wherein an explicit definition is lacking to all by the individual beholder.

Whatever approach the library chooses to take, it must make it abundantly clear to its participating research authors,

1. That they are responsible for protecting their works from copyright infringement
2. Fair use suggests some of their work may be used without notice or permission
3. They retain the copyright ownership of all their works posted within the e-reserves
4. The rules for usage of their works, including datasets and other work product, can be established by them, in concert with the library

INTELLECTUAL PROPERTY PLACED WITHIN THE E-RESERVES

Most libraries are familiar with the typical item that would be deposited in its e-reserves: a research article. The form and sections of a research article would include such materials as an abstract, author notes, footnotes or endnotes, illustrations or diagrams, and other support materials. The method in which these items are stored need only include some declaration of copyright and terms of use of the material. In fact, the very act of making the article available to a reader is itself sufficient to satisfy the copyright registration standard.

Of far more delicate and unknown ground are the research data and collection schemes. Typically, researchers gather data, write a research paper or papers, and then toss the data. As mentioned earlier in this book, the online movement toward an academic commons suggests that some method might be created wherein the collected research materials could be stored and accessed by other researchers. In fact, the effort to format databases in such a way that they can literally "talk" to each other in the course of large meta-analyses is at least as old as the Internet itself.[10]

What can be stored and shared treads on the issues of copyright—which, frankly, are easier to deal with by comparison—and intellectual property, a far stickier issue. An author or publisher holds the copyright, at least in regards to the article from which the data is derived. Within that article there may be charts and tables that include parts of or all (very unlikely) of the data collected, also covered by copyright.

The raw data collected though involves intellectual property rights but not those of copyright. The logic here is that a dataset is not evidence of a "creative" act but rather a gathering and listing of common items, much like a telephone book is a listing of public information. Yes, much effort is put into the gathering of the data. But the courts have not found that such "sweat equity" is a sufficiently creative act to allow protection of data under copyright laws. Thus any data that is actually placed online can be used by any other researcher with impunity, at least in regards to its copyright status. In fact, at the very heart of scholarship is the notion that all research itself is the replication of the data as an exercise to test a proposed theory or outcome. Copyrighting a dataset or lab notebooks would suggest that even the testing of a theory by replicating an experiment or survey would be a violation of law. Testing and retesting of a theory via a duplication of the experiment in question is at the core of scientific inquiry.

However, though copyright does not extend to research data, other laws do. Yet, these other statutes, such as those associated with protecting intellectual property, raise even more questions. As noted by many scholars, the ownership of the research data is an open question. Does the research belong to the sponsoring grant agency? To the university? To the researcher? All of these players—the researcher, university, granting agency, and others with a perceived stake in the potential financial benefits that might be derived from the data—believe they are rightful owners. All have an interest in the data collected and interpreted in the creation of the published work. In fact, it is the interpretation of data that the courts have considered the "creative act" necessary to pass copyright muster. A simple listing of numbers (in quantitative research) or quotes (in qualitative research) are not sufficient to be considered copyrightable.

Of course, what is at stake is some future discovery derived from the collected data not initially found by the first researcher. But, if the initial researcher follows typical patterns and tosses the data, then the question of intellectual property rights is moot. However, simply not planning to use the dataset and leaving it on hard drives in an office is a far cry from placing that dataset in an e-reserve. And, while fair use may set out some boundaries of how much of a work may be cited, anything less than a full dataset is of little interest to other researchers attempting to replicate prior results.

It is the issue of ownership of datasets that poses the highest hurdle. As mentioned earlier, at least three players have a voice in this: the researcher, the university, and the granting agency. Each of these players might expect some portion of whatever new invention or medical breakthrough that is based upon work written or sponsored by any one of them. The researcher might argue that she gathered the data and therefore should reap some benefit. The university might consider the dataset as the work product of a faculty member paid by the institution to produce the research. Finally, the granting agency might expect to benefit from whatever income was generated by research it funded.

Given that all of these arguments have some degree of logic, they must be resolved prior to any posting of research or data on the e-reserves. Clarifying these competing interests places the library in a precarious position. It wants to have an open and trusted relationship with the faculty whose works are sought for the e-reserves. At the same time, however, it is a creature of the university, subject to the authority of central administration. Obviously, the legal standards of the e-reserves within any library must specifically address the ownership and republication or reuse status of the data to be placed there prior to publishing.

For universities facing consistent annual decreases in state funding support, revenue that might flow from these datasets is more than a passing interest: It is vital. As noted by Lewis and Vincler, "Setting aside for the moment the issue of faculty versus university ownership of research, a large area of uncertainty still persists, for although a researcher's scholarly articles representing her findings and reporting her data clearly fall within the purview of copyright law, the fate of the research itself—the data, lab books, and the scientist's expression of 'preliminary ideas'—remains unclear."[11] As a friend of mine once said to me, somewhat cynically, a university has no interest in intellectual property rights as they may apply to research data, unless there's money to be made.

At the same time, states see this research—especially in new areas of international focus such as bioscience—to be a panacea for tight budgets. The lack of clarity over who owns what in terms of research data has left open a door through which many states are seeking to take advantage by declaring their own rights to the work of researchers, which, in total, puts millions of dollars at stake. As noted by Mousavi and Kleiman, "Competition among the states for a share of the burgeoning bioscience industry is fierce."[12] While this competition has largely involved the citing of major research labs, there's no reason to believe it will not eventually spill over into the products of those facilities.

This competition among universities, states, corporations, and finally researchers has led to the "lock down" of research data created by academics. And, across the country, the resulting kaleidoscope of state standards has created a mishmash of legal hurdles and competing interests.

Is this an issue for the millennial library? Not if we accept the old standard of what a library is and should be (and conversely what it isn't and can't be). For many within and without the university, the sole function of academic libraries is the evaluation, labeling, and storage of data for its institution. It must be more if the library is to be the leader in the creation, collection, and distribution of information it is destined to become. Libraries of the future must weigh in with a full-throated call for open access and provide leadership in the effort to find a resolution of who can use raw data and the conditions of that use. It is this collaborative sharing of data that has led many to suggest that a cure for cancer lies within the meshing of existing datasets. No other entity in the university or outside has the "clean hands" of objectivity necessary to lead the tide toward the kind of open, sharing environment necessary to result in the kinds of breakthroughs predicted.

Yet, the lack of clear ownership over faculty-created research data places the entire concept of an open access database (a faculty commons) in the crosshairs of legal action by any number of interested parties. The proprietary nature of data may be so strong that the ability to post those sets, even if they are funded in part or in whole by a federal agency—such as the NIH—may put libraries and universities in a legal hazard. For example, how would a university evaluate what portion of a dataset is appropriate for open access? Would it be left to the research scientist? To those setting NIH standards? To private grantors? To the library e-reserves director?

While we are certainly on solid ground in terms of what research articles can be published, we are far from being so certain in the realm of open access datasets. The complicating issue of ownership and the inability to establish a copyright shield leaves datasets in the realm of property rights law. And, as noted, even this is anything but clear. As legal expert Lester C. Thurow notes, "The world's current one-dimensional system must be overhauled to create a more differentiated one. Trying to squeeze today's developments into yesterday's system of intellectual property right simply won't work. One size does not fit all."[13]

LEVELS OF ACCESS

As mentioned elsewhere, the nature of access to the e-reserves might include open, limited, and restricted subscription, and various levels within each. The access may be read-only, with restrictions preventing downloads or copying. The library, as part of a publishing agreement, might set the degree of access to its e-reserves in concert with the copyright holder, in the case of a finished research paper, or with the intellectual property rights holder, in the case of research data. For unfinished, unpublished research papers that have not yet gone through peer review, the access might be restricted to a defined set of readers selected by the author. Then again, some stated policies by the library might be necessary to ensure the "reviewers" may define how their comments on such unfinished manuscripts may be used. Below is a rubric of possible issues regarding access to articles and data:

Rights Holders	*Faculty*	*University*	*Grantors*	*CRH**
Works, published	√	√	√	√
Works, unpublished	√	√		
Works in progress	√			
Works UGC	√	√	√	√
Datasets	√	√		
Datasets UGC	√	√	√	√

* Copyright Holder(s)

As the rubric indicates, multiple potential rights holders may be present in every act of data collection and sharing, as well as the comparably more pedantic research article publishing. Ideally, it would be to the benefit of all involved if the rights could be clarified and approved prior to publishing. Ensuring that such a desired outcome is achieved often involves some good-faith arbitration. Every phase of publishing must be carefully evaluated by as neutral a party as might be found within the matrix suggested previously. Given the motives of the faculty, university, grantors, and nonfaculty copyright holders, only the library comes close to a nonpartisan status, outside a far more expensive court option. Even the library option, however, might be suspect, given that the library administration typically reports to the university and relies upon the university's legal staff.

The only path to a truly independent, unbiased determination of copyright and intellectual property rights, short of a U.S. District Court judge (or federal trademark court), is a library that can act without answering to the interest of its university administration. Just as the Federal Trade Commission found it liberating to have its own attorneys in the last century, rather than relying on the Department of Justice, a university library with its own lawyers would be more likely to act with more clarity. After all, only the library among all those noted here has no financial motive to cloud its decision-making. And, ostensibly, only the library would be able to judge the merits of the materials involved.

This is not to suggest that all libraries will actually be provided their own legal staff. Just that doing so would solidify the millennial library's position within the university's core mission to teach, research, and serve its students, faculty, and community.

AUTHENTICITY OF RESEARCH

Assuring that the research or dataset presented to the library for posting in its e-reserve is, in fact, an original work would seem to be that of the author. Libraries are typically not at fault for providing access to a publication that contains a libelous statement. The logic is that they cannot be expected to read every publication they place in the public area. This might be extended to issues of plagiarism and misrepresentation of fact.

Yet, university libraries are already being asked to take an active role in tamping down student plagiarism. In fact, recent technology has revealed the degree to which students have cheated by using the words and works of others. As noted by Burke in 2004, such unethical activity is hardly restricted to smaller, less noteworthy schools. Burke adds that having the university library involved in the battle against this activity is plainly logical. "Considering the fact that the library is, at least theoretically, the central location for conducting research in the university, it makes sense that a librarian would be involved in dealing with unraveling the mysteries contained within some problematic student papers."[14]

Tracking down and preventing student plagiarism is one thing. Involving itself with disputes with university faculty over research and data authenticity and ownership is something far more alien to most libraries. Falling back on the safe, limited definition of the library as merely a cataloger of works—a model not so distant from the "common carrier" status of an Internet service provider (ISP)—would work, if this were 1990 and not 2011. Like it or not, libraries are anything but passive actors in the panoply of academic research and publishing. And, like it or not, they will be seen as the first defense for the university in its efforts to protect its reputation. As faculty members guilty of plagiarism may suffer personal embarrassment, the faculty members' university suffers at least as much a blow against its status.

An active millennial library would guard against plagiarism, data theft, and other malfeasance by using the latest software, such as Turnitin, already being used by some faculty to detect student cheaters. The software, of course, could be used to detect faculty acts of plagiarism, if a publisher has the will to do so. And, as libraries move more and more toward a millennial role as academic publishers, they may find it appropriate and dutiful to ensure the work they present on their e-reserves is original. As Wood notes,

> Because librarians have multiple roles as defenders of intellectual and academic freedom, as facilitators of information, and as teachers using the Internet intelligently, librarians can actively promote academic integrity on college campuses.[15]

As noted elsewhere, this requires millennial librarians with nerves of steel. The pressure on faculty to publish is only increasing. Yet, in some ways, if the library makes its new mission as partners in faculty research, it can play a far more active role in ensuring acts of plagiarism—benign or intended—are avoided. This is just one of many side benefits of an active, integrated, involved millennial library. Not only is faculty research facilitated and strengthened, it is validated.

PRIVACY

Frankly, this area of an academic commons is so new, few have commented on it. Can the notes of a researcher be publicized without the author's permission? The closest example that might shed some light (if not an answer) to the question might be the late 2009 uproar over the publishing of "private" e-mails from the Climatic Research Unit (CRU) located on the University of East Anglia's Web server. The e-mails were used by some critics in the global warming debate in an attempt to nullify scientific assertions. CRU was notified that its Web server had been hacked when someone attempted to post them to RealClimate's website. The administrators of RealClimate posted their own feelings on the matter:

> Since emails are normally intended to be private, people writing them are, shall we say, somewhat freer in expressing themselves than they would in a public statement. . . . There is a peek into how scientists actually interact and the conflicts show that the community is a far cry from the monolith that is sometimes imagined. People working constructively to improve joint publications; scientists who are friendly and agree on many of the big picture issues, disagreeing at times about details and engaging in "robust" discussions; Scientists expressing frustration at the misrepresentation of their work in politicized arenas and complaining when media reports get it wrong; Scientists resenting the time they have to take out of their research to deal with over-hyped nonsense. None of this should be shocking.[16]

This is an extreme example and perhaps was controversial more because the general public has a poor understanding of how scientific research is conducted than anything actually in the documents. It may be also that as we move forward it will be common practice to expect all notes, e-mails, and other materials associated with a research project will made public. This exposure might eventually be a boon: It may educate the public about scientific methods. Of course, it could as easily suppress researcher correspondence with a resulting "chilling effect" on the exchange of frank ideas and opinions. For example, the note cited previously was posted anonymously.

Accomplishing an open, honest exchange of ideas within an academic commons is critical to its success. Thus it can be argued that only with an assurance that all such discussions will be held private will the more troubling issues of a research project be resolved. Only with an ironclad rule restricting use of materials, such as e-mail, can researchers feel they can openly discuss with cohorts concerns they have about a project or work product. If this were a world of idealists concerned only with progress, such assurances would be unnecessary. In such an ideal world, ideas would flow and discussions would center on what is for the best outcomes. Obviously this is not an ideal world and the unseen and unseemly skullduggery that is present in and around many projects makes such honest discussions unlikely.

The challenge for the millennial librarians is to manage the academic commons in such a way as to assure the maximum amount of collaboration and honesty, while also providing the maximum amount of privacy possible. This should start with an open statement of policy regarding copyright, intellectual property, and perhaps most important, privacy. Thus far, few in academia have discussed this issue, possibly because they unfortunately take it as a given that what is said in the academic commons stays in the academic commons. Such an assumption is naïve at the least, and potentially damaging at the worst.

Of course, the content that is created within an academic commons, such as e-mail, blogs, and chat rooms, has not been the subject of much, if any, discussion. More to the point, though, are these e-mails and personal notes in chat rooms part of the research project and, thus, owned by the granting agency? Do they belong to a university who has hired the researchers? Are they strictly personal property, not subject to publishing without the author's permission?

As universities rush into the realm of e-reserves and academic commons, they should at the least develop a policy that attempts to address these issues, along with those of copyright law and intellectual property rights. University libraries—as a consortium—might start by enlisting publishers, and major collectors of information (e.g., Google) to convene with the purpose of resolving these issues. Short of an industry resolution, copyright and intellectual property rights will remain a barrier to future growth of an academic commons at all universities. And, pointedly, intellectual property rights are likely to be the larger and more difficult to resolve issue here.

OWNERSHIP ISSUES SURROUNDING THE ACADEMIC COMMONS: TEN MILESTONES

1. As authors look to publish, libraries will be asked more and more to be the copyright and intellectual property rights marshal. This may put library administration in the company of faculty and administrators, as well as granting organizations and government agencies (e.g., NIH). Rather than just being another player, the millennial library must provide leadership through seminars and collaboration.
2. Copyright law is more settled than intellectual property rights. This is hardly saying much however, as some areas of copyright law, such as fair

use, are not close to being well-defined. The millennial library must be a leader here as well, providing information campus-wide on what is and isn't allowed under fair use. Within the academic commons, copyright clearance might be modeled after the Duke University plan, whereby a committee reviews cases that are complex enough to require a "second look."

3. Intellectual property rights is far more difficult to sort through. Competing parties, be they researchers, university administrators, or granting agencies, all have a stake in the datasets involved. The millennial library may act as a catalyst in discussions, but cannot see itself as an arbitrator between these groups. This may be the clearest area that the academic commons might be able to help by fostering discussion, but cannot take an active role in resolving the underlying ownership issues. These issues will likely require court or congressional actions.
4. The millennial library must lobby hard for open access, even in cases of intellectual property right disputes. That is, while it cannot participate in the discussions over who owns the data, it can certainly argue that whoever is determined to own the data should allow for some free access.
5. The rubric offered in this chapter could be a starting point for discussion as to who should be able to access what types of data.
6. The millennial library will expand upon the role many libraries have already taken on: identifying plagiarism. This can be done via software packages such as Turnitin.
7. The privacy issues that may soon start swirling around the publicizing of the notes of researchers should be on the millennial library's radar. Expectations that all e-mails, for instance, might be made public could certainly lead to a "chilling effect" on the conversations among collaborating researchers. The library should establish a set of guidelines for researchers, in concert with faculty and university administrators.
8. The leadership of the millennial library, as it attempts to foster collaboration that leads to better teaching and stronger research, is key to the success of the university in its academic standing. Open discussions, rather than closed-door committees, would create a far more popular outcome that would lead to more participation and buy-in.
9. The first step at any university library considering starting an academic commons might be to work with other universities to create an academic conference to encourage cooperation and actually generate outcomes and standards.
10. It is not an overstatement to pose that failure to address and successfully resolve issues such as fair use, intellectual property rights, and research privacy could stymie the creation of an academic commons. This may be the key area that all millennial libraries must address.

SUMMARY

Today, however, libraries must be part of all discussions regarding academic research at universities. The millennial library must be seen and act as the center of every university. This requires that the library deal directly with two of the fundamental issues surrounding academic commons in the near term: copyright and intellectual property rights.

- How can librarians post faculty-developed information within a learning, teaching, or research commons and still assure the creators of this material that it will be protected from unauthorized use?
- How can librarians ensure that faculty members are not overly restricted in their use of materials, especially a use that would be allowed via the fair use exception?

The two methods by which invention and creativity typically have been protected—copyright and intellectual property rights—are different in derivation and application. Copyright springs from common law. Intellectual property rights are statutory. They differ in other ways:

- Copyright provides a fair use exemption that allows the reuse of some portions of an author's work.
- Intellectual property rights provide no such "automatic" safe harbor.
- Copyright is a more "settled" issue.
- Intellectual property rights is a very unsettled area in practice—especially regarding information gathered in a research project.

And this is the crux of the matter. For now, far more than in the past, a millennial library can store and deliver all manner of notes, voice recordings, even e-mails associated with a research paper, as well as its datasets, all in one place, all accessible. This is a truly profound change. Yes, notes of scientists and writers have been available, but usually not with the published work. E-mails, or what would have been letters, are the stuff of special publishing volumes, often years later, after the death of the author. The ability to publish literally everything opens up the possibility of looking into the very heart of a researcher via her personal notes and e-mails to other researchers. Will this be some sort of new requirement attached to all funding grants? Will it be required that all communication regarding a project will be the property of the grantor, and thus available for publishing?

Copyright, found in Article 1, Section 8, Clause 8 of the U.S. Constitution, provides: "To promote the Progress of Science and useful Arts, by securing for limited Times to Authors and Inventors the exclusive Right to their respective Writings and Discoveries."

- Internationally, copyright is covered country by country, with no broad agreement on the length of time a work is protected.
- The length of time of copyright protection in this country has expanded from fourteen years to the span of the author's life plus seventy years.
- Protecting music, movies, and print rights from unlawful use is the ostensible purpose of copyright laws, both in the United States and internationally.

Section 107 also sets out four factors to be considered in determining whether or not a particular use is fair:

1. The purpose and character of the use, including whether such use is of commercial nature or is for nonprofit educational purposes
2. The nature of the copyrighted work
3. The amount and substantiality of the portion used in relation to the copyrighted work as a whole
4. The effect of the use upon the potential market for, or value of, the copyrighted work

Put simply and directly, no simple test to determine what is fair use has ever been devised or outlined by any higher court. And, it may be the vagueness of the fair use provision that has led many university libraries to set such a broadly and erroneously interpreted policy such as that outlined previously. The degree to which such any maximum allowable policy exists at major universities is unknown, but certainly poses an interesting problem for academics seeking to use materials for "education purposes," a use specifically sanctioned in the Copyright Act.

A case-by-case approach seems to fit well within the strictures of the fair use component of the copyright law. Each "questionable" case is reviewed by a committee at the library to determine if it meets the fair use rules, as determined by the committee. Whatever approach the library chooses to take, it must make it abundantly clear to its participating research authors,

1. They are responsible for protecting their works from copyright infringement.
2. Fair use suggests some of their work may be used without notice or permission.
3. They retain the copyright ownership of all their works posted within the e-reserves.
4. The rules for usage of their works, including datasets and other work product, can be established by them, in concert with the library.

Most libraries are familiar with the typical item that would be deposited in its e-reserves: a research article. The form and sections of a research article would include such materials as an abstract, author notes, footnotes or endnotes, illustrations or diagrams, and other support materials. Typically, researchers gather data, write a research paper or papers, and then toss the data.

The data collected is an intellectual property rights issue not covered by copyright. Copyright does not extend to research data; intellectual property rights do. This is an unsettled area, however. Does the data belong to the research or to the sponsoring grant agency? To the university? To the researcher? All of these players—the researcher, university, granting agency, and others with a perceived stake in the potential financial benefits that might be derived from the data—believe they are rightful owners.

The issue of ownership of datasets itself remains the highest hurdle.

- The researcher might argue that she gathered the data and therefore should reap some benefit.
- The university might consider the data set as the work product of a faculty member paid by the institution to produce the research.
- The granting agency might expect to benefit from whatever income is generated by research it funded.

The legal standards of the e-reserves within any library must specify the ownership and republication or reuse status of the data to be placed there prior to publishing. And, across the country, the resulting kaleidoscope of state standards has created a mishmash of legal hurdles and competing interests. The lack of clear ownership over faculty-created research data places the entire concept of an open access database (a faculty commons) in the crosshairs of legal action by any number of interested parties. The proprietary nature of data may be so strong that the ability to post those sets, even if they are funded in part or in whole by a federal agency like the NIH may put libraries and universities in legal danger.

While we are certainly on solid ground in terms of what research articles can be published, we are far from being near the realm of open access datasets. The complicating issue of ownership and the inability to establish a copyright shield leaves datasets in the realm of property rights law.

As mentioned previously, the nature of access to the e-reserves might include open, limited, and restricted subscription, and various levels within each. The access may be read-only, with restrictions preventing downloads or copying. The library, as part of a publishing agreement, might set the degree of access to its e-reserves in concert with the copyright holder, in the case of a finished research paper, or with the intellectual property rights holder, in the case of research data.

As the rubric provided earlier indicates, multiple potential rights holders may be present in every act of data collection and sharing, as well as even more pedantic research article publishing. Ideally, it would be to the benefit of all involved if the rights could be clarified and approved prior to publishing. Ensuring that such a sought for outcome is achieved often involves some good-faith arbitration.

The only path to a truly independent, unbiased determination of copyright and intellectual property rights, short of a U.S. District Court judge (or federal trademark court), is a library that can act without answering to the interest of its university administration: a university library with its own lawyers would be more likely to act with more clarity. This is not to suggest that all libraries will actually be provided their own legal staff. Just that doing so would solidify the millennial library's position within the university's core mission to teach, research, and serve its students, faculty, and community.

Assuring that the research or dataset presented to the library for posting in its e-reserve is, in fact, original work would seem to be that of the author. Libraries are typically seen as not at fault for providing access to a publication that contains a libelous statement. The logic is that they cannot be expected to read every publication they place in the public area.

However, they are being asked to take an active role in tamping down university student plagiarism. New technology has revealed the degree to which students have cheated by using the words and works of others.

Libraries with an e-reserve may find themselves involved in disputes with university faculty over research and data authenticity and ownership. Like it or not, libraries are anything but passive actors in the panoply of academic research and publishing.

An active millennial library would guard against plagiarism, data theft, and other malfeasance by using the latest software, such as Turnitin, already being used by some faculty to detect student cheaters.

If the library makes its new mission as partners in faculty research, it can play a far more active role in ensuring acts of plagiarism—benign or intended—are avoided. This is just one of many side benefits of an active, integrated, involved millennial library. Not only is faculty research facilitated and strengthened, it is validated.

Can the notes of a researcher be publicized without the author's permission? Are e-mails and personal notes in chat rooms part of the research project and thus owned by the granting agency? Do they belong to a university who has hired the researchers? Are they strictly personal property, not subject to publishing without the author's permission?

As universities rush into the realm of e-reserves and academic commons, they should at least develop a policy that attempts to address these issues, along with those of copyright law and intellectual property rights.

The challenge for the millennial librarians is to manage the academic commons in such a way as to assure the maximum amount of collaboration and honesty, while also providing the maximum amount of privacy possible. This should start with an open statement of policy regarding copyright, intellectual property, and perhaps most important, privacy. Thus far, few in academia have discussed this issue, possibly because they unfortunately take it as a given that what is said in the academic commons stays in the academic commons. Such an assumption is naïve at the least, and potentially damaging at the worst.

NOTES

1. This section and the one following dealing with intellectual property rights are presented in more plain speak than one might find in a legal journal. The effort here is to provide a basic outline of both areas without engaging deeply in the running skirmishes that are part and parcel of both.

2. For example, as related to me by a cohort, Dale Askey of the Kansas State University Libraries, business licensing of products in Germany are far more restrictive, especially in the area of music DVDs that are purchased in the United States and carried in to Germany by a visiting librarian.

3. Thomas Gould, Tomas Lapinski and Elizabeth Buchanan, "Copyright Policies and the Deciphering of Fair Use in the Creation of Reserves at University Libraries," *The Journal of Academic Librarianship* 31, no. 3 (May 2005): 182–197.

4. *Bridgeport Music v. Dimension Films,* 410 F.3d 792 (6th Cir. 2005).

5. "Fair Use," U.S. Copyright Office, www.copyright.gov/fls/fl102.html (22 November 2009) (accessed 11 September 2010).

6. *Basic Books, Inc. v. Kinko's Graphics Corp.* 58 F. Supp. 1522 (28 March 1991).

7. *Basic Books, Inc. v. Kinko's Graphics Corp.*

8. "Fair Use," U.S. Copyright Office; Kenneth D. Crews, "The Law of Fair Use and The Illusion of Fair Use Guidelines," *Ohio State Law Journal* 62 (2001): 602–711; Kenneth Frazier, "What's Wrong with Fair-use Guidelines for the Academic Community?" *American Society for Information Science and Technology* 50, no. 14 (21 January 2000): 1320–1323.

9. Duke University Libraries, "Use and Reproduction Policy," Duke University, library.duke.edu/about/copyright.html (11 September 2010).

10. Judith Preissle Goetz and Margaret D. LeCompte, "Ethnographic Research and the Problem of Data Reduction," *Anthropology and Education Quarterly* 12, no. 1

(Spring 1981): 51–70; R. Kraut, C. Egido, and J. Galegher, "Patterns of Contact and Communication in Scientific Research Collaboration," *Portal: The Guide to Computing Literature* (26 September 1988) (accessed 11 September 2010). Notably, the Kraut, Egido, and Galegher research was presented at a conference in 1988 dedicated to Computer Supported Cooperative Work. Included at this conference was a paper entitled: "Design of a Multi-media Vehicle for Social Browsing." We have been discussing and kicking back and forth the role of technology in social networks for more than two decades.

11. Tammy L. Lewis and Lisa A. Vincler, "Storming the Ivory Tower: The Competing Interests of the Public's Right to Know and Protecting the Integrity of University Research," *Journal of College and University Law* 20, no. 4 (Spring 1994): 417–460.

12. Nader Mousavi and Matthew J. Kleiman, "When the Public Does Not Have a Right to Know: How the California Public Records Act Is Deterring Bioscience Research and Development," *Duke Law and Technology Review* 2005, no. 23 (accessed 11 December 2009).

13. Lester C. Thurow, "Needed a New System of Intellectual Property Rights," *Harvard Business Review* (September–October 1997): 95–103.

14. Margaret Burke, "Deterring Plagiarism: A New Role for Librarians," *Library Philosophy and Practice* 6, no. 2 (Spring 2004).

15. Gail Wood, "Academic Original Sin: Plagiarism, the Internet and Librarians," *The Journal of Academic Librarianship* 30, no. 3 (May 2004): 237–242.

16. The Cru Hack, *Real Climate: Climate Science from Climate Scientists,* www.realclimate.org/index.php/archives/2009/11/the-cru-hack/ (20 November 2009) (accessed 11 September 2010).

Chapter Nine

Selling the Millennial Library and Its Academic Commons to Its Stakeholders

GENERATING BUY-IN AMONG STAKEHOLDERS

Should a library decide to re-create itself as a millennial library, it will face a variety of challenges as it endeavors to embrace all that we have discussed thus far. Winning over the key patrons of the library—students, faculty, and administrators—to any change is always a major task. As the proposed new mission and the services that will be part of a millennial library are rolled out, the library's administration should be prepared to field a variety of responses, both positive and negative. The nature and subject of these responses will be shaped by those who ask them. For university administrators, it is likely to be "How much will this cost?" followed quickly by "Can we make any money doing this?" For university faculty, it could be "Will my published research be valued by my department?" followed by "Do I own the rights to my research, research data, work notes?" For the university students, it is most likely going to be a familiar "What's in it for me?" which, notably, is not that far away from the previously described interests of university administrators and faculty.

Every project faces a point where it must prove that it is relevant and necessary, especially in cash-strapped universities. The millennial library is no different. Wise implementers of new technologies first determine the needs for the innovation. Do students need a new e-mail system? Do faculty need a research commons area? Do university administrators see the library as a research core that fuels academic success? Finding out how the core interest groups of the library feel about the potential of an academic commons not only will guide what areas should be created first, but also the areas that may never be required at all. Done properly, the market research suggested in this chapter will also ensure higher adoption and usage rates, and provide a platform for future technology additions.

The challenges in the implementation of an academic commons are high, whether in refocusing students to use online education resources other than Google, providing the learning tools to teachers that will lead to higher outcomes, or convincing faculty that online collaboration and publishing is not just worthwhile but a vital part of the future of all universities. Without making a case for relevancy and need, the case for funding will always fail. A university has many competing projects, all with outstanding goals and brilliant potential outcomes. The best path for the millennial library is to show it is a key element in the success of all endeavors on a university campus, and that its patrons value its services.

It is not a stretch to suggest that most university libraries are seen as a repository of the past: what has been published. It is rarely seen as a resource for the future: what can be learned, how learning can be supported, and how information can be created, shared, and transformed into knowledge. Breaking through the historic image among university administrators and faculty of a library—not much more than a storage unit with a search function: the saving of journals and monographs, and then the retrieving of journals and monographs—takes more than hoping and wishing. It takes a lot more than a mere statement of resources and what can be accomplished. For students, who often see the library as a warm place to talk with friends, work on projects, or take a nap, integrating the library into their learning is not just critical to the justification of the funding of any library endeavor, it is an ethical imperative. Again, talking to students in vague terms about how they can learn to learn is likely to miss the target.

For the library to become a millennial library, it must see itself as a product with features, benefits, and a marketing plan. Furthermore, in regard to features and benefits, library administrators must understand that the former is what is created and the latter is what is marketed. No library will complete the conversion to a millennial library if it fails to understand that what it sees itself and its features to be are of little value in the battle to convert the image that users (administrators, faculty, and students) have of that campus building with shelves of books.

We are not talking about massive budgets for advertising, posters, and other traditional marketing tools. We would be using these tools, if this were 1980. But, if this were 1980, we would not be talking about an advanced technology library, that is, academic commons. As we move through the second decade of the second millennium, we have at our fingertips new resources, new tools, and new communication channels to make the case for a new library, a millennial library. Harness these resources, tools, and channels properly, and we can make the case not just for funding, but ensure success at every level. Fail to do so and we will remain that remote, dusty building with shelves of books.

It is an argument of whether to focus on the chicken or the egg. The library administration could try to convince the university of the need. This would put the library in the same line of all other funding programs. It could attempt to convince the faculty that they need the library. This would likely be met with skepticism. It could tell students that using the library means access to a variety of resources. This would likely be met with either "so what?" or "who has the time?" Or it could take a more advisedly beneficial path: identify the opportunity, develop a strategy to communicate the benefits to each target consumer, and then allow the users to define what essentially will be the new library brand. In this chapter we will discuss how the millennial library can build its base of support among those outside the library; that is, among the users of the services proposed in the previous chapters. We will then discuss three recent advances in marketing: social networks, viral marketing, and behavior targeting. In addition, we will discuss avenues of potential funding, as well as other long-term issues.

Before we move on, it should be a given that a library staff considering creating an academic commons areas, whether learning, teaching, or research, must be fully online. Every staffer should not only have Twitter accounts, but also Facebook or MySpace pages, their own blog, and other specialized areas such as the research, teaching, sharing, and support site Diigo. They should also have computers ready to Skype, with built-in or inexpensive add-on cameras.

THE MARKETING PLAN

What is offered in the following pages is not what a Fortune 500 company looking to increase brand adoption or incremental sales might create. This plan is slimmed down and focuses on three target consumer/user groups: administration, faculty, and students. This plan will use more modern marketing tools, such as social networks and viral marketing. It will also focus on benefits—such as higher university standing for the administration, higher research success for faculty, and higher grades for students. And, put bluntly, all three of these groups link the success of their activities to financial rewards, pure and simple. If the university can show success, it can expect to at least hold on to the funding it already receives and, possibly, experience an increase. If faculty members succeed in publishing research, they not only can expect success in rank and tenure, but also in grant applications. And, finally, students clearly link their degrees to future success financially (as well as, it is admitted, emotional satisfaction). Each group sees as its ultimate goal an improvement in its current status. A library should not singularly focus its time and energy in addressing what role it plays in creating these successes. Ignoring how to effectively communicate the link that the innovation may have to the success sought by the targeted patrons will very likely leave the library marginalized and unfunded. This can often be the case: a new innovative function is added to the university's network and users are expected to "get it" and adopt it immediately. And, unfortunately, low adoption rates are often met with scorn and disgust among the technical group that installed the new tools: "Why didn't they get it?"

Ensuring they get it starts with understanding the target's needs, not the innovation's features. "How will the new software/service increase success among the patrons who use it?" is a good question. A better one, however, is "Will the patrons see the new software/service as a tool that will increase their success?" Answering this question requires that we first understand the need to be fulfilled by the new software or service, not from the perspective of the software's brochure, but from the potential users.

Step One: Identify the Need or Opportunity

Typically a marketing group seeking to understand what role its product will play in a consumer's life will start with a survey of the target. For a library, this means crafting a survey that reveals the needs of each group. Unfortunately, such surveying is sometimes structured in a way as to ensure a specific goal is reached, one often established prior to the start of the consumer research. In other cases, the survey is loaded with questions about the acceptance or adoption of a particular product or service. Some examples of each of these faults might be a question that asks "The Acme product can increase research success by 75 percent. Would you use the product?" Or, "Students who use Acme product score higher on their finals. Are you interested in using this product?" Both of these are loaded, as is any other form of a question that promises, in vague terms, success without explaining the product or how it works. Perhaps even more troubling, such a survey presumes the target user is already familiar with the Acme product.

Even more troubling are surveys that do not address any issue of need or opportunity. Surveys must first ascertain as to whether the target consumer has failed to find a solution and, if so, why. On the other hand, a question such as "Have you ever collaborated with faculty either within the university or at another institution or institutions on a project?" allows for a simple starting point after which the ensuing questions can explore areas where the person surveyed experienced a need for a product or service. Questions probing this unfulfilled need might include:

- If yes, what was the nature of the need? (The form would include a series of check boxes that would allow multiple answers, such as audio, video, file sharing, etc.)
- Is the patron aware of possible online solutions to facilitate collaboration? (This establishes the level of familiarity the patron might have with online services. If the answer is yes, the form should provide branching to an area where the services could be identified by the patron.)
- Has the patron tried any of these software packages on her/his own? (A simple listing of check boxes would not only establish the degree to which the patron is familiar with software, hardware, and services, but also the level of sophistication of the user.)

Branching questions off questions would probe both the positives and negatives, looking for any need left unfulfilled. For example, a negative response to the initial question—"Have you ever collaborated with faculty either within the university or at other institutions on a project?"—should immediately be followed by a probe into why the person being surveyed had not participated in collaborative work. Was it because of the nature of that researcher's work? Was it because of a lack of interested cohorts within the university or an inability to identify any potential cohorts? A positive response could track the involvement of others outside the university, the use of software, or possible barriers or inefficiencies, such as having to mail materials from one cohort to another.

Surveys are a valuable part of any research project. Yet, they are not the only tools available, and in some cases are not the preferred method. One-on-one interviews can generate very valuable data, sometimes far richer in quality than that of surveys, as we discussed earlier. Focus groups of six to eight potential users can also provide the opportunity for peer discussion of needs. Allowing users and potential users to discuss at some length their needs and expectations can provide valuable insight into how to solve their needs and to effectively market the new service to other potential users. Sometimes what arises from these focus groups is the actual nomenclature that will be relevant to future users—the language particular to students, researchers, and administrators. Using the words and phrases that are most familiar to each of these groups can not only heighten product or service adoption, but also increase the trust factor between the library and its patrons. "You speak my language" translates into "You understand my needs." Focus groups are invaluable in capturing that nomenclature, as well as many other valuable data points.

Whatever the tool used, the research must be free of internal bias or directed even unconsciously to a desired, predetermined goal. This can be extremely challenging to any library staff committee. Unless the committee can be certain that it can act without tampering with the actual data collection and without inserting its own biases, such research should be left to an outside group. This need not be an expensive private contractor. Schools of business or mass communication, if present at the university, can provide assistance. The goals of the consumer research should be to identify existing needs/problems within each of the target groups:

- For students, it may be the information necessary to write an "A" quality research paper.
- For faculty, it may be distance collaboration that leads to a new grant, which in turn leads to publication success and rank or tenure promotion.
- For university administrators, it may be improving teaching that then leads to higher student-learning outcomes, which in turn solidifies the institution's value to its stakeholders and to potential new students.

To measure the perception of the library as a potential solution to these needs or problems:

- For students, the solution may be assistance in finding the right database to search for appropriate references.
- For faculty, it may be the staff assistance in setting up an initial online collaboration site.
- For university administrators, it may be improvements in the tracking of learning outcomes associated with online teaching seminars or other online tools within the teaching commons.

To learn how the target groups assessed the efficacy of solutions, not as presented by the survey or focus group administrators, but by themselves based on what they expected from what they have heard about the academic commons prior to actual use. Is the solution that they anticipated finding one that is present in the commons?

- For students, was the promise couched as "ease" or "fast"? And, if so, was their experience, while an improvement on their past database experiences, not in line with their expectations?
- For faculty, was the technology barrier lowered sufficiently for them to feel comfortable using the online tools?

- For university administrators, were the learning outcomes in line with expectations?

To measure acceptance of online tools of which the patrons may not have experience using:

- For students and faculty, were the success of tutorial sessions measured based on actual online behavior, or the use of subjective and, thus unreliable, offline paper evaluation sheets?
- For university administrators, were the levels of faculty and student involvement in using the new commons sufficient to justify the budget expenditures?

These are just a few areas of potential user expectations of the solution power of the commons and their actual experience within the commons. The promised experience of the academic commons should match the actual patron experience. That is, expectations should be met first. It is all well and good if expectations are exceeded. But over-promising what the patron can accomplish within the academic commons will negate any upset feelings about the project. That is, over-promising creates an impossible standard for the marketing plan to accomplish. Promising the researcher will be awarded a Fulbright only generates disappointment and resentment when the award is not forthcoming. Matching promises to actual experiences starts with avoiding superlatives, such as "the best," and ensures that positive outcomes that will occur are both reasonable and satisfying for the patron. Creating negative outcomes by setting impossible expectations will result in patrons who are unlikely to try again. Furthermore, these disappointed library patrons—faculty or students—are likely to spread their negative feelings to others, a sort of reverse snowball effect that generates many more doubters and fewer and fewer adopters. Perhaps even worse, news of this negative feedback is likely to reach the ears of those providing financial support, such as the university administration.

A well thought-out plan of inquiry should cover all the potential areas of patron use of the library. Perhaps the largest challenge to the library staff is ensuring that the manner in which the needs of students, faculty, and university administrators are measured does not presume any member of this group has any idea of what software solutions are actually available. That is, it would be preferable if the marketing group crafted patron expectations and then met them, rather than having the users create their own set of expectations based on other sources of information encountered prior to introduction to the commons.

Conducted properly, the research results will identify not only what the target patrons feel they are lacking, but also define what opportunities are present to solve the identified needs or problems. This is a critical step; without identifying the opportunity, the end result will be merely another product of a closed-off technology committee with preestablished goals delivering a product that may be very valuable—but just not very useful—for the target consumers.

Step Two: Design a Message Based on That Need or Opportunity

Inside-out thinking is the bane of all marketing efforts. This is the kind of thinking that presumes patrons know as much about technology, for example, as those in charge of installing new software platforms do. Even more deadly to the success of a marketing effort, such thinking defines everything in terms of what the product can do, that is, its features. Does it provide for automatic backup of data? Does it provide rapid search ability? Does it provide easy-to-read instructions for use? While these are valid examples of some of the features of a product that might be used in a library's academic commons, it misses the point: the benefits to the user. Automatic backup of data to a library patron really means, "You will always be able to access your research data. It will be safe and available when you need it." The rapid search feature means "find your material quickly without having to wait and, thus, ensuring that you will meet that term paper, grant, or publication deadline." The "easy-to-read instructions" feature inappropriately included in many ads means "you will be using this software within minutes of accessing it without a struggle." Behind every feature is a benefit that is meaningful to the user of the product or service. Pointing out dozens of details of what the software can do is not nearly as valuable as pointing out the dozens of accomplishments that are possible using the software. After all, the student or faculty person doesn't really care how a software package works, any more than they care how their refrigerator works. They care about what software can do for them (i.e., keep the milk cold). A successful marketing plan cannot ask the target user to translate features into benefits. For example, a family of six isn't in the market to buy a four-door car. They are looking for family transportation. That benefit appears as a four-door feature, but should never be advertised as such.

Identifying the benefits helps the library then identify the opportunity. And, again, the definition of this opportunity must be formed based on what the library patron sees as a solution to a need or problem he or she defines. That is, what is it that the students want to accomplish but can't? Rather than merely suggesting that a particular tutorial might be useful, a message must be crafted to directly address the need or problem. One of the typical situations is the library announcing a series of tutorials on bibliographic software without any hint as to what the tool can accomplish—its benefit. Yes, a package such as RefWorks can manage references and citations. But the advantage to the user is that it saves time. If students suggest in surveys that they find doing term papers difficult because of the vast variety of citation styles, the message addressing this opportunity must specifically answer the need. This requires the library's marketing team to think like students. The resulting message that comes from all surveys, interviews, and focus groups should have a strong emotional context. If faculty work at a school that is four hours away from a cohort university, the appeal might be "Connect with fellow researchers." A better message might be "Stop feeling isolated."

Step Three: Communicate That Solution

When engaging the target groups, it is key that the language used matches that used by each group. This is not one-size-fits-all. Administrators not only have different needs and problems, they also have a different language that they use to express those issues. Involving a well-established administrator in the marketing team to create this message is one possible solution. Testing messages intended for the target groups through the use of focus groups is another perfectly valid approach. The marketing group must make sure it is looking for both positive and negative feedback, not just preening. If the benefit of a service presented in the message—a service the marketing group thought was identified by the target group as much needed—is misunderstood or rejected, then it is likely it is the manner in which the service was presented or the wording used to describe its benefits that has failed. The group must probe deeper in the nature of the rejection. Was it the terms used to describe what could be accomplished with the software? Was it the way in which it was communicated? Was it the tone of the message? Was it where or how the message was delivered?

For example, marketing fast food products in a hospital makes little sense. Just as marketing hospital services in a restaurant would be seen as inappropriate. The marketing of a new support feature that enhances learning, research, and student outcomes must be delivered how, where, and when it will be most effective. Within a new media environment, the marketing team itself can create some of these "places." This requires all library personnel even marginally engaged in conversations with patrons (or potential patrons) to be included in the new approach. This approach goes far beyond the method of using e-mail messages to market a service or product. It requires the marketing to target not the typical demographics or even more exotic psychographics used by advertising agencies to reach and motivate consumers to act. It requires that the marketing follow the behavior of the potential users.

NEW TOOLS: SOCIAL NETWORKING, VIRAL MARKETING, BEHAVIOR TARGETING

As we move from the age of reading to the age of listening and watching—where more and more information will be available in audio or video formats—the need to quickly create simple, direct messages online has also increased. Online mini-films can be used to tutor, provide step-wise instruction, and train users on where to find and how to access information. As we have discussed previously, the creation of such videos has been made far more economically feasible, while at the same time rough-cut videos on YouTube have gained not only more acceptance, but also more trust among university students. Online users do not expect or demand high quality videos; they tend to mistrust those they would describe as "slick." This degree of cynicism is especially high among university students compared to older populations. This issue of mistrust can actually work to the benefit of libraries: they can use the lower-cost of these rough videos to their advantage when marketing to target groups, as we shall discuss later in this chapter.

But videos are only one arrow in our social network quiver. Blogs, Twitter, Facebook, and MySpace also provide inexpensive, highly popular tools to gather and disseminate information. "Conversations" can be set up among the survey team and students, faculty, and administrators in the same or separate "rooms" or threads online. If the surveyors allow the conversation to range far and wide, a vast amount of valuable insights can be gathered. Of course, this means allowing the conversations to roam outside what the research team may have expected. As long as the postings are relevant to the academic commons, the nature of the individual posts should be hands off. That is, rather than engaging in gainsaying or other attempts to quash points and requests—even if these seem unreasonable or unlikely to be part of the academic commons—the surveyors should act only as catalysts. Just keep the conversation moving. It can be quite remarkable when a blog or Twitter conversation goes in a direction completely unexpected by the marketing team. Underlying issues and needs might lead library administration to consider changes or updates not given much attention or importance. Frustrations expressed by a student regarding a research paper may reveal a need for tutoring on choosing the most appropriate research databases. Faculty noting how hard and time-consuming they find it to build a consensus on a grant project may reveal a need to exchange ideas and corrections in real time with cohorts off campus in a secure area. Administrators asking questions regarding ongoing projects may reveal a need for more "instant messaging" on how some group is using the library on a day-to-day basis.

The goal of the research should be to identity areas of needs—services that will actually be used eagerly by the target users. These needs might include reformatting of existing services or adding new services, as well as changing how the services are presented. Yet, because some library patrons are unaware of what they are missing and what an academic commons can do for them, merely posing questions—even in the manner suggested above—may not provide the necessary information.

The solution for this black box phenomena may be simply a matter of watching what patrons do on the library's main site or its commons online area. By using elements of behavior targeting, libraries can track what users are most interested in finding, using, or downloading, as well as what they are not able to access. Behavior tracking, a relatively new marketing research tool, provides data about how users are surfing the library website and what specific areas are getting the most interest. This is much more complex than traditional pageviews and clickthroughs, both of which have been used in online advertising planning for years. Behavior tracking notes which pages the user accesses in relation to other pages in terms of time and repeat visits. But it also can match a stated need, as expressed in a search term, with the actual need of the site user. For example, is the student looking for information regarding children in advertising, but is searching the wrong database? Is the faculty member looking for information on a particular grant, but then fails to find (or even look for) the associated data that could have helped clarify and strengthen the proposal?

Behavior targeting follows the pattern of patron interests and actions, both those that are successful and those that are negative, as suggested previously. What results is a rich set of information about the specific opportunities the library has to reach out and connect with its patrons. This is far more than merely noting that users often need help in search terms. And it is the kind of data that can reveal not only that a patron prefers using one database over another as a matter of habit, but also that this habit results in poor outcomes. Tracking the actual online behavior of library patrons can actually detect possible confusion or avoidance regarding part of the website. This avoidance behavior might be tracked to confusing language or incomplete directions. Even the most simple of user behavior tracking, such as the searching of areas of the website at particular times of the day, may reveal needs and opportunities.

Tracking how patrons are using the library's website should not be taken as a substitute for direct surveying and interviews. Libraries interested in creating solutions rather than merely completing a project must gather as much data as possible. Resources on how to conduct behavior tracking are included in Appendix A.

Creating a Brand and a Brand Statement

With the exception of generics (and maybe even in the case of some of these), all products and services have a brand image. Whether a company or institution asks for it, works to support it, or is even aware of it, the brand exists. This ubiquitous nature of the brand derives from the source of its creation: the user, the consumer, and in the case of libraries, the patron. The brand of a library may be supported by a slogan and may be fed by an ongoing marketing campaign. Yet, it cannot be created by either of these activities. Patrons build an image of their library based on personal experiences and what they hear from others, especially their peers. No amount of advertising will convince them that something they see as a negative is actually a positive, or that the usefulness of a particular resource is any greater than their own experience informs them it is.

Improving a brand and its brand equity, therefore, relies upon what the library marketing group can glean from surveys, interviews, and behavior tracking, not just its marketing plan. The starting point is an understanding of where the library resides in the minds of students, faculty, and administrators. Do students see the library as irrelevant, except as a nice place to talk with friends and take a nap? Do faculty see the library as a barrier, unwilling to provide clear access to necessary materials? Do administrators see the library as a money drain, or a source of potential copyright violations? Each group—students, faculty, and administrators—has different perspectives of "their library." Given that the library means something different to each group, and probably means a variety of things even within each group, a one-size-fits-all approach will not work.

As important as identifying the brand, the marketing group must install a sense of loyalty among the library administration and staff to the brand message. Too many university marketing groups see each year as an opportunity to put out a "new" message or different image. This is precisely the wrong approach to brand building. The message must remain consistent, at least for five years, preferably much longer than that. Every effort must be made to ensure that the message displayed in marketing the academic commons builds brand equity in the minds of the patrons. This brand equity is very much like a bank account. Every deposit must be to the same account, thus growing the identity and trust in the minds of the consumers. Every positive interaction is a deposit that helps the equity grow. Every negative encounter or outcome erodes the account.

This loyalty to brand goes far beyond the issue of protecting the logo from artistic changes, though that too happens far too often in some universities. This is not the time for playtime in the art software sandbox. A consistent design, with consistent color management helps ensure that the patron sees the message as related to prior messages. Certainly different treatments of content can be helpful. But wholesale changes in design and slogans, for example, are foolish attacks on the brand equity.

Connecting to Students

Gardner and Eng in 2005 included in a research paper a survey conducted at the University of Southern California designed to help library administration understand the perception of the USC Leavey Library among undergraduate students.[1] The survey was intended to target existing library users. It included questions regarding the student's status (freshman, sophomore, etc), the frequency that the students had visited the library, how long they stayed, and their reasons for going to the library. Such a survey gives a library an excellent gauge on existing usage, which, of course, could be supplemented by staff walking around the facility and observing what students are actually engaged in doing. In addition, asking if the student is willing to participate in a focus group would open the door for even more data and ideas.

Stopping at existing users, though, would be a mistake. The much larger population for many universities is comprised of students who very rarely, if at all, go to the library either in person or online. They are using alternative sources, such as Google or Google Scholar, to find the information they need for a term paper or report. Attracting these students to the millennial library and all of its components requires making it very clear to them that by simply using a tool like Google Scholar, the student may be missing a broader array of resources. And, it must be made clear that these additional tools could be the difference between a grade they receive and the grade they want, between learning a little and learning a lot, and using their research time wisely. The benefit to the student is academic or scholarly success. What makes the library's academic commons area better than Google? Why is the library's help desk a great first stop for any student visiting the library?

Students who access the library services strictly online from their apartment or dorm room are also a very important population, and one that likely has a far different perspective on potential new services and support. This population is looking for 24/7 support, either via e-mail or, more likely, live chat or instant messaging. The issues these students may have can obviously vary widely, and whoever is on the other end of the wire at the library must be sensitive to the at times confused and unfocused questions posed. This is the time for patience. Carefully walking a student through what may at times seem like pedantic issues can mean the difference between learning and failure. In many cases, a student reaching out for help may not have the capacity to even form a question. They may be frustrated with the required protocol established by the library to access information. They may be unaware of the differences between one database and another. It is not uncommon for faculty to be approached by students unable to find sources for the most common of research paper topics. Carefully and compassionately guiding a student to the right database with the right search terms can open the eyes of a young researcher to the wide variety of applicable options available within a library.

Creating that positive impact with a student from day one is critical. That first interaction with a librarian is the beginning of the library's brand in the mind of the student. A negative or incomplete outcome can leave the brand in a negative or precarious position. A negative brand image is almost impossible to overcome and can take years to reverse. Worse than this, the student with a negative brand image of the library can pass this along to other students, infecting others before their first encounter. These negative attitudes can erode the positive attitudes some students have created on their own or from previous librarian encounters in high school.

Showing real concern for the student's success can create a positive brand image and can help withstand or even reverse negative brand images held by cohorts. Engaging students in special events and other activities that are designed to create positive outcomes can lead to faster brand adoption and build on brand equity. The library cannot afford to miss a brand equity building opportunity and must do all it can to prevent erosion. The end result is a student who turns to the library for help, and having received it, has a better chance to succeed. Building better students is not only a good outcome for the library and the university, but it creates lifetime learners, a society-building success. These successful students can be counted on to spread the word that the library can help, whether the need is a good term paper or long-term research expertise.

Connecting to Faculty

Rather than using a survey to take the temperature of the faculty (a much smaller population), the best approach for the millennial library is personal engagement. This can be in the form of events targeting particular department or schools, or even projects within these schools. Being narrow and specific in its approach to faculty reinforces the sense that the library sees these researchers and educators as unique. Speaking the "language" of a particular department is extremely valuable in winning over faculty to the academic commons. Faculty should come away from these encounters with the belief that the library and specifically its librarians "speak to them" and their special needs. All departments see themselves as unique, just as many faculty feel they are doing work that has little or no connection outside their school or department.

Focus groups are a very effective tool to reach faculty and identify what they see as their needs or problems. Focus groups as a research methodology are, in many ways, opposite to surveys. Gathering small groups of faculty into meetings where they can discuss in plain terms what they are unable to accomplish can obviously provide invaluable information to librarians seeking to establish an academic commons. Such groups can also share success stories than can be leveraged to reach faculty in other departments, schools, and colleges. If a technique, approach, or idea worked in one place, it is likely that it will work elsewhere.

Inviting faculty to receptions, creating a multitude of faculty committees to help the library in specific and relevant areas, and placing librarians in departments one or two days a week are all excellent tools to bridge what is sometimes a wide gap between educators and library personnel. Receptions can be informal, perhaps purposed to introduce a new service or benefit for researchers, or a new tool for educators. Purposeful faculty committees can create buy-in among not only the faculty serving on the committee, but others back in their departments or schools. Giving faculty a sense of involvement in decision making can produce a sense of ownership and concern for the library's welfare. Involving the faculty early in the creation of new services can create a team of promoters who will sell the innovation to their cohorts.

And, as in the case with students, listening carefully and using a great deal of patience can prevent breakdowns between librarians and faculty. From the faculty's perspective, the library may appear to be a vaguely structured group that "doesn't understand" the needs of faculty or even understand the nature of their research. Faculty rarely show the initiative to navigate what they may see as a murky library administrative structure, run by individuals perceived as deaf to the needs of researchers and educators. Part of the gap between faculty and librarians is the specific academic knowledge and expertise known by one side (faculty) and the more generalized—or perceived to be—knowledge base of the other (librarians).

On the other hand, some librarians may feel shut off from faculty and students, asked to respond only to the problems encountered by patrons. Standing behind counters presents a barrier between those who have the specific knowledge need. Creating more positive encounters can lead to a more trusting relationship. Librarians have built very strong and positive bonds when they step out from behind counters and move around the library offering their help to faculty and students, and also going to departments and visiting one-on-one with faculty. It is the trust that can smooth the introduction of new services within an academic commons. Libraries that take the time to build a positive relationship with faculty and students by reaching out to these individuals can also expect to see more support and involvement in the adoption of innovations. Such support is key in the next area, convincing university administrators that an academic commons is not only a good idea, but will have early adoption among students and faculty.

Convincing University Administration

As mentioned earlier, most university administrators are focused on budgets and student enrollments. To reach this group requires a specific agenda be developed that addresses the bottom line value of an academic commons. General discussions of helping faculty and working with students are likely to generate equally vague responses from administrators. When it comes to balancing the books, the university will look at every unit with scrutiny and weigh cost versus need to determine the value of each.

This is where a strong relationship with faculty and students can work to the library's advantage. Students who perceive the library as a solution to their graduation will see a move by the university administration to not support that success as a threat. Faculty who believe the library can enhance their research through facilitating cohort collaboration in grant writing, for example, will see a lack of funding for such an initiative by the university administration as a blow against faculty success. The library can talk all day to administrators about the value of an academic commons. Without a clear image of the value of such an academic commons, the idea becomes just one of many projects at the university that seek funding.

The key here is that the faculty and students feel they are defending their needs to the administrators and making a case for support of initiatives that will lead to more research, teaching, and learning success. The tools provided through an academic commons are not nearly of as great a value as the actual delivery of the resources. Again, we are not talking features here. We are talking benefits. When the served community adopts the concept that Service X will increase their success, that product becomes a "need" for them, not an administration's perceived library "want."

In a very real way, we are talking about the outcomes of buy-ins. We are also presenting a model that requires librarians loosening their grip on the steering wheel of innovation. Coming up with a list of software and notifying faculty and students that they must adopt each on the list will not generate the necessary buy-in to put the university administration on notice. University acceptance of the library as the center of technology will generate turf battles. These battles must be won if the millennial library is to take its place as the leader in learning and research.

THE MARKETING OF THE ACADEMIC COMMONS: TEN MILESTONES

Here are some possible outcomes to the direction we are on with libraries in the new millennium.

1. With the advent of cooperative cataloging, specific monographs will exist at only a few university libraries, and will be shared with other libraries. Duplication of books by multiple libraries will end.
2. All journal research will exist online only.
3. Far less space will be dedicated to the storage of monographs.
4. Library budgets will focus on personnel over software.
5. The role of the library will be to guide students and researchers, and to be a teacher to educators.
6. A library as a physical place of brick and mortar will be supplanted by the millennial library, online and available anywhere at any time.
7. Students will view the library as an asset. Librarians will facilitate, engage, and assist, largely online, but also one-on-one with students.
8. Librarians will be outside the library building, reaching out to faculty wherever they are. A far closer relationship between faculty and librarians will develop as faculty come to see librarians as change agents and solution experts.
9. University administrators will see the commons and the millennial library as an asset and support for the good of faculty and students.
10. Librarians will know where the research data is, how to retrieve it, and how to store it.

SUMMARY

As the library rolls out a proposed new mission and the services that will be part of a millennial library, it should be prepared to field a variety of responses. For university administrators, it is likely to be "How much will this cost?" followed quickly by "Can we make any money doing this?" For university faculty, it could be "Will my published research be valued by my department?" followed by "Do I own the rights to my research, research data, work notes?" For the university students, it is most likely going to be a familiar "What's in it for me?" which, notably, is not that far away from the previously described interests of university administrators and faculty.

Every project faces a point where it must prove that it is relevant and necessary. The millennial library is no different. Do students need a new e-mail system? Do faculty need a research commons area? Do university administrators see the library as a research core that fuels academic success? Finding out how the core interest groups of the library feel about the potential of an academic commons not only will guide what areas should be created first, but also the areas that may never be required at all.

For the library to become a millennial library, it must see itself as a product with features, benefits, and a marketing plan. And, in regard to features and benefits, library administrators must understand that the former is what is created and the latter is what is marketed. No library will complete the conversion to a millennial library if it fails to understand that what it sees itself and its features to be are of little value in the battle to convert the image that users (administrators, faculty, and students) have of a building with bookshelves.

We see features; they see benefits. The library survey plan should focus on the benefits of the academic commons, not the features. This requires that the library marketing staff think like administrators, faculty, and students, each of whom have their own view (or brand) of the library.

- If the university can show success, it can expect to at least hold on to the funding it already receives and, possibly, experience an increase.
- If faculty members succeed in publishing research, they not only can expect success in rank and tenure, but also in grant applications.
- Students clearly link their degrees to future success financially (as well as, it is admitted, emotional satisfaction).

Success of any marketing plan rests on ensuring the targeted groups can answer those issues. "How will the new software or service increase success among the patrons who use it?" is a good question. A better one, however, is "Will the patrons see the new software or service as a tool that will increase their success?" Answering this question requires we first understand the need that would be fulfilled by the new software or service, not from the perspective of the software's brochure, but from the potential users.

Underlying issues and needs might lead library administration to consider changes or updates heretofore not considered of importance. Be ready to answer specific concerns:

- Frustration expressed by a student regarding a research paper may reveal a need for tutoring on research databases.

- Faculty noting how hard and time consuming they find it to build a consensus on a grant project may reveal a need to exchange ideas and corrections in real time with cohorts off campus in a secure area.
- Administrators asking questions regarding ongoing projects may reveal a need for more "instant information" on how some group is using the library on a day-to-day basis.

Identify the areas of needs—services that will actually be used eagerly by the target users. These needs might include reformatting of existing services or adding new services, as well as changing how the services are presented. Understand that some library patrons are unaware of what they are missing and what an academic commons can do for them. In cases like this, simply posing a question might reveal profound needs.

Behavior tracking—the new rock star of marketing—provides data about how users are surfing the library website and what specific areas are getting the most interest. Behavior tracking notes which pages the user accesses in relation to other pages in terms of time and repeat visits. But it also can match a stated need, as expressed in a search term, with the actual need of the site user.

Creating a Brand and a Brand Statement

Consumers create brands. Library patrons create an image of the facility and what it does well and what it does poorly. This is referred to as the brand equity. Every effort should be made to improve on the brand equity. The brand of a library may be supported by a slogan and may be fed by an ongoing marketing campaign. Yet, it cannot be created by either of these activities. Patrons build an image of their library based on personal experiences and what they hear from others, especially their peers. No amount of advertising will convince them that something they see as a negative is actually a positive.

Connecting to Students

Surveys of student perceptions should extend beyond those who actually use the library. The much larger population for many universities is comprised of students who very rarely, if at all, go to the library either in person or online. They are using alternative sources, such as Google or Google Scholar, to find the information they need for a term paper or report. Attracting these students to the millennial library and all of its components requires making it very clear to them that by simply using a tool like Google Scholar, the student may be missing a broader array of resources. Students who access the library services strictly online from their apartment or dorm room are also a very important population, and one that likely has a far different perspective on potential new services and support. This population is looking for 24/7 support, either via e-mail or, more likely, live chat or instant messaging. The issues these students may have can obviously vary widely, and whoever is on the other end of the wire at the library must be sensitive to the confused and unfocused questions posed.

Connecting to Faculty

Rather than using a survey to take the temperature of the faculty, the best approach for the millennial library is personal engagement. This can be in the form of events targeting particular departments or schools, or even projects within these schools. Faculty should come away from these encounters with the belief that the library and specifically its librarians "speak to them" and their special needs.

Focus groups are also a very effective tool to reach faculty and identify what they see as their needs or problems.

Convincing University Administration

To reach this group requires a specific agenda be developed to address the bottom-line value of an academic commons. When it comes to balancing the books, the university will look at every unit with scrutiny. The library must leverage its strong relationship with faculty and students. Students who perceive the library as a solution to their graduation will see a move to not support that success as a threat. Faculty who believe the library can enhance their research through facilitating cohort collaboration in grant writing, for example, will see a lack of funding for such an initiative as a blow against their success.

Ultimate Outcomes

After the academic commons has been built, it must be sold—to its patrons. Carefully developed research will point the way. The starting point should be to build the brand image in each of the target consumer groups: students, faculty, and administrators. Building a brand requires knowing exactly what the existing user base believes about the library, then working from that to create brand equity. The communication starts with identifying how the various consumer targets feel about the library and what they need in terms of academics. A professor may need help with teaching. Students almost always are looking for ways to perform better on exams and essays.

Administrators are looking for leverage to raise the institution's status. All of this requires "outside-in" terms that touch on the consumer's needs, not the library's features.

Hard choices are ahead. Students must come to see libraries as facilitators of success. Researchers must see the librarian as a cohort, helping with the right tools for the right jobs. Administrators must see the millennial library at the center of the university's success, whether that is in learning, teaching, or research. And librarians must walk out from behind their counters—as many are already doing—ready to share new ideas that will help their patrons achieve success.

NOTE

1. Susan Gardner and Susanna Eng, "What Students Want: Generation Y and the Changing Function of the Academic Library," *Portal: Libraries and the Academy* 5, no. 3 (2005): 405.

Chapter Ten

Long-Term Challenges

Politics, Staffing, and the Fourth Commons

WHAT'S AHEAD?

New media technologies have an uncanny way of making many of yesterday's jobs irrelevant and many of today's jobs tenuous. And, at times, the very people responsible for keeping up with the latest software updates and new tools are rendered obsolete by these very same innovations. An illustration of this would be one of the issues surrounding the creation of the Internet itself. When the federal government complained to the company it had tapped to upgrade the nation's communication network in the 1960s—AT&T—that it was dragging its feet, that company's chief executive officer bluntly noted he was being asked to create a technology that would ultimately put his own company out of business. That threat may have been exaggerated. AT&T still exists. Yet the fear that a new innovation may render some human tasks unnecessary is certainly not an exaggeration. One needs to look no further than the auto industry to track the effect of robotics on worker jobs.

Many university information technology groups face a similar issue: Should they install software that renders some portion of their team unnecessary? Should they outsource to private vendors such basic tools as e-mail, and by doing so cut on-campus staff positions? For example, would a private ISP's support to online software users, especially those within a university academic commons area, warrant cutting dozens of library positions? Can online tutorials supplant in-person contact among faculty, students, and librarians?

These questions are important to the academic commons for two reasons. First, the heart of any academic commons—be it a learning, teaching, or faculty commons—is technology. The latest, the best, and the most relevant to the patron groups: faculty and students want what is in greatest demand. Yet, the second reason for giving some thought to the role of new media within a library are the people that make the library a library: librarians. As libraries move forward, the questions of their relevancy in a high technology landscape and amid the swirling, uncertain realities of university funding, puts in doubt any move to create an academic commons. Why can't a university just offer online access, ILL, and be done with it?

The answers are complex. For starters, these technology staffers on the nation's campuses are responsible for much more than just e-mail. They play an important role in making sure university students and faculty have access to various areas of the university—from payroll to distance education—all on a secure network. They are on constant alert for software upgrades, new methods, and innovative ways of addressing challenges. They are not directly part of a library at many universities. They are often called IT, which certainly sounds very much like a library function. But at some universities, such as at Kansas State University, they operate independently of library administration.

The issue is raised because every library considering an academic commons must start first with its relationship with the university's IT group. If the group is independent, it is likely change will occur based on an outside agenda. Such an arrangement may drive the library administration to create its own technology staff. While this may lead to some friction and perceived overlap, the library technology group's task of establishing and maintaining an academic commons may be required, if only to ensure a degree of independence.

In part, the role of such a library technology team would be to help faculty who find the tracking of new media tools a distraction from their teaching and research. For university staff engaged in providing student and faculty support, this constant chasing after the updates and new software solutions can be a real headache. Not only is this a moving target, it is a rapidly moving, ever-changing target.

Library IT professionals are keenly aware of the issues that emerge daily in the realm of new media. They've dealt with change for decades, whether it involved microfilm, electronic databases, or an academic commons. They have witnessed the elimination of card catalogs, the increased use of ILL services, and the irresistible shift from paper to bytes. Every innovation that comes to an academic library forces a reevaluation of not only the services being offered, but also the staff that delivers or maintains these services.

Unless the university and its library are willing to constantly reassess the goals and duties of its technology teams, they will either fall behind the curve in what they provide their patrons (to the harm of students and faculty) or will be forced to justify their existence on a constant basis (to the harm of their staff). The result is ironic: Technology can represent a threat to those very staffers responsible for implementing the latest and greatest renditions.

This uneasy alliance with technology—which is the mother's milk of innovation and progress—is not unique to libraries. Innovation is not always predictable and does not come in smooth patterns. What may have appeared to be the best approach one day, looks less profitable the next. What was a sure thing was that a team would spend ten years planning a new technology rollout, only to see it become obsolete after just one year. The comprehensive planning and long-term software adoption schedules that are features of a university information technology team's matrix are almost impossible to create and maintain in the fluid environment of the inevitable academic commons software and hardware advances. The solutions for needed changes within an academic commons rise far more rapidly and far more often than the longer-term planning pattern of university information technology teams.

Library administration faces the same pressure experienced in any profession: the desire to settle on one path and one solution and then to continue on that path—a kind of inertia—that is almost irresistible. Many university administrative teams favor just such a comprehensive planning approach, especially in terms of budgeting and upgrades. Long-term planning would seem to allow for smooth, predictable change to be managed most efficiently. If change would just behave itself and be predictable, a comprehensive approach might work. But change is clearly unpredictable: The Internet landscape is littered with the remains of ideas, products, and companies rendered unnecessary. Consider data storage devices: tape replaced by disk, replaced by larger disk, replaced by CD-ROM, replaced by DVD, replaced by memory sticks, replaced by, at some point, presumably, the cloud. A hot item this year can be overtaken by an even hotter idea next year. In such a rapidly changing environment, an incremental approach to change is likely to be better suited to accommodate the latest software and hardware options. Such an approach, which has its home in policy studies, argues that a plan that looks only a short distance ahead, allows for "course corrections." The philosophy is grounded in the belief that not all of the possible variables necessary for a comprehensive approach can be identified sufficiently to justify a comprehensive, multiyear plan. Given the constant updating of software (e.g., Microsoft) and the introduction of entirely new platforms (e.g., Google, Google Scholar, Google Books, Google apps, and the tens of thousands of mobile apps), a step-wise approach would not only seem appropriate but the only possible reliable option. Whatever limits we may have felt in the 1990s that put bounds on anticipated bandwidths and CPU speeds, advances in both after the turn of the century have made the ancient wish for high-speed to handheld devices now a reality. When it comes to computers and networks, speeds are reaching the point that almost anything can be accomplished, including the kind of academic commons proposed here. One need only review the text of "Did

You Know," a high school student project created in 2006, to feel the speed at which change in technology is upon us. Or consider that a new blog was being created every 30 seconds in 2006.[1] Or the recent predictions of the death of the Web itself, as suggested in the chart below.

Table 10.1. Is the Web Dying? (Domains and Internet Statistics for September 1, 2010)

All	*New*	*Deleted*	*Transferred*	*TLD*
122,278,599	77,938	93,307	85,694	All TLDs
89,507,345	52,963	57,963	61,174	.COM
13,315,010	8,041	8,344	8,011	.NET
8,696,108	5,929	5,731	4,800	.ORG
6,926,182	7,837	17,957	9,902	.INFO
2,114,721	1,645	1,803	881	.BIZ
1,719,233	1,523	1,509	926	.US

TLD= Top-level domains

Source: Whois Source, www.whois.sc/internet-statistics/

What has been put forth in the past nine chapters is that millennial librarians are uniquely qualified to meet the needs to constantly update technology, constantly consider new options, and constantly communicate this to faculty and students. As we have argued, these librarians are not just the storage agents of information. They are the managers of a new relationship between their patrons and information, some information located within the library, some located elsewhere; some data created by faculty on campus, some created in concert with others off campus; and some research made available instantly, created by the interaction with the academic commons itself. Part of the process that allows faculty and students to find that information relies upon librarians to constantly look for better solutions, new research tools, improved teaching matrixes. This is not a time for the slow-footed. However, it is also not the time for willy-nilly launches into new services. The best millennial libraries will be those that can balance the need for flexibility and nimbleness with the critical ability to identify and foster good ideas, while identifying and eliminating the bad ones. Over time, the best library technology practices will rise to the top, research on these options will be shared using the academic commons itself, and the very same interaction expected to happen within the commons among academics will occur among those librarians seeking to create, refine, and maintain a commons, be it learning, teaching, or research.

The need to remain nimble applies to every area of a university. It is not suggested here that the ability to adopt new ideas is any more important among millennial librarians than it is, say, within a school of medicine. However, the ways in which researchers in a medical school collaborate with cohorts to create breakthroughs in cures will rely heavily on the activities within an academic commons. In this way, all streams of progress will increasingly flow through the millennial library and its staff. We will look at three factors that will have significant impacts on the success or failure of a millennial library: the committee charged with creating and directing the academic commons, changes in technology, and the long-term relevance of the commons to its patrons.

THE MILLENNIAL LIBRARY COMMITTEE

The most valuable committee the library administration could form would be one that knows its mission is progress and that such progress comes, at least in part, through a willingness to constantly change and adopt new procedures. That is, the committee must be focused on looking at every option, including outsourcing—if that is the best path—and avoid creating walls around "most favored" projects. The key here is to create best practices, not best staff relations—though there are no reasons why both cannot be achieved. Such a committee starts from the premise that software, once installed, can be replaced almost immediately by a better option. Of course these changes create more work for library staff and more resistance even from library patrons who have become familiar with the former software. Thus, these decisions must be made carefully and with compassion for those involved. But, if the ultimate advantage of switching to a new online platform is powerful, then all those affected by the change must feel they are part of the decision process. Rather than acting dictatorial, the millennial committee will seek to convince and persuade both the library staff and its patrons that the change is beneficial in the long run by clearly laying out the advantages of the new idea. This last point is so very important. Rather than hiding behind the features of the new software, for example, the millennial committee will work hard to show the specific benefits to its patrons and users—students and faculty.

Any committee that avoids change merely creates a barrier to progress. A locked-in-place or even slow-to-change committee policy will put students and faculty at a disadvantage. Students will not be given access to the best tools to learn and create. Faculty will be working with lower-standard platforms for teaching and research that not only will affect their own careers, but also hamper the progress of their students and the academy. This is a very important point: The new role of the library, that is, specifically the millennial library, is to serve as a conduit for progress. Progress in learning, teaching, and research. Whatever else the library administration may feel its duties are, addressing the need for the best tools to reach the highest standards in these three areas must remain paramount.

Given that software and hardware generally are considered out of date within two years after release, the need to keep all options open is obvious. This constant state of change should be reflected in the tenure of committee members themselves. Rotating in new members will keep the committee's perspectives fresh and relevant. Such rotations will also keep the millennial committee from "capture" by those with which it works in closest proximity: the library staff. However, while the committee must press for progress and updates, any hint of a constant state of distress or mistrust must be avoided. If the committee acts with openness and is aware that one of its roles is to evaluate all possible upgrades, the changes will be implemented more smoothly, quickly, and perhaps most importantly, successfully.

Committee members must include individuals from outside the library. These can be faculty, students, and administrators. They can also be staff from other universities who bring a unique view of library service. These committee members from outside the library should be selected based on their knowledge of online learning, teaching, and research tools. Such a committee should not include those students or faculty who have no interest in the advances that are central to the goals of this group. If a faculty member sees no use for new media, then he can hardly be expected to offer much in the way of insight or even support. This is a committee of the willing and the committed.

In a survey of faculty at a Midwest university, I found that faculty in the hard sciences—engineering, medicine, biology, chemistry—and the social sciences were the most interested in new online resources that could help their research and teaching. Those in the humanities were less interested. Those in the business school felt they had already created the necessary platforms for their work. It would be interesting to see if this pattern among schools and disciplines is repeated at other universities.

The task of choosing the committee should be that of the dean of libraries, rather than a university-wide electoral process or appointment by the faculty senate. Again, the value of such a committee is in its willingness to address the needs of the library and the academic commons, and the degree that it is comfortable with the certainty that change will be constant. The issue of change has been stressed repeatedly here because it is not in the tradition of some universities to see change as positive or necessary. Yet, no other endeavor will rely as heavily on change as the creation of a sustainable academic commons. Those universities that embrace change as the key element in their academic commons will reap the largest benefits.

The Technology: The Need for a Library-centric Commons

As we have said many times, this is a rapidly moving target. This is what has caused me the greatest stress in writing this book. With the certain knowledge that within moments of this work being published, new ideas, new platforms, and new software will be announced, this book is nonetheless offered as a guide. The fear of being "behind the curve" in the world of software is a reasonable one, and based on the certainty that we are always just a little behind, and that new tools of learning, teaching, and research are only days (hours?) away.

All of the academic commons we have discussed to this point—learning, teaching, and research—have been about, in part, keeping library patrons up to speed on new technology that will enhance their efforts, be it term papers, class syllabi, or academic papers. A millennial library committee may decide from its research that one more might be necessary before the others are even considered. A fourth commons should be considered by any university library to serve its own faculty: the LibTech commons. This fourth commons would serve the library's own faculty, and also might be most efficiently created and maintained by the staff at several universities acting in concert.

This multi-university millennial library commons would be the leaders in identifying the best new software packages and hardware devices. Most of these new software packages and hardware devices would be installed to assist patrons in the learning, teaching, and research commons, of course. But a separate class of software and hardware is now being created to help library technicians create and maintain their academic commons. This library-centric technology is also evolving rapidly, as are the various committees and support agencies within library science. We are in the midst of a blooming of sorts. More and more interest is being focused on the role of the university library in all areas of an institution's daily activities, as the library is being asked to participate actively in a university's success. For example, Capterra lists more than seventy-five options specifically intended to assist library technicians.[2] Included are tools such as Surpass meant to automate daily activities within a library.[3] First Systems is a platform intended to help librarians in "knowledge and portal management."[4]

Capterra is not the only software support center for librarians. EDUCause, a nonprofit "whose mission is to advance higher education by promoting the intelligent use of information technology" provides support to technology teams within universities. Some of the support is directed at elements of the academic commons suggested in this book, such as teaching and pedagogy. Other elements are more technically focused, targeting other activities within a university, such as user authentication.[5] ITIL Foundations offers software to support help desk activities.[6] Many more sites support library technology. (See Appendix B.)

Marshall Breeding of Library Technical Guides argued in 2000 that the current pace of change within library technology required its own online newsletter column, Library Technology Guides, based in part on his work at Vanderbilt University's library.

> One of the biggest challenges that a [library] systems office faces involves managing the problems and requests that come in from library staff and users. The incoming flow of tasks often seems relentless, and without an effective set of procedures, processes, and tools, a systems operation can really get bogged down. In this column I'll focus on some processes we have implemented at Vanderbilt to deal with this issue.[7]

Keeping up with all the possible options facing an academic commons in this coming decade might be more than one library can handle. And, in some ways, it would be ironic to suggest that students and faculty need their own academic commons, but librarians do not. They do. A LibTech commons, created specifically to help the library staff around the world stay current with the latest technology releases, could also provide ideas to overcome the other challenges we have discussed in the previous chapters. Rather than relying upon what could be found by a single library staff operating alone, the LibTech commons could unite library professionals into one global knowledge base.

Members would include all librarians, globally sharing ideas and suggesting revisions and updates of existing services and projects. More than a blog or message board, the LibTech commons could include collaborative platforms similar to those provided by a millennial library to its campus students and faculty. New ideas could be tested, reviewed, critiqued, and shared, all within a secure or open access online environment, and all available to librarians around the world.

Librarians, just as students, teachers, and researchers, need an online resource they can count on to be up-to-date, and a site that can be maintained by the users themselves. This lowers the amount of time any one library technology expert must spend tracking down new software and devices. We have an excellent model for this: Linux. Created in the early 1990s, Linux server software was the product of Linus Torvales and many other programmers who quickly jumped into the project, volunteering their time to improve the code of this worldwide project.[8] The LibTech commons would be very similar, with a hosting available at an open access site, such as ibiblio.org (nonprofit), or Scarecrow Press (private), and volunteers scattered across the globe at hundreds of university libraries providing the necessary information updates, dialogue, and evaluations.

Over time the site would become a natural place for those creating new support software and devices to "register" their ideas, thus reducing the need for any one librarian or committee to hunt down innovations alone. Open access and for-profit software creators could upload information and links to subject-specific feedback areas, such as interactive online whiteboards, or simple blogs for written or video comments. Users might review the proposed software or service after it is made available. A board or committee established by the LibTech commons users might also weigh in with its opinion. Either way, the new ideas would make their way to those most interested, evaluated by these users, and adopted or rejected by those participating on an individual basis.

Such a single global academic commons for librarians might be the first step to one unified library that crosses political boundaries. In many ways, this is far more than the database arrangements already in place. For example, PloS is "a nonprofit organization of scientists and physicians committed to making the world's scientific and medical literature a freely available public resource." Part of the mission of PloS is to actively seek "opportunities to work cooperatively with any group (scientific/scholarly societies, physicians, patient advocacy groups, educational organizations) and any publisher who shares our commitment to open access and to making scientific information available for the good of science and the public."[9] More than reflecting the ideas surrounding meta-databases we discussed previously, platforms such as PloS are actively seeking ways to break down the walls separating science and its users. In a similar fashion, the LibTech commons would provide a clearinghouse for software and hardware, best practices, and all of the issues raised in this book. It would be a one-stop answer center, as well as a place for collaboration among library researchers, just as the research commons is for nonlibrary academics.

In many ways, the active use of ILL by cooperative institutions reflects an effort to provide some elements of expanded coverage, as might be accomplished by joining two libraries into one. This is not to suggest that the day will come when we have one administrative structure overseeing one global library. But that may happen, and the creation of one global LibTech commons might represent the first step. Imagine a single repository for all updates and new ideas for information management. Such a cauldron of interaction among librarians across the globe might result in breakthroughs in areas of information science and the gathering and sharing of datasets mentioned earlier. Perhaps no one library could ever encapsulate the spirit of the Library of Alexandria, but hundreds or thousands of libraries acting in concert might. To a great degree, the ease with which libraries share and support each other in current activities is a very real manifestation of a single, massive Alexandrian cloud, available on every computer screen worldwide created by individuals perpetuating the tradition of online communities that stretches back to USENET groups of the 1970s. At the same time, the LibTech commons could be only one of multiple online catalogs, each addressing a specific area of learning, teaching, or scholarship.

LONG-TERM ISSUES OF ACCURACY: LINK ROT AND DOIS

As mentioned in chapter 1, research has shown that half of Web links—internal or external—will fail within four to six years on most websites. This "link rot half-life" is especially critical in academic research. In the era of printed volumes of research, citation to a particular page or a particular research article was simply a matter of getting it right the first time. Cite the journal or monograph, and abide by the particulars of any of the hundreds of citation styles and the job is done.

In the case of online research publishing, citations to pages within the same journal or to outside sources are a great deal more worrisome. How can a researcher reading an article online find the cited material if the link to that citation no longer functions?

At least two possible solutions have been proposed. The digital object identifier (DOI) provides a permanent (or nearly permanent) address for a URL by using a numeric string that can be associated with any electronic object, such as a research article or monograph. Unlike a standard website address, the structure of which can be manipulated by a site owner, the DOI provides a mechanism for locating the current URL for a document. Created by the International DOI Foundation, DOI offers a more stable mechanism for linking to online content. The International DOI Foundation developed and implemented this solution to link sustainability in the late 1990s. It has been proliferated to a range of publishing applications since 2000. At last count in 2009, approximately 43 million DOI names had been assigned by some four thousand organizations.

A second popular option, Permalink, was developed by early blogger Matthew Haughey in response to concerns that links to online journal sites would fail.[10] Many online journal sites are built using a database, employing an underlying software such as MySQL. Dynamic Web pages within databases were notoriously known to shift at the addition of new files, creating link rot, or failed bookmarks and links used at external sites. By using Permalink, the citations would remain valid. Establishing an unchangeable set of characters that could include the author's name, title, subject, or other identifiers would work well to preserve the link itself. Permalink cannot preserve the actual content, as in the case of a file being deleted. But it can ensure that while the file remains online, the file can be found. The key element with Permalink is its ability to keep a link valid, even if a Web page address is renamed or moved within the site database. The Permalink remains unaltered, making it possible to create a link citation with some assurance it will remain valid for years to come.

Unfortunately, several versions of Permalink by various vendors have been created and marketed. To date, major blogging sites and software manufacturers have not agreed on one standard. And if you enter a blog site, such as theseoblogger.com/seo-blogs/wordpress/wordpress-seo-tutorial-permalink-structure/, you find that while most posters use "postname" in their Permalink, others prefer by title, date, and other references. It is best for the technologists involved with the LibTech commons to work this issue out to a standard agreeable within their group. Here are two blogs that might be accessed to start a library technology team down the road to a choice of the type of Permalink they would prefer:

Postname: The SEO Blogger. Discusses the use of Permalink within WordPress in a blog where a majority of the authors prefer using postname.[11]

Title: Modern Software Experience. A good discussion of the history of Permalink and the growing use. The author prefers using the "title" in the Permalink, but admits, "There are no official Permalink standards."[12]

An alternative to Permalink, persistent uniform resource locator (PURL), allows for "a level of indirection that allows the underlying Web addresses of resources to change over time without negatively affecting systems that depend on them."[13]

Bottom link, the choice of what type of tool to preserve links within an e-reserve is squarely the responsibility of the library technology group. Bringing that discussion within the library commons would help clarify the disparate opinions and might result in the agreeable adoption of one standard. As it is, the situation is unsettled.

KEEPING THE COMMONS RELEVANT TO ITS PATRONS

The pressure can be overwhelming to stay current. Since starting this book, I have witnessed the rollout of many new platforms and software, many bearing directly on the topic of this book. I have seen a breakthrough deal between

Google and book publishers and its (temporary?) demise. I have witnessed the creation and closing of academic commons. How can anyone keep up with all these changes? Any committee formed to consider the creation of a faculty commons, for instance, would face a constantly shifting landscape of new products that offer, literally, a premade, login-and-launch online collaborative environment. These packages—for some—may render the concept of an academic commons into a commodity, shifting users away from any necessity to understand what is happening behind the screen, where the data is being stored, or how the interactions are supported in real time. An example of a product moving into a commodity status might be website construction itself. Ten years ago, if a student asked me if Web design might be a good career choice, my answer would have been an unequivocal "yes!" Today, a website can be purchased from a well-established, brand-name vendor for as little as $5 a month, with hundreds if not thousands of design templates available. This is the transformation of a craft into a commodity, at least at one end of the spectrum. Yes, high-powered php-driven sites require more high-tech expertise, and these sites are anything but a commodity. But the ability for an average company to set up a simple Web presence is undeniably simpler and cheaper than when the first Web editor burst on the scene a dozen years ago.

The problem with commodity-sized academic commons platforms is the same with the generic $5-a-month website designs: they are generally one-size-fits-all in performance and user experience. This might satisfy some library administrators who feel the pressure—but not the need—to establish an academic commons. It is unlikely such a vanilla academic commons will satisfy that university's library patrons. In some ways this is similar to a personal experience I had with a city website where schedules for softball games were posted as word processing files, not HTML. When I inquired as to why the information was not converted to HTML, the reply was "we were told to get it on the site. It's on the site." A similar experience occurred while I was managing a state board of regents website. If the protocol is loosely defined, the solution will take the path of least effort.

The constantly shifting copyright and intellectual property rights standards that are circling over the administration of all academic commons are another area of great concern. Within a few months, Google Books, for example, went from no progress in handling copyright, to seemingly a completed deal, to a court decision stalling major portions of the project. Intellectual property rights are no less sticky, with a variety of players vying for control of the data, as also discussed earlier.

Perhaps more than any project on campus, creating an academic commons—learning, teaching, research, or all three together—requires that those involved be aware this is not a launch-and-walk-away project. For this reason, a library administration needs to carefully consider the composition of the team that will establish the academic commons website, as well as all the other services we have discussed thus far. And, of no less importance, it must be just as concerned when choosing those expected to run this operation. Those involved in both the construction and management must be flexible thinkers, ready to shift to new, better options. This is not a common quality among universities, where the comprehensive approach seems preferred: "set a path and go." This might be an acceptable model for choosing the variety of flowers for the university gardens, but only if that choice is made one year at a time. Building an academic commons is similar in nature: step-wise decisions must be open to modification as the software and hardware markets change.

One of the toughest jobs for library administration interested in establishing an academic commons is lack of up-to-date training among its staff, and, less frequently, a lack of willingness among some employees to learn new software or new ways to interact with patrons. While almost all libraries can boast of individuals within their staffs that can cruise the software of ILL or online catalogs and databases, the line often stops there. In some libraries, technologically aware staffers become a sort of elite that other, less "techie" staffers use as a buffer. Why learn any of these new ideas when there are people to whom we can route technology questions and research requests?

This diversion technique would be less damaging to the value of a library to its university if the demand for answers were to remain constant and predictable. But students are rapidly moving away from the traditional desktops that most of us are familiar with and into a realm of fully mobile, always connected computing. Following these students as they switch on their iPods, Droids, and iPads requires a library's staff be at least aware of the nature of these new computing devices, if not completely comfortable in their uses. This changeover to handheld reading devices is especially clear when one considers the rapid evolution of the iPad itself. The marriage of a device with the thousands of apps created to expand its capabilities opens up wide vistas of possibilities in education.

An even more difficult challenge is the demand by faculty for librarians to know where everything is and be able to deliver all the information immediately. As noted by Jonathan Shaw in *Harvard Magazine* in 2010: "The skills that librarians have traditionally possessed seem devalued by the power of online search, and less sexy than a Google query launched from a mobile platform."[14]

This does not differ by much from the common problem among university faculty who are older and less interested in learning new tricks. As one science professor was heard to say in a discussion about the university possibly requiring students to have portable computers, "If they have laptops in my class, they'll be looking at online porn." This reflects the fear some faculty have of new technology in their classrooms. This fear cannot be allowed to exist in a millennial library. Requiring that all staff members at a library (or professors at a university) open a Twitter account or create a Facebook page may seem unrealistic, yet students are more and more relying on Facebook to share ideas with friends. Faculty are using Twitter to converse with cohorts. Instant messaging is rampant. The options available to communicate within a university are exploding, moving rapidly away from static websites (and the Web itself) and more toward social networks (and non-Web apps). To remain in touch and relevant to patrons, millennial librarians must eagerly embrace new communication tools. Relying on e-mail will no longer be enough to engage students and faculty in conversations about the academic commons.

The concept of a librarian as a collector and retriever of information is still very relevant, especially within an age of information that is out of control. Again, as noted by Shaw, the "vision of future librarians as digital-information brokers rather than stewards of physical collections is already taking shape in the scientific disciplines. . . . In fields faced with information overload—such as biology, coping with a barrage of genomic data, and astronomy, in which an all-sky survey telescope can generate a terabyte of data in a single night—the torrents of raw information are impossible to absorb and understand without computational aids."[15]

The trouble is, as discussed earlier in this book, undergraduates are generally ignorant about how to find the best information online or off, and graduate students are little better. As noted by Palfrey in *Born Digital:* "We need them to be guides in this increasingly complex world of information and we need them to convey skills that most kids actually aren't getting at early ages in their education. I think librarians need to get in front of this mob and call it a parade, to actually help shape it."[16]

THE FUTURE

Here are some possible (likely?) outcomes to the direction we are on with millennial libraries in the near term—within this decade, or sooner.

Clustering of Libraries to Serve Common Needs

With the advent of cooperative cataloging, specific monographs will exist at only a few university libraries and will be shared with other libraries. Duplication of books by multiple libraries within a geographic area will end. These clusters of libraries will cooperate through their own LibTech commons to create and maintain their learning, teaching, and research commons. Information, specifically research and data sharing, will flow freely between all of these commons. Over time, the cooperation between libraries—now seen in shared storage facilities—will extend to areas of administrative functions. Distant management of staff, similar to that of a manufacturing company with multiple plants and one central financial office, could result in cost-savings, even within multiple university libraries.

Journal Publishing Online

The millennial library will facilitate more online journals, as well as more open access research. Over time, individual libraries will develop an area of specialty in their holdings, such as rural community development or leadership studies. Eventually, the nature of journal publishing will evolve into individual articles published by researchers, edited and proofread by the same professionals now in that field, both inside and outside of commercial publishing houses. The rating of these articles will be conducted by editorial boards operating in much the same fashion they do today, except with more participation in an online rating system. The actual nature of publishing will include collaborative work on the part of cohorts, as well as the inclusion of UGC from invited commentators. All of this activity will take place within an academic commons constructed and managed by millennial librarians.

Print Monographs Will Slowly Disappear from Library Shelves

Print journals are already being withdrawn from many university library shelves. Monographs are sure to follow, at some point. As the demand for space increases within universities and their libraries, less space will be dedicated to the storage of print monographs. Already, university staffs are evaluating what journals and monographs are available online and simply removing the print versions from their stacks. The rise in the use of handheld e-readers (along with their increased sophistication) will lessen the need for bound copies of the classics (pre-1923, as of 2010). As issues of copyright are resolved, more and more books will be converted to electronic format. The major portion of new books is likely to be print and, in some part will also be stored electronically. But the economics of print will drive more and more new publishing online exclusively, eventually. As of today, online books represent a miniscule portion of published monographs and the adoption rate on digital readers feels much like the experience we had with computer standards in the 1980s: all over the board. Until some agreeable standards and some more evolved readers are created, the replacement of paper with bytes will remain slow (but steady).

Library Budgets Will Support Staff over Software

The millennial library budgets of the future will focus more and more on staff and less on software. Part of this trend can be associated with cloud computing, but also the dire need for trained librarians to keep track of the vast amount of data that will be available online. In addition, working with students and faculty will require more personnel, despite the likely increase in video tutorials and other online technologies. As education continues to move to distance education platforms, the demand for staff to support these new learners will increase. If a university values its library staff to support its online learning efforts, the inclusion of a library fee for every student enrolled would be one way the additional staff could be funded. This makes far more sense than a library user fee, which would very likely drive down actual use of the learning, teaching, or research commons. Those universities that find innovative ways to fund larger library staffs in tough economic times will reap the benefits of higher graduation rates, successful (and grateful) alumni, and a higher quality and quantity of faculty research. A university library is no place to scrimp. As noted by a Harvard researcher: "Even at Harvard, [where] we spend millions of dollars [annually for access to the databases,] many of the medical staff, graduate students, and residents don't know how to use. . . . " he pauses. "Well, it's worse than that. They don't know that they exist."[17]

The Millennial Librarian as Guide

The role of the librarian will be that of guide to students and researchers, and teacher to educators. As the amount of information increases past 2 trillion Web pages in a few years (perhaps months), the need for a professional hunter will increase. Universities and researchers will covet a librarian trained in the science of the search. This emerging science—searchology—will also become an art form. The best searchers will work with academics to create the best research outcomes. It is likely, as well, that some of the very best searchers will break away from the academy to offer their services in the private sector, at a premium. The art of finding the best answers will be much sought after and rewarded. In a way, this shift to an independent search professional is occurring today within journalism. As more and more former newspaper and television reporters are fired, many of them are setting up their own information gathering and dissemination operations. What some are seeking are online editors to brush up their copy, as well as online proofers to correct their typos and grammar. This is a result of an industry's collapse. Independent searchologists would reflect the opposite trend: the rise of a new industry within an increasingly successful and important profession.

The Library as an "edu" Institution

A library as a physical place of brick and mortar will be supplemented by the millennial library, online and available anywhere, any time. Given the expectation of a sharp increase in distance education, the library will be required to staff its online portals 24/7. The global student community will require access to these learning experts, search experts, and academic commons experts around the clock. This will include live chat sessions, as well as e-mail and Twitter. The academic commons will be available everywhere at any time. Thus librarians will also be required to assist learners and researchers at any time of the day (or night).

Students to View the Library as an Asset: Perhaps a Fifth Commons for Professionals

Millennial librarians will facilitate, engage, and assist, largely online, but also one-on-one with students. This relationship will very likely continue well after the student graduates. As students come to see the millennial library as a key part of their professional success, they will request the library continue to help them, whether they are scientists, writers, or artists. The need for information will demand a portal—a professional commons—that the millennial library will be uniquely situated to provide. This fifth commons will work exclusively with professionals in the private sector, helping them progress and improve their skills by finding the best information and best tutorials online. This service could be provided via an app sold or offered with a small subscription fee, and given the implications of Anderson's Long Tail Theory, could be a source of significant income for the library in the future. The basis of the fee, of course, is not the information—that's free. It is the ability to find the information that will require the app, fee or not. And, in the future as it is today, the best information searches will be conducted by millennial librarians.

Roaming Librarians

Librarians will be outside the brick-and-mortar building, reaching out to faculty and students wherever they are: in classrooms, offices, departments, dorms, and dining halls. Subject librarians will visit their departments, setting up shop literally in the building on a regular schedule. Generalists and research specialists will meet with students across campus, rather than waiting for the students to come to the library. Professors will be visited in their offices and given advice on new research resources, as well as feedback on new teaching resources. A far closer relationship between faculty, students, and librarians will develop as faculty come to see librarians as change agents and solution experts. Students and faculty will come to identify a particular librarian or small group of librarians as "their guides."

The Library Must Be Seen as the Core Unit of the University

University administrators will see the academic commons and the millennial library as an asset, even more than many do today. The identification of academic commons online resources as beneficial to the education of students and the improvement of faculty teaching and research will underscore the prime role of the library in the success of the university. They will also come to see the multiple collaboration of several university libraries as a net plus. This may take time, but as we see more and more collaboration among universities to deliver online education,[18] universities will come to see a similar collaboration among multiple library staffs to generate more learning, higher teaching standards, and higher quality research.

All Information Will Flow through the Millennial Library

Whether it is researched by university faculty, taught in university classrooms, or published by university authors, the millennial library will be the crossroads of all information. Facilitating online conversations among researchers, training educators in new classroom techniques, and helping students become better learners, librarians will act as a integral part of daily life at the university. These highly trained information science professionals will know the best practices in teaching and learning, and will know the location of the best research data, how to retrieve it, and how to store it.

SUMMARY

The adoption and dissemination of new technology can have devastating effects on existing industries and their workers. Yet, for some industries, such as information science, innovation must be embraced despite its potential impacts. As libraries move forward they must be seeking out, evaluating, and adopting new technologies. This will require a constant eye on retraining library staff to use new tools and teaching others to do the same. Failure to embrace the best software on the part of librarians will lead to a drop in best practices, to the detriment of faculty and students.

What has been put forth in the past nine chapters is that millennial librarians are uniquely qualified to meet the need to constantly update technology, constantly consider new options, and constantly communicate this to faculty and students. Part of the process that allows faculty and students to find that information relies upon librarians constantly looking for better solutions, new research tools, improved teaching matrixes. Over time, best library technology practices will rise to the top, research on these options will be shared using the academic commons itself, and the very same interaction expected to happen within the commons among academics will occur among those librarians seeking to create, refine, and maintain this new "place" that will exist both online and offline.

The millennial committee will work hard to show the specific benefits to its users—students and faculty. Committee members must include individuals from outside the library. These can be faculty, students, and administrators. They can also be staff from other universities who bring a unique view of library service. In a survey of faculty at a Midwest university, I found that faculty in the hard social sciences were the most interested in new online resources that could help their research and teaching. Those in the humanities were less interested.

All of the academic commons we have discussed to this point—learning, teaching, and research—have been about, in part, keeping library patrons up to speed on new technology that will enhance their efforts, be it term papers, class syllabi, or academic papers. The university library committee should consider creating a fourth area to serve its own faculty: a LibTech commons. A LibTech commons, created specifically to help the library staff around the world stay current with the latest technology releases, could also provide ideas for the other challenges we have discussed in the previous chapters. Members would include all librarians, globally sharing ideas and suggesting revisions and updates of existing services and projects. More than a blog or message board, this LibTech commons could include collaborative platforms similar to those provided by a millennial library to its campus students and faculty. The site would be updated and maintained by the users themselves. This lowers the amount of time any one library technology expert must spend tracking down new software and devices. The LibTech commons would be hosted at an open access site, such as ibiblio.org (nonprofit) or Scarecrow Press (private), and volunteers scattered across the globe at hundreds of university libraries providing the necessary support.

Over time the site would become a natural place for those creating new support devices to "register" their ideas, thus reducing the need for any one librarian to hunt down innovations alone. Users might review the proposed software or service after it is made available. Such a single global LibTech commons for librarians might be the first step to one unified library that crosses political boundaries.

Half of a site's Web links—internal or external—will fail within four to six years on most websites. This "link rot half-life" is especially critical in academic research. For online research publishing, citations to pages within the same journal or to outside sources are worrisome. How can a researcher reading an article online find the cited material if the link to that citation no longer functions? At least two possible solutions have been proposed. DOI and Permalink are reliable solutions to concerns that links within online journal sites will fail.

Those involved in both the construction and management of an academic commons must be flexible thinkers, ready to shift to new, better options. The concept of a librarian as a collector and retriever of information is still very relevant, especially within an age of information that is out of control. However, undergraduates are generally ignorant about how to find the best information online or offline, and graduate students are little better. Only millennial librarians can stem this tide.

THE FUTURE

1. Libraries will cluster to serve common needs.
2. Journal publishing online will increase rapidly.
3. Print monographs will slowly—very slowly—disappear from library shelves.
4. Library budgets will support staff over software.
5. The millennial librarian will become a new scientific category: searchologist.
6. The library will become an online institution.
7. Students will increasingly view the library as an asset.
8. Millennial librarians will roam throughout the university.
9. The library will be valued by faculty as a partner in research, and by administrators as a partner in raising the reputation of the institution.
10. All information will flow through the millennial library.

The success of an academic commons at any university rests heaviest on its founding committee. This committee should reflect the university, but also should reflect those who are dedicated to the success of a commons. This is no time for gainsaying and pushback. Rather than acting dictatorial, however, the millennial committee will seek to convince both library staff and its patrons that any suggested change will be beneficial in the long run. And, the membership of the committee itself must change to prevent a buy-in to any one approach or any one software platform.

What is required as we move forward is bold leadership that takes on the ancient barriers, calms the doubts and fears of those more comfortable with paper, and universities willing to look past petty competition to the common good of humanity. For what is at stake in these commons, for students (learning) or for faculty (teaching and research), is progress on a scale we have never experienced. Fostering the sharing of resources and ideas, the academic commons could play the central and most important role in making the global university not only possible, but a success. And, it is this global learning institution that will be needed, if we are to succeed.

NOTES

1. A. Lenhart and S. Fox, "Bloggers: A Portrait of the Internet's New Storytellers," *Pew Internet & American Life Project* (19 July 2006), www.pewinternet.org/pdfs/PIP%20Bloggers%20Report%20July%2019%202006.pdf (accessed 10 July 2010).
2. www.capterra.com/library-automation-software?gclid=CLaSgu_i7aICFQLEsgodmkqIew
3. www.surpasssoftware.com/products.htm
4. www.optimus-prime.com
5. www.educause.edu
6. www.itilfoundations.com/software/helpdesk/
7. www.librarytechnology.org/ltg-displaytext.pl?RC=8992
8. www.linux.org/info/linux_timeline.html
9. www.plos.org
10. codex.wordpress.org/Using_Permalinks
11. theseoblogger.com/seo-blogs/wordpress/wordpress-seo-tutorial-permalink-structure/
12. www.tamurajones.net/MarkingPermalinks.xhtml
13. "Persistent Uniform Resource Locator," purl.org.
14. Jonathan Shaw, "Gutenberg 2.0: Harvard's Libraries Deal with Disruptive Change," *Harvard Magazine* 2010, no. 5 (May–June 2010), harvardmagazine.com/2010/05/gutenberg-2-0 (accessed 10 July 2010).
15. Shaw, "Gutenberg 2.0: Harvard's Libraries Deal with Disruptive Change."
16. John Palfrey and Urs Gasser, *Born Digital: Understanding the First Generation of Digital Natives* (New York: Basic Books, 2008), 365.
17. Shaw, "Gutenberg 2.0: Harvard's Libraries Deal with Disruptive Change."
18. The Great Plains Interactive Distance Education Alliance is one of the oldest and most successful distance education platforms in the world. More than a dozen universities in the Great Plains and elsewhere have agreed to allow students to matriculate at their schools, as well as others, receive their degree from the school of their choice, and pay uniform fees. www.gpidea.org.

Appendix A

Resources for Survey Techniques and Analysis

Allan, Graham, and Chris Skinner, eds., *Handbook for Research Students in the Social Sciences.* Falmer Press: London, 1991.

Assael, Henry, and John Keon, "Nonsampling vs. Sampling Errors in Survey Research," *Journal of Marketing* 46 (982): 114–123.

Babbie, Earl R. *Survey Research Methods.* Belmont, Calif.: Wadsworth, 1973.

Basic Tools for Process Improvement. Washington, D.C.: Department of the Navy, 1996, www.tql-navy.org.

Bangura, A. K. *The Limitations of Survey Research Methods in Assessing the Problem of Minority Student Retention in Higher Education.* San Francisco: Mellen Research UP, 1992.

Belson, W. A. *Validity in Survey Research.* Brookfield, Vt.: Gower, 1986.

Biemer, Paul P. "Nonresponse Bias and Measurement Bias in a Comparison of Face to Face and Telephone Interviewing," *Journal of Official Statistics* 17 (2001): 295–320.

Bollinger, Christopher R., and Martin H. David. *Sample Attrition and Response Error: Do Two Wrongs Make a Right?* Madison: University of Wisconsin Center for Demography and Ecology, 1995.

Brassard, M., and D. Ritter. *The Memory Jogger II: A Pocket Guide of Tools for Continuous Improvement and Effective Planning.* Methuen, Mass.: GOAL/QPC, 1994.

Braverman, M. "Sources of Survey Error: Implications for Evaluation Studies," *New Directions for Evaluation: Advances in Survey Research* 70 (1996): 17–28.

Busha, Charles H., and Stephen P. Harter. *Research Methods in Librarianship: Techniques and Interpretation.* Orlando: Academic Press, 1980.

Campbell, Angus, and Georgia Katona. "The Sample Survey: A Technique for Social Science Research," in *Research Methods in the Behavioral Sciences*, ed., Theodore M. Newcomb. New York: Dryden Press, 1953, 14–55.

Cannell, Charles F., and Floyd J. Fowler, "Comparison of a Self-Enumerative Procedure and a Personal Interview: A Validity Study," *Public Opinion Quarterly* 27 (1963): 250–264.

Carr, H. H. "Is Using Computer-based Questionnaires Better than Using Paper?" *Journal of Systems Management* 19 (1991): 37.

Cochran, William G. *Sampling Techniques,* 3rd ed. Boston: Harvard Press, 1977.

Converse, Jean M., and Stanley Presser. *Survey Questions: Handcrafting the Standardized Questionnaire.* Thousand Oaks, Calif.: Sage, 1986.

Cook, Thomas D., and Donald T. Campbell, *Quasi-Experimentation: Design and Analysis Issues for Field Settings.* Boston: Houghton Mifflin, 1979.

Culbertson, Amy, Archester Houston, Debbie Faast, Michael White, Monica Aguirre, and Carol Behr. *The Process Improvement Notebook.* Pub. No. 97-01 Washington, D.C.: Department of the Navy, TQLO, 1997.

Curtin, Richard, Stanley Presser, and Eleanor Singer. "The Effects of Response Rate Changes on the Index of Consumer Sentiment," *Public Opinion Quarterly* 64 (2000): 413–428.

Curtin, Richard. "Changes in Telephone Survey Nonresponse over the Past Quarter Century," *Public Opinion Quarterly* 69 (2005): 87–98.

Developing and using questionnaires, GAO/PEMD-10.1.7. Washington, D.C.: Government Printing Office, 1993.

Diamond, Shari S. "Methods for the Empirical Study of Law," in *Law and the Social Sciences*, eds. Leon Lipson and Stanton Wheeler. New York: Russell Sage Foundation, 1986.

Federal Quality Institute, *Self-assessment Guide for Organizational Performance and Customer Satisfaction.* Washington, D.C.: U.S. Government Printing Office, 1993.

Fowler, F. J. "Survey Research Methods," in *Applied Social Research Methods Series,* vol. 1. Newbury Park, Calif.: Sage, 1993.

Fox, J., and P. Tracy. *Randomized Response: A Method for Sensitive Surveys.* Beverly Hills, Calif.: Sage, 1986.

Garvin, D. A. "What Does 'Product Quality' Really Mean?" *Sloan Management Review* 26, no. 1 (Fall 1984): 25–43.

Goree, C., and J. Marszalek. "Electronic Surveys: Ethical Issues for Researchers," *The College Student Affairs Journal* 15, no. 1 (1995): 75–79.

Groves, Robert M., and Robert L. Kahn. "Surveys by Telephone: A National Comparison with Personal Interviews," in *Handbook of Survey Research*, eds. Peter H. Rossi, James D. Wright, and Andy B. Anderson. Orlando: Academic Press, 1983.

Groves, Robert M., Stanley Presser, and Sarah Dipko, "The Role of Topic Interest in Survey Participation Decisions," *Public Opinion Quarterly* 68 (2004): 2–31.

Hayes, B. *Measuring Customer Satisfaction.* Milwaukee: ASQC Quality Press, 1992.

Henry, G. T. *Practical Sampling.* Newbury Park, Calif.: Sage, 1990.

Hsu, J. "The Development of Electronic Surveys: A Computer Language-Based Method," *The Electronic Library* 13, no. 3 (1995): 195–201.

Hyman, H. H. *Secondary Analysis of Sample Surveys.* New York: John Wiley & Sons, 1972.

Kish, Leslie. *Survey Sampling.* New York: Wiley, 1965.

Leeuw, Edith de. "To Mix or Not to Mix Data Collection Modes in Surveys," *Journal of Official Statistics* 21 (2005): 233–255.

Monette, D. R., T. J. Sullivan, and C. R. DeJong. *Applied Social Research: Tool for the Human Services,* 2nd ed. Fort Worth, Tex.: Holt, 1990.

Resource Manual for Customer Surveys. Washington, D.C.: Executive Office of the President, 1993.

Scholtes, P. *The Team Handbook.* Madison: Joiner Associates, 1998.

Schuman, Howard, and Stanley Presser. *Questions and Answers in Attitude Surveys: Experiments on Question Form, Wording and Context.* Thousand Oaks, Calif.: Sage, 1981.

Simon, J. *Basic Research Methods in Social Science: The Art of Empirical Investigation.* New York: Random, 1968.

Spendolini, M. J. *Customer Satisfaction Measurement.* Laguna Beach, Calif.: MJS Associates, 1992.

Sproull, L. S. "Using Electronic Mail for Data Collection in Organizational Research," *Academy of Management Journal* 29 (1986): 159–169.

Sudman, Seymour, and Norman M. Bradburn. *Response Effects in Surveys: A Review and Synthesis.* Chicago: Aldine, 1974.

Tourangeau, Roger, and Tom W. Smith. "Asking Sensitive Questions: The Impact of Data Collection Mode, Question Format, and Question Context," *Public Opinion Quarterly* 60 (1996): 275–304.

Wells, D. L. *Strategic Management for Senior Leaders: A Handbook for Implementation.* Washington, D.C.: Department of the Navy, 1996.

Wells, D. L., and L. M. Doherty. *A Handbook for Strategic Planning.* Washington, D.C.: Department of the Navy, 1994.

Zimmerman, Richard E., Linda Steinmann, and Vince Schueler. "Designing Customer Surveys That Work," *Quality Digest* 16, no. 10 (1996): 22–28.

Appendix B

Research and Collaboration Tools

Rather than attempt to provide the end-all, be-all of listings, let me offer some suggestions and a few websites that undoubtedly will be updated as new software packages and server platforms are released. At the same time, let me offer my own site (faculty.jmc.ksu.edu/gould/commons/updates). This site will be updated on a regular basis and will include other websites that offer options and updates.

Some universities, such as Cornell and Yale, have bundled their software platforms to serve a particular collection. In the case of Cornell, several databases connect students and faculty to expanded features through independent software applications via password-protected accounts. ARTstor and other similar collections of images are made accessible to campus patrons using a third-party platform offered by Luna Imaging (www.lunaimaging.com/insight/index.html). This certainly is not the only arrangement Cornell makes to provide resources to its faculty and students, but it is a very good example of the repackaging of existing data into a very accessible format.

As we look at the various software packages that libraries might consider adding to their in-house desktops and cloud-computing centers, please keep in mind that this is in no way an exhaustive list, nor is it a static list: new products are rolled out seemingly on an hour-to-hour basis. Also keep in mind that as we move toward a cloud computing environment, many software options will move to open access. Consider the following open access (free) options for existing proprietary software as proposed by investintech.com:

Table B.1. Supporting Software and Online Platforms, as of January 1, 2011

Application	*Online Alternative*
Microsoft Office 2007	Google Docs
Adobe Photoshop CS3	Splashup
Microsoft Visio 2007	Gliffy
Adobe Acrobat 8.1	iConv
Apple Aperture 1.5	Flickr
Microsoft Office Outlook 2007	Gmail
Adobe Dreamweaver CS3	app2you
Desktop calculators	InstaCalc
MS Outlook	FaxZERO
Website analysis software	Google Analytics
MSN Messenger	meebo
Desktop Task Lists	Ta-da List
Microsoft OneNote 2007	Stikkit
Apple MindManager 7.0 Mac	Bubbl.us
MS Excel 2007	chartAll
MS PowerPoint	Preezo

Invest in Tech is not the only website dedicated to open access software support. One of the most popular is Gizmo (www.techsupportalert.com), a site that covers the release of new "freeware" packages. For example, a poster to Gizmo compiled a list of open access software for the visually impaired (www.techsupportalert.com/content/computer-aids-visually-impaired.htm). The list includes more than a dozen options that are either inexpensive ($14) or free. This is not to suggest that any of these are up to the industry's gold standard (Dragon or Jaws); it does suggest that efforts in that direction are well underway. Similar online forums at Gizmo and other sites deal with

Browsers
CD/DVD burning
Disk utilities
File transfer
GIS
Graphics
Math, science and engineering
Music
Reference
Scanning
Statistics
Website building

This just scratches the surface of the various software applications that are available for inclusion in learning, teaching, and research commons. What is even more impressive is that as more and more developers turn to creating small applications, also called "apps," for mobile computing devices, even more collaborative platforms will emerge.

Flowr (theflowr.com/) is an example of this. Offered in a free, limited format, a handful of collaborators can share information in a closed, private one gigabyte network. Even the full version, with unlimited users and 10 GB of space is only $5 per user.

Many libraries are already engaging in creating online resources to assist in the creation of archives, such as that at the Indiana University Digital Library Program (www.dlib.indiana.edu/research/index.shtml). IU's site includes links to various collections and teaching tools. A few are included below.

Digital Audio Archives Project (DAAP) Audio Collection: Using the performance archive of the Indiana University Cook Music Library as a test bed, the goal of DAAP is to reduce the cost of building a digital audio library. The project will design and create an effective and economical workflow management system for digitizing analog audio tapes and building a Web-accessible digital audio library. This project is funded by an IMLS National Leadership Grant as a partnership with Johns Hopkins University.

Digital Libraries Education Program: Indiana University and the University of Illinois at Urbana-Champaign received funds from the Institute of Museum and Library Science (IMLS) to create the first research-based, comprehensive master's-level and post-MLS degrees focusing on digital libraries.

Ethnomusicological Video for Instruction and Analysis Digital Archive Video Collection: The Ethnomusicological Video for Instruction and Analysis (EVIA) Digital Archive project is a joint effort of Indiana University and the University of Michigan to establish a digital archive of ethnomusicological video for use by scholars and instructors. The EVIA Digital Archive intends to preserve video recordings and make them accessible online for teachers and researchers around the world.

Institute for Digital Arts and Humanities Text Collection Image Collection Audio Collection Video Collection: The Institute for Digital Arts and Humanities links a network of disciplinary experts and highly technical faculty and support staff who work in interdisciplinary teams on collection-building, tool-building, and the development of appropriate methods for study and analysis of collections. The expertise of the faculty from the School of Informatics and Computer Science, School of Library and Information Science and highly qualified professional staff at the Digital Library Program and University Information Technology Services work together with the disciplinary expertise of the arts and humanities faculty to redefine research and scholarship in the arts and humanities on the IU Bloomington campus.

IU Digital Library Technical Infrastructure: The Digital Library Program is in the midst of a two-year project to update its software and hardware infrastructure supporting digital collection storage, preservation, and access. With funding from University Information Technology Services (UITS), the DLP is implementing a central digital repository using Fedora software and developing and implementing Web tools for cataloging, searching, browsing, and using digital images, text, and other types of media.

METS Navigator Image Collection: METS Navigator is a METS-based (Metadata Encoding and Transmission Standard) system developed by the Indiana University Digital Library Program for displaying and navigating sets of page images or other multi-part digital objects.

The project includes several other examples of collaboration hosted within the library's server. Also included are links to examples of collaboration with outside groups, such as the Digital Library Federation and the National Science Digital Library.

SOCIAL MEDIA TOOLS

Networks

Facebook (www.facebook.com)
MySpace (www.myspace.com)
LinkedIn (www.linkedin.com)
Twitter (twitter.com)
FriendFeed (friendfeed.com)
Ping (ping.fm)

Blogs

Blogger (www.blogger.com)
LiveJournal (www.livejournal.com)
WordPress (wordpress.com)
Tumblr (tumblr.com)

Collaborative

Wetpaint (www.wetpaint.com)
PBwiki (pbwiki.com)
Google Docs (docs.google.com)
Zoho (creator, docs, wiki, etc. – www.zoho.com)

Data Sharing

Diigo (www.diigo.com)
Delicious (delicious.com)
StumbleUpon (www.stumbleupon.com)
Digg (digg.com)

Photography

Flickr (www.flickr.com)
Shutterfly (www.shutterfly.com)
Photobucket (photobucket.com)
Picasa (picasa.google.com)

Video

YouTube (www.youtube.com)
Hulu (www.hulu.com)
Vimeo (vimeo.com)
Seesmic (seesmic.com)
Ustream (www.ustream.tv)
Skype (www.skype.com)

Some Links to Software Tracking Sites

C-Net, one of the older and well-established software ranking sites on the Web, tracks updates and new releases for both MacOS (download.cnet.com/mac/) and PCs (download.cnet.com/windows/?tag=hdr;snav). Some others include:

Brothersoft: www.brothersoft.com/
FileHippo: www.filehippo.com/
Free Downloads Center: www.freedownloadscenter.com/
Freebyte: www.freebyte.com/links/software.html
FreeWare: ttp://www.freeware-guide.com/
FreewareFiles: www.freewarefiles.com/
Simtel: www.simtel.net/
Softpedia: www.softpedia.com/
TopDownloads: www.topdownloads.net/
Tucows: www.tucows.com/
ZDNet: downloads.zdnet.com/

And, of course, some sites compile and rank software sites, such as Smashing Apps: www.smashingapps.com/2009/09/19/top-10-free-software-download-sites.html.

Whatever site your team relies upon, the team needs to know that new sites will come online and some existing ones will disappear. This is one of the features of the net. What is required is a constant eye on new software that can benefit students and faculty, software that can assist in writing, teaching, and conducting research. Over time, the academic commons will come to be seen as a one-stop clearinghouse for new ideas and new tools.

A millennial library team might consider allowing users to maintain and update a site within the academic commons that would provide the latest ideas in software. Of course, the problem that would likely arise immediately would be false information posted for malicious reasons, as well as information posted by those with a fiduciary interest. Both of these activities could do irreparable damage to the site's reputation and lower trust among those who need it most. Such an arrangement of allowing outside input through a UGC format would require constant oversight and management to ensure the "bad" posts are filtered. In a way, this UGC model is very much like the platform that Wikipedia has made a success.

Appendix C
Library Case Studies

This appendix presents descriptions of academic commons for a collection of libraries that updates original data prepared by Anne C. Moore, Associate Director, User Services, W.E.B. Du Bois Library, University of Massachusetts. It was published in *Transforming Library Service Through Information Commons*, eds. D. Russell Bailey and Barbara Gunter Tierney (Chicago: American Library Association, 2008). In addition, I have included some of the recent work at Ohio University, which provides an example of spatial change and service coalescing. All are excellent examples of how libraries have come to embrace their new role as millennial libraries.

This collection of cases suggests that, in some libraries, little has changed since 2006, while at others much has changed, and at even others, great change is in the works as this book is being written. The selection is not intended to represent a statistically robust sample but it does cover both small and large institutions and provides a snapshot of rapid change. As library administrators seek to implement the academic commons services offered in this book, they may find the examples of these libraries to be helpful.

Data for Ohio University, the first library included here, is based in part on a conversation with Ohio University's Alden Library's Jan Maxwell on July 2, 2009. Several elements of the University of Ohio's Alden Library Academic Commons are quite interesting, starting with the special emphasis on the nature of the separate faculty commons. Maxwell, interim dean of the library during the construction of the faculty commons in 2007, put significant importance on marketing research that included focus groups, blogs, and even tracking letters to the editor in the campus newspaper gathered by the library staff in advance of deciding what services would be included. During this same period, Maxwell notes, the university's provost had a handful of special faculty support services that needed a home. What resulted was a separate floor of the library dedicated to faculty support, including everything from research services to group teaching techniques. Since the opening of this faculty-focused service area, it was noted that traffic was much higher during the summer, which took the library staff by surprise. On reflection, it became clear that faculty were using the services of their commons area when they had the most time to dedicate to research, which is likely to be the same at most universities. Maxwell also notes a byproduct of the learning commons: noise. "This would at times disturb some undergraduates and graduate students and faculty," she said. Even though the library had a policy that every other floor was considered a quiet zone, controlling the chatter was "impossible without putting staff actually on those floors." Other librarians who were interviewed as part of the research into this book also commented on the noise of a learning commons, some suggesting it was proof that the area was actually producing what was expected: collaboration.

I have augmented this interview with information gathered from the learning and faculty commons located within the university library's website, as shown in the following:

The learning commons, a collaborative endeavor with Academic Technology and University College, provides the following services in a technology-enriched environment:

- Up-to-date technology: computers (both Mac and Windows), scanners, printers (including color), photocopiers, production tools, loan of laptop computers
- Library services: reference librarians who can help you find information for your research
- Writing assistance: the Student Writing Center can help with the writing process
- A café, student lockers, new books display, and much more. . . .

Additional resources and services include:

Reference Collection	Open access
Multimedia Center (12 seats)	Open access
Computer workstations	Open access
Group study rooms (Nine, 5–10 seats each)	Reserve Online

Rollins Room for Student Leadership (up to 20 seats)	Reservation required
Shostak Assistive Technology Room (2 seats)	Available upon request
Laptop Loan Program (32 laptops, 3 hr. limit)	First come, first served
Public Fax (past the elevators)	Restricted to sending

THE FACULTY COMMONS

Opening in the fall of 2007, the faculty commons combines a number of faculty support services in one spot:

The Center for Academic Technology: The Center for Academic Technology is an academic support facility available to faculty interested in instructional innovation. Faculty seeking assistance in designing, developing, and assessing instructional resource materials and technology-based tools and applications can visit the Center for Academic Technology (CAT) in the new faculty commons located on the third floor of Alden Library.

The Center for Teaching and Learning: Faculty Commons, Alden Library 301: The Center for Teaching and Learning (CTL) works collaboratively with university colleagues to enhance the connection between teaching and learning. The center offers workshops, discussion series, individual consultations, and other programs and resources for faculty, teaching associates, and instructional staff.

Through center programs and activities, colleagues across the university share teaching and learning ideas and expertise with one another, learn of new developments in the scholarship of teaching and learning, and strengthen teaching skills and strategies. At the heart of such efforts is a core value of enhancing—potentially transforming—students' intellectual growth and skill acquisition, and promoting their development as individuals and as engaged citizens.

Goals of the Center for Teaching & Learning

- Respond to the teaching and professional development needs of faculty, instructors, and graduate students at different points in their careers

(*continued*)

- Encourage mentoring relationships within the teaching and learning community
- Promote leadership roles of faculty and other colleagues in teaching and learning initiatives, including graduate students as future faculty
- Strengthen linkages between the center and other programs and units across the university that also are integral to the teaching and learning missions of the university
- Foster collaborative initiatives in the scholarship of teaching and learning
- Highlight excellence in teaching and learning at Ohio University

Source: www.library.ohiou.edu/find/

The remaining eight libraries are based on data included in Moore's dataset and updated by more recent numbers provided to me by library administrators. See Tables C.1 through C.8.

Table C.1. Brigham Young University

Library Website	www.lib.byu.edu	
IC Website	www.lib.byu.edu/departs/gen/ic/index.html	lib.byu.edu/sites/informationcommons/
Carnegie Classification	Research Universities (high research activity)	
	2006*	2010**
# Undergraduates	26,928 full-time; 3,314 part-time	30,558 full & part-time
# Graduate Students	1,484	3,164
# Faculty	1,600 faculty, 1,300 administrative, 1,200 staff	1,500 faculty, 2,500 administrative & staff
Highest Degree Offered	Doctorate	
# Volumes	3,538,205	4,080,079
# Titles	3,398,058	3,468,357
# Periodical Titles	27,161	71,634—In 2006 the number reported changed from subscriptions to number of titles.

# FTE Librarians	73	71
# Other FTE Staff	102	110
Library Annual Budget	$24,341,029	$27,167,004
Annual Circulation	825,744	622,098
Annual Gate Entries	3,221,551	3,008,715
IC Opening Date	February 24, 2004	
IC Name	Harold B. Lee Library Information Commons (aka No Shhh! Zone)	
IC Service Model Type	Partially integrated services	
# Computer Workstations	63 individual, 5 public, 52 group, 4 consultation, 6 multimedia, 2 in study rooms= 132 total	62 individual, 5 public, 68 group, 4 consultation, 10 multimedia, 2 in study rooms= 151 total
What's on Desktop	IE, Firefox, MS Office 2003, Photoshop (Elements)/ Omni Page Pro/Adobe Acrobat Pro, Nero, multimedia software, macromedia suite	IE, Firefox, MS Office 2003, Photoshop/ Omni Page Pro/Adobe Acrobat Pro, Nero, multimedia software, macromedia suite
IC Architect	None; repurposed existing general reference space	
Hours	Mon.–Fri. 7am–12am, Sat. 8am–12am	
IC Area	19,250 sq. ft	19,250 sq. ft
# Physical Service Points in IC	3: Reference, Computer Assistance, Multimedia Assistance	2: Reference/ Computer Assistance, Multimedia Assistance
Average # IC Users in a typical month	42,596 computer log-ins (doesn't include numbers using the space to study without logging in)	Not reported
Print reference materials in the IC?	Yes, but very few. Most have been moved to other subject-specific reference areas.	Only a few behind the service desk. None in open, public shelves.

*2006 data compiled by Michael Whitchurch, Information Commons Section Head. Published in D. Russell Bailey and Barbara Gunter Tierney, *Transforming Library Service Through Information Commons* (Chicago: American Library Association, 2008).

**2010 data provided by Whitchurch.

Table C.2. University of Arizona

Library Website	www.library.arizona.edu	
IC Website	www.library.arizona.edu/ic/index.html	
Carnegie Classification	Research Universities (very high research activity)	
IC Name	Main Library Information Commons	
IC Service Model Type	Partially integrated services	
	2006*	2010**
# Undergraduates	28,368	30,346
# Graduate Students	7,387	6,989
# Faculty	1,502 FTE (teaching faculty)	1,585
Highest Degree Offered	Doctorate	
# Volumes	4,844,241	5,722,280
# Periodical Titles	36,060	68,095
# FTE Librarians	51.75 active FTE, 5.0 vacant FTE, 56.75 total	40.75
# Other FTE Staff	105.75 active FTE, 9.0 vacant FTE, 114.75 total	93.63
Library Annual Budget	$21,723,566	$27,022,959
Annual Circulation	231,924 circulations and 158,879 renewals	150,215
Annual Gate Entries	1,549,543	2,083,933
IC Opening Date	2002	
# Computer Workstations	267	738****
What's on Desktop	Internet browser, propriety research databases, word processing, spreadsheet, desktop publishing, graphics, mathematics/statistics, multimedia, presentation; for complete listing see www.library.arizona.edu/ic/infocommons-software.html	
Hours	Mon.–Thurs. 12am–11:59pm; Fri. 12am–9pm; Sat. 9am–9pm; Sun. 11am–11:59pm	
IC Area	29,000 sq. ft.	
# Physical Service Points in IC	3: IC reference desk, photocopy desk, and multimedia zone service area	
Average # IC Users in a typical month	90,000	25,000 est. use and 56,613 "entering main library"*****
Print reference materials in the IC?	Yes, limited reference materials are available	

*2006 Data provided by Leslie Sult, Instructional Design Librarian. Published in D. Russell Bailey and Barbara Gunter Tierney, *Transforming Library Service Through Information Commons* (Chicago: American Library Association, 2008).

**2010 Update: John C Miller-Wells, Library Information Analyst, Access & Information Services Team, including Michael Brewer and Alex Rizra, staff at the University of Arizona Library.

***"We actually have three 'information commons' but the ones in our Science and Fine Arts libraries are just repurposed space with computers, not a newly designed space like the IC in the Main library." Michael Brewer, Team Leader for Instructional Services, University of Arizona Libraries, September 15, 2010.

****738 public workstations across our libraries' information commons and other public user areas.

*****No accurate counts available.

Table C.3. University of Calgary

Mackimmie Library		
	2006*	2008–2009**
# Undergraduates	23,071 FTE	Unchanged
# Graduate students	5,127 FTE	Unchanged
# Faculty	2,209 FTE	Unchanged
Highest degree offered	Doctorate	
# Volumes	2,535,714	Unchanged
# Titles	1,644,207	Unchanged
# Periodical Titles	353,872	Unchanged
# Librarians	43 FTE	Unchanged
# Other Staff	155 support, 22 casual	Unchanged
Annual Budget	$22,619,301	Unchanged
Annual circulation		
initial loan	349,609	261,993
renewals	1,294,321	970,057
reserve loans	106,473	39,788
Gate Entries	14,065***	
Workstations	230	
IC Area	42,043	
Physical Service points	3	
Average users	5,000 (in a typical month)	
Print references in the IC? Yes		

*In 2006, Susan Beatty, Head, Information Commons, prepared a report published in D. Russell Bailey and Barbara Gunter Tierney, *Transforming Library Service through Information Commons* (Chicago: American Library Association, 2008).

**In a phone conversation with Beatty in August 2010, she noted that the Information Commons would be moving in 2011 into three floors of the new six-floor Taylor Family Digital Library. This new facility will offer more focused services to students and faculty, including writing and research consulting. Students will be offered drop-in writing assistance, and faculty will be able to access a massive online archive of teaching, learning, and research video materials.

(*continued*)

Table C.3. University of Calgary (*continued*)

The new Academic Commons area at the new building "will offer books and online resources, a large Learning Commons with café, workrooms, film and audio rooms, editing and recording suites, multimedia labs, quiet study areas, and seminar and consultation space for academic growth."

The library's staff is working with an ongoing and dynamic list of potential new services that may be offered in the Taylor Library, including:

- Live display of currently available workstations
- Room availability display system
- Plasma screens for displaying researcher, student work or other information
- Large format scanner and plotter/printer (digitization of maps)
- Circulating Laptops/Netbooks
- Circulating FLIP video cameras
- Surface Tables (SMART Tables)
- Disposable cameras
- Ipods
- Smart Boards, collaborative for team work
- Smart Boards for teaching
- Dual monitor desktop computers
- 3D visualization room
- Digital video globe
- Geo Wall
- Team collaboration software
- Data wall
- Audio booth
- Digitization lab
- Multi-media stations

(lcr.ucalgary.ca/tfdl-teams/technology)

Beatty added that the library was in the process of creating a "high density library storage" facility that would hold 1.5 million volumes, leaving 500,000 print titles to be housed in the new library. Beatty also noted the new facility would be called the Learning Commons, not the current term, Information Commons.

****Single day, peak-period sample

Table C.4. University of Georgia

Library Website	www.libs.uga.edu	
Carnegie Classification	Research Universities (very high research activity)	
	2006*	2010**
IC Website	www.slc.uga.edu	www.mlc.uga.edu
# Undergraduates	25,002	26,142 (enrolled fall 2009)
# Graduate Students	8,456	8,743 (enrolled fall 2009)
# Faculty	2,956 faculty (instruction/research/public services), 3,559 administrative/other professional	2,890 faculty (instruction/research/public services), 3,926 administrative/other professional
Highest Degree Offered	Doctorate	Doctorate
# Volumes	4.2 million	4.6 million
# Periodical Titles	48,000	7,000 print and 48,000 electronic full-text journals

# FTE Librarians	70 for entire library, 6.5 for IC	64 for entire library (5 for IC)
# Other FTE Staff	200 for entire library, 3 for IC	142 for entire library, 3 for IC
Library Annual Budget	$22,600,000 (no separate budget for IC operation)	$11,605,389 for FY2007–2008 (no separate budget for IC operation)
Annual Circulation	469,062 (FY2006)—includes circulation and physical reserves	394,866 (FY2009)—includes circulation and physical reserves***
Annual Gate Entries	922,437 for Main Library and Science Library, 1.8 million for IC (FY2006)	1.5 million for IC (FY10)
IC Opening Date	36,372	
IC Name	Student Learning Center	Zell B. Miller Learning Center
IC Service Model Type	Primarily integrated services	
# Computer Workstations	500 PCs	558 PCs and 50 Macs
What's on Desktop	Internet, propriety research databases, office suites, word processing, spreadsheet, charting/graphing, desktop publishing, graphics, mathematics/statistics, multimedia/presentation	
Hours	Mon.–Thurs. 7:30am–2am; Fri. 7:30am-9pm; Sat. 10am–7pm	Mon.–Thurs. 7am–2am; Fri. 7am–7pm; Sat. 10am–7pm; Sun. 11am–2am
IC Area	ca. 200,000 sq. ft. divided roughly in half: Electronic Library (2,240 seats) and classrooms (2,200 seats)	
# Physical Service Points in IC	6	6
Average # IC Users in a typical month	200,000 during fall/spring semesters	220,000 during fall/spring semesters
Print reference materials in the IC?	Yes, a small collection of ca. 60 titles.	

*Data for 2006 prepared by William G. Potter, University Librarian and Associate Provost. Published in D. Russell Bailey and Barbara Gunter Tierney, *Transforming Library Service Through Information Commons* (Chicago: American Library Association, 2008).

**Data for 2010 prepared by Caroline C. Barrett, Libraries General Operations.

***Circulation number provided by Daron Mitchell, Office Supervisor, Circulation Services.

Table C.5. University of Massachusetts–Amherst

Library Website	www.library.umass.edu	
Commons Website	www.umass.edu/learningcommons/	
Commons Name	Umass Amherst Learning Commons	
Carnegie Classification	Research Universities (very high research activity)	
Service Model Type	Primarily integrated services	
	2006*	2010**
# Undergraduates	20,392	20,410
# Graduate Students	4,254	4,556
# Faculty	1,147	1,254
Highest Degree Offered	Doctorate	Doctorate
# Volumes	3,204,025	3,331,482
# Periodical Titles	41,308	59,328
# FTE Librarians	55	45
# Other FTE Staff	75 (does not include 46 FTE student assistants)	85 (does not include 57 FTE student assistants)
Library Annual Budget	$14,113,346 (FY2006) for library (plus $410,000 ongoing base budget for IC)	$14,765,404 (FY2010) for library (includes $576,034 ongoing base budget for IC)
Annual Circulation***	408,867	296,062
Annual Gate Entries	726,000	1,143,989
Commons Opening Date	Oct. 21, 2005	
# Computer Workstations	58 library public PCs; 122 authenticated (106 PCs and 16 Macs); 17 Gateway M280 tablet PCs	40 Public PCS; 241 authenticated (174 PCs and 67 Macs); 52 circulating laptops (PCs)
What's on Desktop	Browsers, Microsoft Office, licensed software of all types, including graphics, multimedia, statistical and GIS programs	(See list below)****
Hours	During academic semesters, the entire building is open: 11am. Sun–9pm. Fri; 9am–9pm. Sat. (142 hours per week)	
Commons Area	23,500 sq. ft. (renovated space)	30,000+ sq. ft. (renovated space)
# Physical Service Points in the Commons	4 on floor (plus 1 on the fly); 5 on other floors	5 on floor; 5 on other floors

Average # Commons Users in a typical month	60,000	95,332
Print reference materials in the Commons?	Yes, the main print reference collection for the library (18,000 volumes)	Yes, the main print reference collection for the library (12,000 volumes)

*Original data prepared by Anne C. Moore, Associate Director, User Service. Published in D. Russell Bailey and Barbara Gunter Tierney, *Transforming Library Service Through Information Commons* (Chicago: American Library Association, 2008).

**Updated by: Leslie Button, Terry Warner, Dianna Williams and Sarah Hutton. Special thanks to University of Massachusetts Amherst Library administration for their work in creating and updating this information.

***Includes Integrated Sciences and Engineering Library and Music Reserve Lab in other buildings.

****The Amherst library administration provided a very specific list of software provided in their Learning Commons for 2010 update:

Authenticated PCs: Windows 7*
U.C. Davis Nutritional Analysis Suite
McAfee VirusScan Enterprise 8.7.0i*
Dragon Naturally Speaking 10 (Assistive Technologies Center only)
Jaws 11 (Assistive Technologies Center only)
Kurzweil 1000 12 (Assistive Technologies Center only)
Kurzweil 3000 12
ZoomText 9.1
Firefox 3.6*
Microsoft Internet Explorer 8*
ArchiCAD 12
AutoDesk 3ds Max Design 2010
AutoDesk AutoCAD 2010
AutoDesk AutoCAD Architectural Desktop 2010
Autodesk Revit Architecture 2010
Google SketchUp 7.1
Graphisoft ArchiCad 12
Rhinoceros 4.0 SR8
Visual Analysis 7.0
Adobe Acrobat Professional 9*
Adobe Acrobat Reader 9
Adobe Bridge CS5
Adobe Dreamweaver CS5*
Adobe Fireworks CS5
Adobe Flash CS5
Adobe Illustrator CS5
Adobe InDesign CS5*
Adobe Photoshop CS5*
Inspiration 9
Microsoft Expression Studio 4
Microsoft Office Access 2010*
Mac OS 10.6*
McAfee Security 9*
Mozilla Firefox 3.6*
Safari 5*
Google Earth 5
Google SketchUp 7
Adobe Acrobat Pro 9*
Adobe Acrobat Reader 9*
Adobe Bridge CS5
Adobe Dreamweaver CS5*
Adobe Drive CS5
Adobe Flash CS5
Adobe Flash Player 10.1
Adobe Fireworks CS5
Adobe Help 3
Adobe Illustrator CS5
Adobe InDesign CS5*
Adobe Photoshop CS5*
Apple iWork Keynote '09*
Apple iWork Numbers '09*
Apple iWork Pages '09*
Apple Preview 5
TextWrangler 3.1
Inkscape 0.46
Microsoft Office Excel 2008*
Microsoft Office Word 2008*
Microsoft Office PowerPoint 2008*
OpenOffice.org 3.2
PixelGlow Graphviz 2.26
Scribus 1.3
Tams Analyzer 3.7
Apple iCal 4*
Apple Mail 4*
Adobe Media Encoder CS5
Adobe Media Player 1.1
Microsoft Office Excel 2010*
Microsoft Office InfoPath 2010*
Microsoft Office PowerPoint 2010*
Microsoft Office Publisher 2010*
Microsoft Office Word 2010*
Microsoft Visio 2010
Eclipse SDK 3.5
Java J2SE
JES 4.3
Python 3.1
Squeak 4.1
Visual Studio .Net 2005
Library Applications
n3D 4.1
Image J
SciFinder Scholar 2006
Solero 8
Wink 2

(continued)

Table C.5. University of Massachusetts–Amherst (*continued*)

ArcGIS 9.2
Google Earth 5.2
Mathematica 7
Matlab 2010
ProTeXt
GhostScript
GhostView
Audacity 1.3
iTunes 8
ISO Recorder
Picture Viewer 7.6
QuickTime Player 7.6*
Roxio 10
VLC Media Player*
Windows Media Player 11*
Windows Movie Maker
Adobe Authorware
Adobe Flash*
Adobe Shockwave*
Chime Plug-in
Sun ODF Plug-in (MS Office)
FileZilla*
SecureCRT 6.5*
WinSCP 4.2*
Logger Pro 3.8
Minitab 16
PASW Statisticis 18 (formerly SPSS)
R 2.11
Apple Final Cut Express 4
Apple Garageband '09
Apple iDVD '09
Apple iMovie '09
Apple iPhoto '09
Apple iTunes 9.2
Apple iWeb '09
Apple Quicktime Player 10
Audacity 1.3
Finale 2008 (Fine Arts Center 444 only)
Flip4Mac WMV Player 2.3
QLab 2.3
RealPlayer 12*
VideoLan VLC 1.1*
Second Life Viewer 2
Fetch 5.6*
JellyFiSSH 4.5*
Terminal 2.1*
Logger Pro 3.8
Mathematica 7
R (and R 64) 2.11
Tex BibDesk 1.5
Tex Excalibur 4
Tex LaTeXiT 2.1
Tex TeXShop 2.33
Apple Boot Camp*
Stuffit Expander 14*
SAS 9.2
Stata Intercooled 11
SYSTAT 13
7-Zip*

Table C.6. University of Minnesota–Twin Cities

Library Website	www.lib.umn.edu	
IC Website	www.lib.umn.edu/about/undergrad/infocommons/	
Carnegie Classification	Research Universities (very high research activity)	
Highest Degree Offered	Doctorate	
# Undergraduates	28,957	29,926
# Graduate Students	14,107	14,148
# Faculty	2,495	2,825
	2006*	2009
# Volumes	6,200,669	
# Periodical Titles	36,900	
# FTE Librarians	0.25	0.25
# Other FTE Staff	0.75	0.75
Annual Circulation	591,397	
Annual Gate Entries	373,628	
IC Opening Date	11/11/2004	

IC Name	Information Commons	Smart Learning Commons
IC Service Model Type	Single-staffed by librarians, paraprofessional, or students—somewhat integrated services	
# Computer Workstations	35	
What's on Desktop	Internet, propriety research databases, office suites, word processing, spreadsheet, charting/graphing, desktop publishing, graphics, mathematics/statistics, multimedia/ presentation	*
Hours	Staffed: Mon.–Thurs. 9am–10pm; Fri. 9am–6pm; Sat. 12pm–6pm; Sun. 12pm–10pm. Building: Mon.–Thurs. 8am–12am; Fri. 8am–9pm; Sat. 10am–10pm; Sun. 12pm–12am	
IC Area	1,735 sq. ft.	
# Physical Service Points in IC	1	1
Print reference materials in the IC?	Yes, computer help books. IC shares the first floor of Wilson Library with the reference collection, so there are many print resources nearby (just not physically within the IC). Students can bring materials into the IC without checking them out.	

*Original data prepared by Carolina Crouse, Information Literacy Librarian. Published in D. Russell Bailey and Barbara Gunter Tierney, *Transforming Library Service Through Information Commons* (Chicago: American Library Association, 2008).

**Updated by Scott Spicer, Media Outreach and Learning Spaces Librarian University of Minnesota Libraries–Twin Cities

***Wilson SMART Learning Commons Software List

General-Use Computers:

- Microsoft Office 2008
- Trellian web page
- Photoshop Elements 2
- SPSS 12 (Statistics, 1 computer)

Multimedia Computers:

- Adobe Creative Suite 3 Design Premium*
  - Adobe Acrobat Pro 9
  - Adobe Illustrator CS3
  - Adobe InDesign CS3
  - Adobe Dreamweaver CS3
  - Adobe Photoshop CS3 Extended
  - Adobe Flash CS3
  - Adobe Fireworks CS3
- Apple iLife 08*
  - iPhoto 08
  - Garageband 08
  - iWeb 08
  - iTunes
  - iDVD
  - Quicktime
- Apple iMovie '06, '08 iMovie Guide*
- Final Cut Express*
  - LiveType
  - Adobe Premier Elements*, **
  - Adobe Photoshop Elements
- Microsoft Office 2007/ Mac 2008*
  - Excel, Excel Guide
  - Word
  - PowerPoint

*CS3 Design Standard on 2 Macs

**Premiere on 1 PC production station

Source: Scott Spicer
Media Outreach and Learning Spaces Librarian
University of Minnesota Libraries–Twin Cities

Table C.7. University of Southern California

Library Website	www.usc.edu/leavey/	
IC Website	www.usc.edu/leavey/ic/	
Carnegie Classification	Research Universities (very high research activity)	
IC Name	Lower IC: Leavey, Upper IC: Dorothy Leavey	
IC Service Model Type	Primarily integrated service-reference/computing combined	
IC Opening Date	1994	
	2006*	2010**
# Faculty	3,100 full-time, 1,400 part-time	3,249 full-time, 1,486 part-time
Highest Degree Offered	Doctorate	Doctorate
# Volumes	Leavey 39,000, USC libraries 3.9 million, e-books 280,351, e-journals 37,712, databases 53,756	Leavey 39,000, USC libraries 4 million, e-books 431,899, e-journals 87,805, databases 1,382
# Periodical Titles	Leavey 271, USC libraries 37,800	Leavey 271, USC libraries 98,700
# FTE Librarians	5	5
# Other FTE Staff	9	14
Library Annual Budget	$1,390,000	$1,390,000
Annual Circulation	130,000	130,000
Annual Gate Entries	1.5 million	1.34 million
# Computer Workstations	250 PCs and Macs for both Commons: 88 PCs and 43 Macs in Lower IC, 74 PCs and 1 Mac in Upper IC, 20 PCs in PC classroom (learning room A), 24 Macs in Mac classroom (learning room B)	282 PCs and Macs for all Commons: 112 PCs and 42 Macs in Lower IC, 72 PCs in Upper IC, 6 PCs and 6 Macs in Multimedia Commons, 20 PCs in PC classroom (learning room A), 24 Macs in Mac classroom (learning room B). In addition, 5 public access Kiosk computers: 2 Kiosk computers in main lobby, 2 Kiosk computers in Lower IC, 1 Kiosk computer in Upper IC. Also, 13 Scanners: 12 scanners in Multimedia Commons, 1 scanner in Lower IC.

What's on Desktop	Library research resources, proprietary databases, Internet, Microsoft Office, spreadsheet, Web publishing, Adobe suite, mathematics/ statistical package (SPSS, SAS, Minitab, etc.) graphics, charting, multimedia/presentation and class applications, e.g., SAP 2000, ARCVIEW, Screen Writer, AUTOCAD, Finale, EP Budgeting, EP Scheduling, Mathlab	Library research resources, proprietary databases, Internet, Microsoft Office, spreadsheet, Web publishing, Adobe suite, mathematics/ statistical package (SPSS, SAS, Minitab, etc.) graphics, charting, multimedia/presentation and class applications, e.g., SAP 2000, ARCVIEW, Screen Writer, AUTOCAD, Finale, EP Budgeting, EP Scheduling, Mathlab
Hours	24/7 during fall and spring, cutbacks in summer	24/7 during fall and spring, cutbacks in summer
IC Area	Lower IC 18,998 sq. ft., Upper IC 9,892 sq. ft.	Lower IC 18,998 sq. ft., Upper IC 9,892 sq. ft.
# Physical Service Points in IC	Lower IC 2, Upper IC 1	Lower IC 1, Upper IC 1
Average # IC Users in a typical month	Lower IC 23,100; Upper IC 22,320	Lower IC 41,370; Upper IC 40,380
Print reference materials in the IC?	Yes, basic undergraduate reference collection.	Yes, basic undergraduate reference collection.

From the Leavey Library Website (15 Sept 2010):

Computers in the Information Commons (lower-level and second floor) are for the use of USC faculty, staff, and currently enrolled students only. Computers require a USC login and are available on a first-come, first-served basis. No game playing is allowed. Any computer left unattended for more than 10 minutes will be given to the next person in line.

Computing Facilities

Leavey Library supports a full range of computing activities. The Lower Commons, located on the lower level of Leavey, has 39 iMAC and 71 PC computers. The Dorothy Leavey Memorial Commons, or Upper Commons, is located on the second floor and has 70 PC computers and 40 study carrels with network connections for laptop computers. All computers in both Commons have USB ports and CD/DVD drives.

(*continued*)

Table C.7. University of Southern California (*continued*)

Additional computer workstations are available in the Learning Rooms (on the Lower Level). These computers are available when the rooms are not in use for a class:

Learning Room A: 20 PC computers

Learning Room B: 24 iMac computers

In the Lower Commons, an Express Station is available for a maximum of 5 minutes to send print jobs or for short computing sessions (such as checking E-mail). Public access stations, which have Internet access but no productivity software, are available on the first floor of Leavey as well as in the Lower Commons.

Listings of software installed in Information Technology Services computing centers and the Information Commons: Macintosh PCs

Printing

USC Libraries provides printing options from all library research terminals, Leavey Library Information Commons and Multimedia Lab computers. For more details about printing in Leavey please see our Technology page.

Research and Computing Consultation

Leavey librarians, staff and student navigation assistants (SNAs) are available to assist patrons with research using a combination of print, electronic and Internet resources. They can also assist with computing questions regarding productivity software and E-mail.

Simple reference questions can be answered by phone at (213) 740-6938 (Leavey Reference Desk). For chat or e-mail reference go to Ask-a-Librarian. If you have in-depth computing questions, please call the Customer Support Center at (213) 740-5555.

Reference librarian hours for the fall and spring are 11 a.m.– 7 p.m. Monday–Thursday, 11 a.m.–4 p.m. Friday and 1 p.m.–7 p.m. Sunday. Student navigation assistants are available whenever the library is open to assist with research and computing questions.

The ITS Customer Support Center walk-in area is located in Leavey Library's Lower Commons at the Reference and Computer Consultation Desk. Services such as account assistance, software support, and statistical software distribution are available here between the hours of 9 a.m. and 5 p.m., Monday through Friday. For more information, please see the CSC site: www.usc.edu/its/csc/

Reference Collection

Leavey has a wide variety of print and electronic reference resources that are available to aid your research. The reference collection is located in the Lower Commons in bookcases along the perimeter of the room and behind the reference desk. For more information please see our Book & Journals page.

Collaborative Workrooms

Both commons have rooms available for group study. The Lower Commons has 19 rooms, designed for groups of five to 12 people. The Upper Commons has 13 rooms, designed for three to four people. All workrooms provide a white board, dry erase markers and network connections for laptops. Workrooms 3K through 3X in the Lower Commons have PC computers. Reservations may be made in advance at the reference desks in the Upper and Lower Commons. You must make reservations in person; reservations are not taken over the phone. You will need to show your USCard while using the room. Other important information on reserving and using the workrooms is on the Collaborative Workroom Policies page.

Writing Consultation

In cooperation with the Writing Center, writing consultants are available Monday through Thursday from 7–9 p.m. in room 3Z (lower level, northwest corner) during the fall and spring semesters.

Adaptive Technologies Room

The adaptive technologies room is located in room 3AA in the Lower Commons. Leavey Library and the Center for Academic Support and Disability Services and Programs work together to provide users with disabilities equal access to computing resources through a variety of adaptive technologies. For more information on the available technologies and on the training program for their use, please contact the Academic Support and Disability Services and Programs Office at (213) 740-0776.

Source: www.usc.edu/libraries/locations/leavey/ic/

*2006 data compiled by Shahla Bahavar, Reference Coordinator, USC Libraries. Published in D. Russell Bailey and Barbara Gunter Tierney, *Transforming Library Service Through Information Commons* (Chicago: American Library Association, 2008).

**2010 data compiled Bahavar.

Table C.8. University of Southern Maine

Library Website	library.usm.maine.edu	
Carnegie Classification	Master's Colleges and Universities (larger programs)	
Highest Degree Offered	Doctorate	
IC Name	Information Commons	
	2006*	2010**
# Undergraduates	8,622	7,618
# Graduate Students	2,352	1,770
# Faculty	399	390
# Volumes	352,325	369,000
# Periodical Titles	63,801	35,000
# FTE Librarians	15	14.75
# Other FTE Staff	24	33
Library Annual Budget	$2,968,326 (no separate budget for IC)	$4,060,000.00
Annual Circulation	28,426	26,500
Annual Gate Entries	206,600	309,077
IC Opening Date	September 6, 2005	Portland 2005; Gorham 2005, expanded 2008 and 2010; Lewiston/ Auburn 2009
IC Service Model Type	Partially integrated services	Blended services Gorham: Fully integrated services Lewiston-Auburn: Partially integrated services Portland
# Computer Workstations	Portland 15, Gorham 14, Lewiston-Auburn 13	Lewiston Auburn 36 pcs, 2 Macs; Gorham 38 pcs, 2 Macs; Portland 25. 1 Mac
What's on Desktop	Internet, proprietary research databases, Microsoft Office suite, subject-specific offerings via computer lab software packages, course management software	Internet, URSUS Library catalog, proprietary databases, Microsoft Office Suite, subject specific software packages, course management software, Adobe Photoshop

Hours	All hours that each library is open: Portland and Gorham: Mon.–Thurs. 8am–11pm; Fri. 8am–6pm; Sat. 10am-6pm; Sun. 10am–10pm. Lewiston-Auburn: Mon.–Thurs 8am–8pm; Fri. 8am–4:30pm; Sat. 9am–3pm; Sun. closed	All hours that each library is open: Portland: Mon.–Thurs. 7:45am–11pm; Fri. 7:45am–8pm; Sat. 10am–8pm; Sun. 10am–11pm: Gorham Mon.–Thurs. 7:45am–11pm, Fri. 7:45am–8pm, Sat. 11am–7pm, Sun. 12pm–11pm: Lewiston–Auburn: Mon.–Thurs 8am–8pm; Fri. 8am–4:30pm; Sat. 9am–3pm; Sun. closed
IC Area***	Portland 8,694 sq. ft., Gorham 1,665 sq. ft., Lewiston-Auburn 920 sq. ft.	Gorham 2,100 sq ft; Lewiston Auburn 7,000 sq ft; Portland 8,694 sq ft
# Physical Service Points in IC	1 at each of three campuses	
Average # IC Users in a typical month	Portland 782, Gorham 297, Lewiston-Auburn 212	Portland 785; Gorham 950; Lewiston-Auburn 415
Print reference materials in the IC?	Yes, each campus library has its own print reference collection.	

*Data for 2006 prepared by Barbara J. Mann, Coordinator, Information Literacy Program, and David Nutty, Director of Libraries. Published in D. Russell Bailey and Barbara Gunter Tierney, *Transforming Library Service Through Information Commons* (Chicago: American Library Association, 2008).

**Data for 2010 prepared by David Nutty, Director of Libraries.

***In 2008, the wall between the library and the adjacent computer lab in Lewiston-Auburn was removed to create an inviting space for students to study, research, or use computers in a wireless environment. Group study spaces, new computers and furniture, a centralized help desk, and a computer classroom for library instruction now make up the new Commons @ LAC.

****The Commons@Gorham Library was first opened in 2005, expanded in 2008 and remodeled and expanded in 2010. The computer lab on this campus was incorporated into the library in 2005 to initially establish the Gorham Commons. Since then, the Commons@Gorham Library has been refined and a blended service model was introduced in 2010.

Index

About the Author

Thomas H. P. Gould teaches mass communications—mainly advertising and new media—at Kansas State University. He is editor of the *Online Journal of Rural Research & Policy* and an e-zine focused on Kansas. His fascination with the act of publishing was provoked by such works as *The Annotated Sherlock Holmes* by William Baring-Gould (1960). His research focus on academic publishing is part of a long-term effort to understand the past, present, and future of the various parts—such as peer review—of a rapidly changing professional activity. He lives and works in Manhattan, Kansas, located in the heart of the Flint Hills, and enjoys hiking in the Rockies, so long as the end of the day includes a hot shower, good food, long conversations with Carol, and a warm, soft bed.